Minority Protection

Standards and Reality

Minority Protection

Standards and Reality

IMPLEMENTATION OF COUNCIL OF EUROPE STANDARDS IN SLOVAKIA, ROMANIA AND BULGARIA

Anna K. Meijknecht
Lecturer in European and International Public Law
Tilburg University, The Netherlands

T•M•C• Asser Press
The Hague

Published by T·M·C·ASSER PRESS
P.O.Box 16163, 2500 BD The Hague, The Netherlands
<www.asserpress.nl>

T·M·C·ASSER PRESS' English language books are distributed exclusively by:

Cambridge University Press, The Edinburgh Building, Shaftesbury Road,
Cambridge CB2 2RU, UK,
or
for customers in the USA, Canada and Mexico:
Cambridge University Press, 40 West 20th Street, New York, NY 10011-4211, USA
<www.cambridge.org>

ISBN 90-6704-191-2

PREFACE

Although the development and adoption of new international standards concerning the protection of minorities can in many cases be seen as an important political achievement, it is only a small step towards the actual solution of minority problems. The real challenge for the international community, States and minorities lies in the implementation of these international standards in the everyday reality of the minorities in question.

To what extent do minorities benefit from international standards concerning their protection? The question seems simple and obvious, but the answer turns out to be complex and difficult. This study deals with this question by transgressing the dividing line between the law and the reality which underlies it. It gathers information from sources which are familiar to lawyers and legal scholars, such as: international legal documents, national legislation, and policy documents, on the one hand, and, on the other, sources which relate to the 'reality' of minorities, such as: interviews, field reports concerning human rights violations, statistical data concerning sociology and the economy.

This approach made it possible to analyse the whole path of implementation: from the international level to the grass-roots level, and resulted in both practical and more analytical observations and recommendations concerning the improvement of the protection of minorities.

As a matter of fact, this is the way in which legal research should be carried out: looking behind the standards, however important they are, and seeing what happens to them on a day-to-day basis. Isn't this what it's all about? More specifically in this case: to what extent do minorities themselves really profit from all the words devoted to them? The book written by Dr. Anna Meijknecht is, amongst many other things, a great lesson in modesty for all those who think that problems are solved as soon as the 'legislator' has spoken. Chapeau!

Tilburg, June 2004

Prof. Dr. Willem VAN GENUGTEN
Professor of International Law,
Tilburg University
Chairman of the Board
of the Netherlands School
of Human Rights Research

ACKNOWLEDGEMENTS

Can minorities attain the status of 'subjects of international law'? This was the central question in my doctoral dissertation. The present book deals with the opposite question: Does international law reach its subjects? In other words: What is the use of international standards concerning minority protection for the actual improvement of the living conditions of minorities?

Fascinating, but also sobering, was the search for information concerning the living conditions and problems of minorities in Slovakia, Romania and Bulgaria. Together with Dr. Marcia Rooker, I travelled through Romania and Bulgaria, visiting minority organisations and Roma ghettos, conducting interviews with people involved in the protection of minorities. Marcia's expertise and interest in the situation of the Roma, which she shared with me in numerous discussions, proved to be an invaluable source of inspiration for this book.

This study is one of four projects in a research programme entitled 'Grondslagen van een Europese Rechtsorde: Concurrentie, Convergentie en Cooperatie' ['Foundations of an European Legal Order: Competition, Convergence and Cooperation'], funded by the Netherlands Organisation for Scientific Research within its programme for strengthening legal research (SaRO). The project itself was called: 'Bescherming van nationale minderheden: van normen naar implementatie' ['Protection of National Minorities: from Standards to Implementation']. The project was carried out within Tilburg University's department of European and International Law as well as within the Netherlands School of Human Rights Research.

I am greatly indebted to Professor Willem van Genugten who was the initiator of this research project. His idea to look 'behind the law' resulted in the present project. I wish to extend my gratitude to the board of referees for this book: Professor Asbjørn Eide, Professor Cees Flinterman, and Dr. Nena Trifunovska, whose insights, advice and practical remarks were of great value. Thanks are also due to Peter Morris for the English correction of the manuscript and to Marjolijn Bastiaans of T.M.C. Asser Press.

I dedicate this book to Timon, Marit and Emma.

The Hague, May 2004 Anna MEIJKNECHT

TABLE OF CONTENTS

Part II
NON-DISCRIMINATION

ABBREVIATIONS

CEDIME	Centre for Documentation and Information on Minorities in Europe
CEDIME-SE	Centre for Documentation and Information on Minorities in Europe-Southern Europe
CM	Committee of Ministers of the Council of Europe
COE	Council of Europe
COE PA	Council of Europe Parliamentary Assembly
DAHR	Democratic Alliance of Hungarians in Romania
ECHR	European Convention on Human Rights
EDRC	Ethnocultural Diversity Resource Center (Romania)
ERRC	European Roma Rights Center
EU	European Union
EurCourtHR	European Court of Human Rights
HRC	Human Rights Committee
HRP	Human Rights Project
HHRF	Hungarian Human Rights Foundation
HCNM	High Commissioner on National Minorities
IHF	International Helsinki Federation for Human Rights
ICCPR	International Covenant on Civil and Political Rights
ICERD	International Convention on the Elimination of All Forms of Racial Discrimination
ICESCR	International Covenant on Economic, Social and Cultural Rights
ILO	International Labour Organization
NGO	Non-Governmental Organization
NCCD	National Council for Combating Discrimination (Romania)
OSI	Open Society Institute
OSI AP Report	Monitoring the EU Accession Process Report of the Open Society Institute
OSCE	Organization for Security and Co-operation in Europe
RFE/RL Newsline	Radio Free Europe Newsline
RCRC	Resource Center for Roma Communities
ROMANI CRISS	Roma Centre for Social Intervention and Studies
SMK	Hungarian Coalition Party (in Slovakia)
SR	Slovak Republic
UDHR	Universal Declaration of Human Rights

UDMR	Hungarian Democratic Federation of Romania
UN	United Nations Organization
UNDP	United Nations Development Program
UNPO	Unrepresented Nations and Peoples Organisation

Part I
INTRODUCTION

Chapter 1
PURPOSE AND OVERVIEW OF THIS STUDY

1.1 Purpose

The situation of minorities and the way they are treated by their State is increasingly relevant as one of the requirements for admission to international organizations, in particular the Council of Europe and the European Union.[1] However, international principles with regard to minority protection, once they are laid down in an international legally binding document, must pass several stages before they can become effective. The first stage is called 'national Constitutions and legislation', the second, 'State practice and policy' and the third, 'the actual situation of minorities (reality)'. The following comment by Gabriel Andreescu, Strasbourg Ombudsperson for National Minorities in Romania, illustrates how the different stages can become gaps:

> 'It is important to monitor the differences between legal provisions and the actual practices. In Romania there is a significant difference between the value of some provisions and the fact that they are not enforced in practice. This difference is highlighted by the proliferation of hate speech and by the discrimination of Roma in the labour market. The distance between legislation and practice is due to the weakness of the rule of law.'[2]

This study intends to deal, from a comparative perspective, with the implementation of international minority rights in national legislation, State practice and reality. Since they share several characteristics, which

[1]For instance, until 1998, the insufficient protection of minorities by the Slovak government was considered by the European Union as failing to fulfil the political requirements for candidate membership of the European Union. See: Ondrej Dostál, 'Národnostné menšiny', in: Kollár, Miroslav, Meseznikov, Grigorij (eds.), *Slovensko 2000, Súhrnna správa o stave spoločnosti*, Bratislava, 2000, p. 176.

[2] Gabriel Andreescu, Strasbourg Ombudsperson for National Minorities, Romania, *Shadow Report*, October 1999, Comment on Art. 4, paras. 1 and 4, <www.minelres.lv/reports/romania/romania_NGO.htm>.

enables a comparison to be made, the cases of Slovakia, Romania, and Bulgaria have been selected for this study. These three States share the following: the fact that they have several relatively large groups of national minorities with a kin-state; the fact that they all have a large Roma community; and a difficult socio-economic situation which is partly due to a recent communist past, and to the requirements posed in the transitional period towards a free market economy. Finally, all three States are Member States of the Council of Europe and have ratified the Council of Europe Framework Convention on National Minorities (hereinafter: Framework Convention)[3] which entered into force more than five years ago, on 1 February 1998. Chronologically speaking, the Framework Convention was ratified by Romania on 11 May 1995, by Slovakia on 14 September 1995, and by Bulgaria on 7 May 1999.

The purpose of this study is to describe and analyse in the case of Slovakia, Romania and Bulgaria, the practical results of the obligations and commitments concerning the protection of minorities following from the Framework Convention. In other words, the purpose is to assess how the standards of the Framework Convention function in reality.

This study will describe and evaluate the situation of minorities in Slovakia, Romania and Bulgaria in the light of two specific international obligations concerning minority protection: non-discrimination and linguistic rights, both of which are embodied in the Framework Convention. It should be emphasised that this study does not intend to give a detailed description of the minority situation of each minority in each of the States mentioned, but that the focus will be on these two standards of the Framework Convention and that this study will examine what happens to these standards in 'practice' and 'reality'. 'Practice' is what the State does, this includes national legislation and other administrative or legal measures taken by the State with regard to minorities. 'Reality' means everyday life and the situation of the beneficiaries (or subjects) of those international standards, thus, the minorities themselves.

First, the standard of non-discrimination and the State practice based on this international standard will be assessed through an analysis of international documents and national legislation and measures with regard to minorities. 'Reality' will be described with regard to the Roma minori-

[3] For the complete text of the Council of Europe Framework Convention on the Protection of National Minorities, see Annex I.

ties in Slovakia, Romania and Bulgaria, the Muslim minority in Bulgaria, and the German and Hungarian minorities in Slovakia in relation to the Beneš Decrees. Although there are many other minorities in this region of Europe which have to cope with discrimination, I have chosen to describe only the situation of some minorities, whose situation is, unfortunately, illustrative of several specific forms of discrimination.

Second, international standards and State practice with regard to linguistic rights as embodied in Articles 10-14 of the Framework Convention will be discussed. The way these standards function in reality will be analysed on the basis of the situation of the Hungarian minority in Slovakia and the Hungarian minority in Romania and the Roma in Slovakia, Romania and Bulgaria.

1.2 Political Commitments with Regard to Minorities Following from the Opinions of the Parliamentary Assembly of the Council of Europe

In this study several documents and sources of information will be used in order to determine a) the international obligations with regard to minorities as established by the Council of Europe, b) the practice of States with regard to the implementation of these standards, c) the situation in 'reality' as experienced by minorities themselves and as described by different observers, and d) the supplementary measures proposed – and sometimes taken – by States to overcome urgent minority problems.

As far as the determination of international obligations/standards is concerned, it must be taken into account that the Parliamentary Assembly of the Council of Europe imposed specific political commitments on States when they applied for membership of the Council of Europe in the early 1990s, thus, several years before the Framework Convention was concluded. This sub-section will provide an overview of the specific commitments with regard to minorities which Slovakia, Romania and Bulgaria accepted when becoming members of the Council of Europe.

The democratisation process in Central and Eastern Europe led to Bulgaria's accession on 7 May 1992 and to Romania's accession on 7 October 1993; membership of the Slovak Republic replaced Czechoslovakia's accession from 1991 on 30 June 1993.

The admission process usually begins with a request to the Secretary General of the Council of Europe, who transmits it to the Committee of Ministers for consideration. The latter consults the Parliamentary Assembly, which in turn commences an enquiry into whether the candidate fulfils all the necessary requirements. This is done by an 'on the spot' investigation by parliamentary committees and also, since the 1990s, by fact-finding missions. Although not a statutory provision, it has also become customary to require the acceptance of the European Convention on Human Rights and Fundamental Freedoms by any new candidate. Slovakia has already considered itself bound by the Convention since 1 January 1993; Romania ratified it on 20 June 1994; and Bulgaria on 7 September 1992. The three States ratified most[4] of the additional Protocols to the European Convention on Human Rights and Fundamental Freedoms and recognized Articles 25 and 46 of the European Convention. At present this means that they recognize the jurisdiction of the European Court of Human Rights. Since 1 November 1998, the date when Protocol 11 to the European Convention entered into force, the jurisdiction of this Court has been compulsory.

The Opinion adopted by the Assembly then determines the invitation from the Committee of Ministers to the State to become a full member. Generally speaking, Opinions are expressed by the Parliamentary Assembly of the Council of Europe on questions put to it by the Committee of Ministers, such as the admission of new Member States to the Council of Europe, but also on draft conventions, the budget, and the implementation of the Social Charter. The Parliamentary Assembly of the Council of Europe is not a legislative organ. Opinions of the Parliamentary Assembly are not legally binding.

Recent Parliamentary Assembly Opinions on applications for membership of the Council of Europe refer to specific commitments entered into by the authorities of the candidate States concerning issues related to the basic principles of the Organization. The Assembly considers that the honouring of these commitments is a condition for the full participation of parliamentary delegations of new Member States in its work. Subsequently, the honouring of commitments entered into by the authorities of new Member States is closely monitored by the Political Affairs Commit-

[4] Bulgaria did not sign Protocols 9, 10 and 12; Protocol No. 12 has not been signed by Romania and Slovakia; and Protocol 13 has not been signed by Slovakia (June 2004).

tee and the Committee on Legal Affairs and Human Rights and reported to the Bureau at regular six-monthly intervals until all undertakings have been honoured.[5] The Committee on the Honouring of Obligations and Commitments by Member States of the Council of Europe (Monitoring Committee) took over the monitoring procedure in 1997.

The specific political commitments for the States in question are listed in the following Opinions:

- Opinion No. 175 of the Parliamentary Assembly of the Council of Europe on the application by the Slovak Republic for membership of the Council of Europe, adopted on 29 June 1993.
- Opinion No. 176 of the Parliamentary Assembly of the Council of Europe on the application by Romania for membership of the Council of Europe, adopted on 28 September 1993.
- Opinion No. 161 of the Parliamentary Assembly of the Council of Europe on the application by Bulgaria for membership of the Council of Europe, adopted on 5 May 1992.

1.2.1 **Slovakia**

The specific political commitments which Slovakia entered into are listed in Opinion No. 175 (1993) of the Parliamentary Assembly of the Council of Europe on the application by the Slovak Republic for membership of the Council of Europe. They mainly concern the protection of the rights of minorities. In general, three commitments on the part of the Slovak Republic can be deduced from the text of Opinion No. 175 and the Framework Convention:

- The first commitment is to base Slovak policy regarding the protection of minorities on the principles laid down in Recommendation 1201 (1993) on an additional protocol on the rights of national minorities to the European Convention on Human Rights (para. 8 of Opinion No. 175).

  As far as Recommendation 1201 on an additional protocol on the rights of national minorities to the European Convention on Human

[5] COE PA Order No. 488 (1993), on the Honouring of Commitments Entered Into by New Member States.

Rights is concerned, it has not (yet) resulted in the adoption of an additional protocol. Recommendation 1201 is not legally binding. Yet, Article 15 para. 4 of the Treaty of Good Neighbourliness and Friendly Cooperation between the Slovak Republic and the Republic of Hungary provides that the norms and political commitments enshrined in Recommendation 1201 shall be applied, in respect of *inter alia* persons belonging to the Hungarian minority in the Slovak Republic, 'as legal obligations'. The Slovak Republic has ratified this Treaty with Hungary after a long discussion on the meaning of the territorial autonomy mentioned in Article 11 of Recommendation 1201.

Article 2 of the Framework Convention, states that 'the provisions of this framework Convention shall be applied (...) in conformity with the principles of good neighbourliness, friendly relations and co-operation between States'. On 9 December 1998, the Slovak Government approved the Protocol between the Ministry of Foreign Affairs of the Slovak Republic and the Ministry of Foreign Affairs of the Republic of Hungary concerning the creation of a mechanism facilitating the application of the Treaty. On its basis, 11 mixed expert commissions would gradually be set up, one of which will engage in national minority issues. The Slovak Government assigned the ministries responsible the task of ensuring that the mixed commissions started to operate by the end of January 1999.

- The second commitment is to adopt legislation granting to every person belonging to a minority the right to use his/her surname and first names in his/her mother tongue and, in the regions in which substantial numbers of a national minority are settled, the right for the persons belonging to this minority to display in their language local names, signs, inscriptions and other similar information, in accordance with the principles contained in Recommendation 1201 (1993) (para. 9 of Opinion No. 175). These commitments correspond with Art.11-14 of the Framework Convention.
- The third commitment is to continue to eliminate from Slovak legislation all the laws or decrees adopted by previous governments which are likely to contain elements discriminating against a group of persons or an ethnic, national community living on its territory, particularly those concerning 'collective guilt' (para. 11 of Opinion No.

175). These commitments correspond with Article 4 of the Framework Convention and Article 14 of the ECHR.[6]

In 1999 the Monitoring Committee (rapporteurs G. Magnusson and J. Sinka) presented a thorough report on the Honouring of Obligations and Commitments by Slovakia[7] in which the developments in Slovakia were assessed in an 'essentially positive' way. Consequently, the draft recommendation proposed, *inter alia,* to close the then current monitoring procedure and recommended to the Committee of Ministers to 'address the minority issues mentioned in the text when monitoring the implementation of the Framework Convention on the Protection of National Minorities'.[8] The minority issues mentioned were the consequences of the law on the State language, the need for a law on the use of minority languages, and the measures to address the problems of the Roma population.

1.2.2 **Romania**

The specific political commitments which Romania entered into are listed in Opinion No. 176 (1993) on the application by Romania for membership of the Council of Europe. In general, the following commitments on the part of Romania can be deduced from the text of Opinion No. 176: Although the Assembly

> 'appreciates the written declaration of the Romanian authorities in which they commit themselves to basing their policy regarding the protection of minorities on the principles laid down in Recommendation 1201 (1993) on an additional protocol on the rights of national minorities to the European Convention on Human Rights', it further:
>
> - calls 'upon the Romanian Government to return property to the churches and to permit the establishment and operation of church schools with a particular view to teaching children of minority groups their mother tongue' (para. 8 of Opinion No. 176).
> - urges the Romanian authorities 'to implement improvements in conditions of detention. It also calls upon the competent Romanian

[6] See Chapter 7 of present study which deals with the Beneš Decrees.

[7] Monitoring Committee, Doc. No. 8496, 6 September 1999, Honouring of Obligations and Commitments by Slovakia, (rapporteurs: Magnusson, Sinka).

[8] Monitoring Committee, Doc. No. 8496, 6 September 1999, p. 5.

political leaders to reconsider in a positive manner the issue of releasing those persons imprisoned on political or ethnic grounds' (para. 9 of Opinion No. 176).

- proposes that the Romanian authorities and the Romanian Parliament: adopt and implement as soon as possible, in keeping with the commitments they have made and with Assembly Recommendation 1201, legislation on national minorities and education;
- makes use of all means available to a constitutional State in order to combat racism and anti-Semitism, as well as all forms of nationalist and religious discrimination and incitement thereto.
- Finally, the Assembly recommends that Romania ratifies the European Charter for Regional or Minority Languages as soon as possible.[9]

In 1997, the Parliamentary Assembly observed in a resolution that Romania had 'made considerable progress towards the fulfilment of her obligations and commitments since joining the Council of Europe on 7 October 1993' and 'it takes note of the Romanian authorities' resolve to further the rights of national minorities and especially to amend the 1995 Education Act so as to allow mother tongue instruction for members of national minorities'. However, the Assembly still urged Romania 'to be firmly committed to fighting racism, xenophobia and intolerance, particularly in respect of the Rom population, while committing itself to basing its policy regarding the protection of minorities upon the principles laid down in Recommendation 1201 (1993)'. Concretely, the Assembly asked Romania to 'promote a campaign against racism, xenophobia and intolerance and take all appropriate measures for the social integration of the Rom population'.[10]

---

[9] The European Charter for Regional or Minority Languages was ratified by Slovakia in September 2001 with several reservations (http://conventions.coe.int/treaty/EN/cadreprincipal.htm). The European Charter for Regional or Minority Languages was signed by Romania on 17 July 1995, but has not been ratified. In 2003, the Department for Inter-ethnic Relations at the Ministry of Public Information yet prepared a Bill to ratify the European Charter for Regional or Minority Languages. This Bill has been sent to the ministries for opinion and comment. The European Charter for Regional or Minority Languages has not been signed by Bulgaria.

[10] COE PA Resolution 1123 (1997), on the Honouring of Obligations and Commitments by Romania.

Finally, considering that Romania has honoured her most important obligations and commitments, the Assembly decided to close the monitoring procedure. In its recommendation to the Committee of Ministers the Assembly added that 'in view of the remaining obligations and commitments, which Romania is bound to fulfil within a year, the Assembly recommends that the Committee of Ministers aid Romania's efforts to, *inter alia*, carry out a campaign against racism, xenophobia and intolerance.[11]

1.2.3 **Bulgaria**

The political commitments which Bulgaria entered into when applying for membership of the Council of Europe are listed in Opinion No. 161 (1992). However, this Opinion contains no references at all to minorities and only provides general information (similar texts can be found in the Opinions concerning Slovakia and Romania) to the effect that 'the Republic of Bulgaria is able and willing: i. to fulfil the provisions of Article 3 of the Statute (...) ii. to collaborate sincerely and effectively in the realisation of the aim of the Council of Europe as specified in Chapter I of the Statute of the Council of Europe thereby fulfilling the conditions for accession to the Council of Europe as laid down in Article 4 of the Statute'.

After two reports by the Monitoring Committee on Bulgaria's honouring of obligations and commitments[12], the Parliamentary Assembly of the Council of Europe was 'convinced that Bulgaria is committed to democratic reform and welcomes, *inter alia*, the ratification of the Framework Convention for the Protection of National Minorities'. However, with regard to minorities the Assembly also expressed its concern about 'the insufficient implementation of minorities' constitutional rights as regards education and information in their mother tongue through electronic media' and 'continuing cases of police brutality, particularly towards Roma'.[13] Notwithstanding those and several other points of

---

[11] COE PA Recommendation 1326 (1997), on the Honouring of Obligations and Commitments by Romania.

[12] Monitoring Committee Doc. 8616, 26 January 2000, Honouring of Obligations and Commitments by Bulgaria (rapporteurs: Atkinson and Gjellerod).

[13] COE PA Resolution 1211 (2000), on the Honouring of Obligations and Commitments by Bulgaria.

criticism of Bulgaria's honouring of obligations and commitments, the Assembly considered the current monitoring mechanism procedure to have been closed.[14] Consequently, after January 2000, further specific monitoring of Bulgaria's developments in the field of minority rights takes place within the monitoring mechanism of the Framework Convention.

1.2.4 **Conclusion**

Summarizing, the Opinions of the Parliamentary Assembly of the Council of Europe as adopted concerning the requests of Slovakia, Romania and Bulgaria for accession to the Council of Europe in the early 1990s, are rather cautious. Probably, in accordance with the political situation and the euphoria at that time – the Eastern-European Countries had just opened up – a very harsh criticism of the human rights situation in those States was not feasible. Also with regard to minorities, the Opinions are rather diplomatic and do not refer to the situation of specific minorities. Nevertheless, between the lines one can see the Assembly's concern as regards the Roma in Romanian prisons; concerning the consequences of the Beneš Decrees for the Germans in Slovakia; and with regard to the linguistic and cultural rights of the Hungarians in Slovakia and the Csangos in Romania.

The subsequent reports of the Monitoring Committee and the resolutions and recommendations of the Parliamentary Assembly are more explicit in their criticism of the way in which Slovakia, Romania and Bulgaria will honour their obligations and commitments, and frequently refer, in the case of Slovakia, Romania as well as Bulgaria, to the situation of the Roma and problems with the implementation of the linguistic rights of minorities.

The Opinions of the Parliamentary Assembly and the subsequent reports of the Monitoring Committee were part of a long process of political standard-setting and awareness of minority problems within the Council of Europe[15], a process which has (so far) resulted in the drafting

---

[14] *Idem.*

[15] In October 1990, part of this process was Recommendation 1134 of the Parliamentary Assembly where it recommended that the Committee of Ministers should draw up a protocol to the ECHR or a special Convention on the rights of minorities. In January 1993

and adoption, as well as the entry into force, of a legally binding document: the Framework Convention. The political requirements with regard to the protection of minorities laid down in these Opinions are incorporated by the legal standards of the Framework Convention. The work and reports of the Monitoring Committee are, as far as minority issues are concerned, continued by the monitoring mechanism of the Framework Convention.

1.3 The Council of Europe Framework Convention on the Protection of National Minorities: the Monitoring Mechanism

As described, this study will specifically deal with some of the standards concerning the protection of minorities as established within the Council of Europe's Framework Convention on the Protection of Minorities. The present section will discuss the monitoring mechanism of the Framework Convention and will list the relevant documents which relate to this monitoring mechanism, thus, the State Reports of Slovakia, Romania and Bulgaria. The subsequent Chapters of this study will elaborate on the contents and standards of the Framework Convention.

As far as the monitoring mechanism of the Framework Convention is concerned, Article 24 of the Convention determines that 'the Committee of Ministers of the Council of Europe shall monitor the implementation of this Convention by the Contracting Parties'.

This monitoring consists mainly of a system of reports which States have to transmit to the Secretary General of the Council of Europe. Subsequently, the Secretary General transmits this information to the Committee of Ministers. The aim of the first report, which has to be transmitted 'within a period of one year following the entry into force of this framework Convention in respect of a Contracting Party', is to provide full information on legislative and other measures which the Party

---

the Assembly adopted Recommendation 1201 containing a draft additional protocol on the rights of minorities to the ECHR. Although subsequent recommendations (see, for instance, Recommendation 1492 adopted in 2001) confirmed the need for an additional protocol, no major developments can be expected in the short term. See for more details, G. Pentassuglia, *Minorities in International Law*, Strasbourg, Council of Europe Publishing, 2002, pp. 127-129.

has taken in order to give effect to the undertakings set out in the Framework Convention. The purpose of the subsequent reports is to complement the information included in the first report.

In order to ensure the efficiency of monitoring the implementation of the Framework Convention, it provides for the setting up of an Advisory Committee. The task of this Advisory Committee is to assist the Committee of Ministers when it evaluates the adequacy of the measures taken by a Party to give effect to the principles set out in the Framework Convention. It has been up to the Committee of Ministers to determine, within one year of the entry into force of the Framework Convention, the composition and the procedures of the Advisory Committee, the members of which shall have recognised expertise in the field of the protection of national minorities.[16] The Advisory Committee held its first meeting in June 1998. In 2003, the Committee consisted of 18 members.[17]

As far as Slovakia, Romania and Bulgaria are concerned, special attention will be paid in this study to the documents listed hereunder which relate to the monitoring system of the Framework Convention:

- Report submitted by the Slovak Republic pursuant to Article 25 paragraph 1 of the Framework Convention for the Protection of National Minorities.[18]
- Report submitted by Romania pursuant to Article 25 paragraph 1 of the Framework Convention for the Protection of National Minorities.[19]
- Report submitted by Bulgaria pursuant to Article 25 paragraph 1 of the Framework Convention for the Protection of National Minorities.[20]

[16] Articles 24 and 25 Framework Convention; Explanatory Report to the Framework Convention sub 93-96; Rules adopted by the Committee of Ministers on the monitoring arrangements under Articles 24 to 26 of the Framework Convention for the Protection of National Minorities (Resolution (97) 10, adopted by the Committee of Ministers on 17 September 1997 at the 601st meeting of the Ministers' Deputies).

[17]The composition of the Advisory Committee, its rules of procedure, and its meeting reports and can be found at <http://www.coe.int/T/e/human%5Frights/Minorities/>.

[18] ACFC/SR(1999)008, received 4 May 1999 (hereinafter: Slovak State Report, 1999).

[19] ACFC/SR(1999)011, received 24 June 1999 (hereinafter: Romanian State Report, 1999).

[20] ACFC/SR(2003)001, received 9 April 2003 (hereinafter: Bulgarian State Report, 2003).

- Opinion on Slovakia of the Advisory Committee on the Framework Convention for the Protection of National Minorities.[21]
- Opinion on Romania of the Advisory Committee on the Framework Convention for the Protection of National Minorities.[22]
- Comment of the Government of the Slovak Republic to the Opinion of the Advisory Committee on the Implementation of the Framework Convention for the Protection of National Minorities in Romania.[23]
- Comment of the Government of Romania to the Opinion of the Advisory Committee on the Implementation of the Framework Convention for the Protection of National Minorities in Romania.[24]
- Resolution of the Committee of Ministers on the implementation of the Framework Convention for the Protection of National Minorities by Slovakia.[25]
- Resolution of the Committee of Ministers on the implementation of the Framework Convention for the Protection of National Minorities by Romania.[26]

The State reports as submitted by the different States and the Comments of States on the Opinions of the Advisory Committee are rich sources of information on national legislation and standards and sometimes on national practice, as perceived by the different governments. As far as Bulgaria is concerned, the Bulgarian Government submitted its State report to the Council of Europe in 2003. Already in 1998, however, the Bulgarian Helsinki Committee published a Shadow report, which was adopted by the Committee of Ministers on 30 September 1998 at the 642nd meeting of the Ministers' Deputies[27]. In 2003, the Bulgarian Helsinki Com-

---

[21] ACFC/INF/OP/I(2001)001, adopted on 22 September 2000 (hereinafter: Advisory Committee Opinion on Slovakia, 2000).

[22] ACFC/INF/OP/I(2002)001, adopted on 6 April 2001 (hereinafter: Advisory Committee Opinion on Romania, 2001).

[23] GVT/COM/INF/OP/I(2001)001, published 6 July 2001 (hereinafter: Slovak Comment, 2001).

[24] GVT/COM/INF/OP/I(2002)001, published 10 January 2002 (hereinafter: Romanian Comment, 2002).

[25] Resolution Res CMN(2001)5, adopted on 21 November 2001 (hereinafter: CM Resolution on Slovakia, 2001).

[26] Resolution Res CMN(2002)5, adopted on 13 March 2002 (hereinafter: CM Resolution on Romania, 2002).

[27] <www.bghelsinki.org>.

mittee published an Alternative report which comments and supplements the Bulgarian State Report of 2003. Alongside the Bulgarian Report of 2003, relevant information from the Shadow report and the Alternative Report will be used in this study.

The Opinions of the Advisory Committee and the Resolutions of the Committee of Ministers represent, in turn, the standards of the international community with regard to minority protection as reflected in the Council of Europe.

Apart from the above-mentioned international documents the following sources of information have been used in order to establish 'practice' and 'reality' with regard to minorities:

- The Constitutions and national legislation concerning non-discrimination and linguistic rights have been used as far as necessary to supplement the already detailed information on national legislation and implementation in the above-mentioned Reports submitted by the States to the Council of Europe. Further, especially with regard to the Roma, the different measures which are proposed and taken by the different governments have been analysed. These measures are the Slovak 'Strategy for the Solution of the Problems of the Roma National Minority and the Set of Measures for Its Implementation'[28], the Romanian 'Strategy of the Government of Romania for Improving the Condition of Roma'[29], and the Bulgarian 'Framework Program for Equal Integration of Roma in Bulgarian Society'[30].
- The actual situation of minorities ('reality') has been assessed through interviews with minority representatives and State representatives and analyses of the documentation of national and international (non-)governmental organizations such as the United Nations Development Program (UNDP), the Centre for Documentation and Information on Minorities in Europe (CEDIME), the European Roma Rights Center (ERRC), Amnesty International, and of the EU monitoring accession reports of the Open Society Institute. Finally, also information from the Radio Free Europe Newsline has been used.

---

28 <www.government.gov.sk/INFOSERVIS/DOKUMENTY/ROMSTRAT/en_romstrategia.shtml>.

29 </www.gov.ro/engleza/obiective/afis-index-diversedoc-eng.php?idrubrica'2>.

30 A full text of the Framework Program is available from the HRP at: hrproject@mbox.cit.bg.

1.4 Overview of this Study

Part I, entitled 'introduction' covers the first two Chapters of this study. Chapter 1 contains a general overview of the political commitments and legal obligations as established by the Opinions of the Parliamentary Assembly of the Council of Europe and the Framework Convention, respectively, for Slovakia, Romania, and Bulgaria. Chapter 2 will deal with the meaning and effect of population censuses, because their results are often used as a basis for the attribution of rights or the denial of rights to minority groups.

The remaining Chapters of this study have been divided into three parts: Part II (Chapters 3, 4, 5, 6, 7 and 8) and Part III (Chapters 9, 10, 11, 12 and 13) will discuss two of the standards of the Framework Convention in further detail: Part II will deal with non-discrimination, in particular the Roma minority in Slovakia, Romania and Bulgaria, and the Turkish minority in Bulgaria while Part III will discuss the linguistic rights of minorities, specifically in relation to the Hungarian minority in Romania and Slovakia and the Roma. Part IV will contain a summary, overall conclusions, observations and recommendations.

Chapter 2
COUNTING MINORITIES

2.1 The Freedom to Identify or Not to Identify: Article 3(1) Framework Convention

From time to time States organize population censuses in order to establish, inter alia, the composition of the population and to give citizens an opportunity to identify or not to identify themselves as members of a minority group. Such a census, however, is more than a statistical instrument and in itself it often has a certain effect. Apart from the practical problems which the organization of a census must overcome, such as bilingual questionnaires and a classification of the different minorities, a census is able to awake nationalistic sentiments, often expressed by different 'census awareness campaigns'. Ultimately the results of a census can also lead to different interpretations and can be used for different purposes.

As follows from Article 3(1) of the Framework Convention on National Minorities 'every person belonging to a national minority shall have the right freely to choose to be treated or not to be treated as such and no disadvantage shall result from this choice (...)'. However, it must be emphasised that, according to the Explanatory Report, the freedom to choose in Article 3 'does not imply a right for an individual to choose arbitrarily to belong to any national minority' and that '[t]he individual's subjective choice is inseparably linked to objective criteria relevant to the person's identity'.[31] Section 2.4 will describe how the aspects of an 'arbitrary choice' and of the 'objective criteria' become relevant when the Roma population needs to be determined.

[31] Explanatory Report to the Framework Convention on the Protection of National Minorities (hereinafter: Explanatory Report), sub 35.

2.2 Practical Problems with a Census

In May 2001, a census was held in Slovakia.[32] During this census, for the first time since 1945, bilingual census questionnaires (Slovak-Hungarian, Slovak-Ruthenian, Slovak-Ukrainian and Slovak-Romanes) were prepared to cover regions with significant minority populations. The Slovak *Minority Language Law of 1999* specifies a 20 % threshold; however, bilingual census papers were not used in cities with large Hungarian communities such as Bratislava/Pozsony (over 20,000 ethnic Hungarians) or Kosice/Kassa (over 10,000 ethnic Hungarians). Further, some infringements were reported in some Galanta/Galáánta District settlements where the Hungarian population amounts to 40 %, and in Hornéé Saliby/Fels oszeli (70 %) census takers did not have bilingual questionnaires available, as was reported by the Hungarian-language daily ÚÚj Szóó.[33]

Another practical problem was the formulation of different rubrics which had to cover the different minorities. In the absence of a definition of 'minorities' in the Framework Convention and in Romanian, Slovak or Bulgarian legislation, States have a margin in determining which groups qualify for the status of 'minority'. In Romania, for instance, in the 1992 census[34] the 'other nationalities' rubric included persons who had declared themselves to be Csangos (2,062 persons in 1992). Since they did not constitute a separate minority according to the census list, they were not entitled to the same rights as the other minorities on the list.

Remarkably, these facts were interpreted in different ways: the Romanian Government held that with regard to the freedom to identify, or not to identify, oneself with the name used to designate a particular ethnic group, 'the provisions of Article 3 of the Framework Convention on National Minorities have been rigorously adhered to by the Romanian authorities'. [35]

However, the opinion of the Advisory Committee was that:

> 'since Romanian law says nothing about the conditions for recognition of minorities, it appears that some authorities take the view that the Csangos do not

[32] For the results of this census, see Annex II.

[33] Hungarian Human Rights Foundation (HHRF) – ÚÚj Szóó (Bratislava/Pozsonvi), 22 May 2001.

[34] See Annex II.

[35] Comment of Romania sub 17: comments on Article 3.

> constitute a minority, and are not therefore entitled to the same rights as the minorities listed earlier. The Advisory Committee took the view that, given the historic presence of the Csangos in Romania and the specific elements of their identity, the Romanian authorities should favourably consider the extension of the Framework Convention to persons stating that they are members of this community and should explore this question in consultation with the representatives of the Csangos.'[36]

The reaction of the Romanian Government to this Opinion of the Advisory Committee seems to lack any logic: First, in its Comments on the Opinion of the Advisory Committee, the Government of Romania confirmed that 'the persons who declared themselves to be Csangos are also included among "other nationalities as an ethnic/national group"' and then it repeats that 'the provisions of Article 3 have been rigorously adhered to by the Romanian authorities'.[37] Subsequently it is stated that 'during the next population census, to be carried out in March 2002, the intention is to ensure that all persons belonging to national minorities have the right freely to choose and declare their membership of an ethnic/national group to state another name for a national group'.[38] In the end, the census of 2002 did not mention the Csangos as a separate group.

Also in a Bulgarian census of 1992[39] the different rubrics caused some confusion: the census showed great diversity within the group of Muslims. Some identified themselves as ethnic Bulgarians whose religion is Islam (70,251), others as Muslim Bulgarians, Bulgarian Mohammedans or Pomaks (65,546), and still others as Turks whose mother tongue is Bulgarian (25,540). It might be logical to classify all three categories as 'Pomaks' as the majority of those people are descendants of Bulgarians who were forcibly converted to Islam during the 14th to 19th century of Ottoman domination. Greek academics and activist movements promote the thesis of the existence of a Pomak nation, but such views are not popular in Bulgaria. Quite a few Muslims even find the term 'Pomak' offensive. The inconsistency of such ideas is also confirmed by the large-scale voluntary conversion of Pomaks to Christianity.[40]

---

[36] Advisory Committee Opinion on Romania, 2001, sub 18. See Chapter 9.

[37] Romanian Comment, 2002, sub 18.

[38] *Ibid.*, sub 21.

[39] The census of 2001 had only one rubric of 'Turks', see Annex II.

[40] See Chapter 6.

In order to prevent such practical problems in the future the Advisory Committee advised that the respective governments should consult minorities - especially through the Council of National Minorities (in Romania), which has already shown an interest - on the organization of a census, and particularly the content of the forms. It also favours the idea of recruiting and training observers from minority groups, who could play a useful role in making minorities understand the importance of the census.[41]

2.3 Effects of a Census

The effect of a census might be that it awakes different emotions and voices. The census of 2001 in Slovakia serves to provide some examples: At a press conference Viliam Obenhauser, Vice-President of the Slovak National Party, called on the population to declare themselves to be Slovak, regardless of their native language, during the national census which was then in progress. 'Those who consider the Slovak Republic as their homeland are of Slovak nationality,' he contended.[42] Minority organizations also launched their own census awareness campaigns urging those belonging to minorities to freely declare their nationality.[43] Csemadok (the main cultural organization of Hungarians in Slovakia), for instance, launched a census-awareness campaign entitled 'Declare Yourself!' The aim of the program, which included billboards, leaflets and town meetings throughout the country, was to encourage ethnic Hungarians to declare their nationality during the 2001 census. In the previous 1991 census, more than 567,000 persons declared themselves to be ethnic Hungarians, while 612,000 indicated Hungarian as their native language.[44]

In 1991, in the census held across Czechoslovakia, only 80,000 people living in Slovakia declared themselves to be of Roma origin. However, estimates of the true figure range as high as 500,000. As far as the Roma are concerned, Roma leaders were unhappy about the fact that of the

[41] Advisory Committee Opinion on Romania, 2001, sub 21.

[42] ÚÚj Szóó (Bratislava/Pozsonvi), 26 May 2001. <www.hhrf.org/monitor/105slo.htm>.

[43] HHRF, 25 May 2001, ÚÚj Szóó (Bratislava/Pozsonvi), 26 May 2001.

[44] HHRF, 2 May 2001, ÚÚj Szóó (Bratislava/Pozsonvi) 10 and 16 May 2001 and Magyar Nemzet (Budapest), 10 May 2001.

22,000 officials working on the 2001 census only 100 were Roma. Edmund Mueller of the office for the legal protection of Roma in Košice, said that he thought the government would manipulate the census figures, just as had been done in the previous one in 1991. Roma leaders therefore launched a 'just census' campaign demanding that there should be 617 Roma census officials, one for every Roma settlement in Slovakia. They dismissed suggestions that there would not be enough qualified Roma to fill their 'quota', arguing that many Roma have a driver's licence, which is evidence that they are literate and therefore competent to conduct the census. The Roma leaders would be satisfied if some 300,000 Roma declared themselves to have Roma nationality, which would be a great deal more than the 76,000 who did so in the previous census. The Slovak government met one of the Roma demands: in localities where over one fifth of the population were Roma the census forms are to be both in Slovak and Roma.[45] The biggest problems arose in South Slovakia where many Roma traditionally states their nationality to be Hungarian.

Also in Romania the official authorities have to cope with the fact that some people try to use the census for political or personal ends: Under article 90 of the Romanian Public Administration Law of 2001[46], if a national or ethnic minority makes up over 20 % of the population of a given administrative unit, they have the right to street signs, schools, and official proceedings in their own language. The 1992 census figures showed that 23 % of Cluj's population was composed of ethnic Hungarians. However, the then mayor of Cluj, Mr. Funar, who is known for his hostility to ethnic Hungarians, believed that the Hungarians do not make up more than 10 % of the population of Cluj. Unlucky for Mr. Funar, in 2002 a new law came into effect in Hungary: the Status Law, which gives special privileges to Hungarians living as national minorities in Romania and other countries bordering Hungary.[47] The Roma of Cluj are for the most part of ethnic Hungarian descent and there has been a rush of Roma, as well as ordinary Hungarians, to apply for Hungarian identity cards which was made possible by the Hungarian Status Law. Nevertheless Mr. Funar tried to persuade the Roma of Cluj to admit that they are Roma when the census collectors visit them and has even threatened to person-

[45] CTK-Czech News Agency, 1 May 2001; RFE/RL Newsline, 31 April 2001.

[46] Law No. 215 on Local Public Administration, 23 April 2001.

[47] See Chapter 7.

ally visit anyone in the town who claims to be Hungarian on the census form, in order to verify their claim.[48] This story is not only indicative of the effects which a population census might have on human, especially Mr. Funar's, behaviour, but also of the result of such a census. In particular, the numbers belonging to the Roma population as a rule demonstrate a discrepancy between the official result and the 'reality' estimates.

2.4 The Result of a Census

As the following data show, doubts can also be cast on census results:

In the *Slovak Republic*, official data (2001 census) report 89,920 people to be of Roma identity, or 1.7 % of the population. However, the Minority Rights Group estimates the number to be between 480,000 to 520,000, or 9-10 % of the total population. This would make the Roma the second largest minority in the Slovak Republic, after the Hungarians. It would also mean that Slovakia has one of the highest per capita populations of Roma in the world.[49]

Also in *Romania* there is a remarkable discrepancy between the official statistics in the census figures and the estimates made by representatives of national minorities, especially where the Roma minority is concerned. Official data (1992 census) count 409,723 Roma, or 1.8 % of the population. Different expert estimates place this figure at around 1.5 million, or 6.5 % of the population. Other estimates report between 1.4 million and 2.5 million Roma, making this group the largest Roma population in Europe and possibly the world. The Romanian government issued the following comment on this fact:

> 'As regards the data submitted by the organizations representing the various minorities – and particularly those representing the Roma/Gypsy minority – these are no more than the subjective views of their authors, as the respective estimates are based on statistical surveys or other sources of evidence. The measures taken for carrying out the 2002 census will help secure more accurate results, especially given the growth of awareness of their identity among the Roma/Gypsy minority, a process fostered by the measures the Romanian

---

[48] Nick Thorpe, BBC News Online, 27 March 2002.

[49] European Roma Rights Center (ERRC), *Time of the Skinheads, Denial and Exclusion of Roma in Slovakia*, 1997, p. 9.

Government has taken since 1992 to preserve and promote this minority's ethnic, cultural and linguistic identity.'[50]

Also in *Bulgaria*, there is a discrepancy between the census data and a series of surveys by independent authors. Official data (2001 census) report 365,797 people to be of Roma identity or 4.7 % of the population. Different experts' estimates (data from sociological polls, labour offices, the social assistance service, Ministry of Interior) vary between 600,000 and 750,000, without showing any essential changes over the last few years. This suggests not only that the real number of Roma is far larger, but also that the number of people who identify themselves as being Turks should be modified.

The UNDP mentions a number of factors which both complicate the task of determining the size of Roma populations and result in official demographic data systematically undercounting the number of Roma. The first reason reflects the desire to avoid the 'ghetto stigma', especially in countries where the word 'Roma' has become synonymous with poverty, marginalisation, and exclusion. Fears of anti-Roma discrimination in the labour market, and in education and health systems, are a second reason. Measurement difficulties also stem from the fact that, in social surveys, Roma populations (especially when Roma communities are relatively small and live among other minority populations) tend to identify themselves as being affiliated with local ethnic or religious majorities. As described in Bulgaria, Roma living in areas populated primarily by ethnic Turks tend to identify themselves as Turks, even though they may not speak Turkish.[51] However, the phenomenon of 'preferred ethnic self-identity' – the public declaration of another, non-Roma, ethnic identity – is widespread among the Roma, and the censuses in Slovakia and Romania indicate that this is not only a typical Bulgarian phenomenon. In Romania and Slovakia many Roma consider themselves to be Hungarians.

---

50 Romanian Comment, 2002, sub 2.

51 United Nations Development Program (UNDP), *Avoiding the Dependency Trap*, Bratislava, 2002, pp. 24-25. Through this report, the UNDP and the International Labour Organization (ILO) have undertaken a comprehensive quantitative survey of the Roma minorities in five Central and Eastern European Countries (Bulgaria, the Czech Republic, Hungary, Romania, and the Slovak Republic).

Although Article 3 of the Framework Convention contains a very broad concept of self-identification stating that 'every person belonging to a national minority shall have the right freely to choose to be treated or not to be treated as such', the practice of choosing a preferred ethnic identity as, for various reasons, applied by many Roma, clearly exceeds the scope of this broad concept. According to the Explanatory Report to the Framework Convention, Article 3 'does not imply a right for an individual to choose arbitrarily to belong to any national minority'. Subsequently, the Explanatory Report contains some criteria: 'the individual's subjective choice is inseparably linked to objective criteria relevant to the person's identity'. Considering the fact that a definition of minorities is lacking in all international and national documents concerning minorities, what are these objective criteria? Moreover, how objective are 'objective criteria? '[52]

Clarifying in this respect is the distinction made by the UNDP between, on the one hand, the 'extended self-determination approach to self-identification'. This refers primarily to cultural and behavioural dimensions of individual identity, which 'complement ethnic self-identification with opinions of professionals working with Roma or with Roma issues (teachers, social workers, doctors, police etc.) or opinions of the interviewers (whether of market research or scientific studies)'.On the other hand, UNDP points to the existence of an identity which is imposed by a social context.

> 'This identity is imposed by the surrounding majority culture. Within the imposed identity pattern, a person from a distinct group is not regarded as an individual with individual characteristics (education, income, etc.), but instead as a carrier of group characteristics. According to these views, it does not matter how educated a Roma may be: being Roma automatically implies illiteracy. Imposed identification is a major factor behind refusals to self-identify as Roma.'[53]

Summarizing, Article 3 of the Framework Convention imposes on States the obligation that minorities shall have 'the right freely to choose to be treated or not to be treated as such and no disadvantage shall result from

[52] A.K. Meijknecht, *Towards International Personality: The Position of Minorities and Indigenous Peoples in International Law*, Intersentia, Antwerp, 2001, pp. 77-86.

[53] UNDP, 2002, p. 24.

this choice'. The explanatory report, however, seriously limits the scope of the words 'freely to choose' by stating that this choice may not be arbitrary.

Censuses organized once in a while by States enable all citizens to exercise their right (not) to identify themselves as belonging to a minority. States prefer a low number of Roma (and of other minorities as well, see the example of Mr. Funar) in the census because of the census effect: a low census number implies less measures, less attention to complicated minority problems and, most importantly, less expenditure. Individual Roma contribute to this low census number: when asked 'to identify or not to identify', many Roma prefer not to identify themselves as Roma but, for several reasons, as Hungarians or Turks. For the Roma as a group, however, this attitude has a reverse effect: an official low number of Roma means less money and less attention and consequently less opportunities. The consequences are that the census results are unreliable and that census results, especially the number of Romas, are often amended by experts and non-governmental organizations.

As far as Roma are concerned, the words 'freely to choose' and 'no disadvantage' in Article 3 are unrealistic. First, the limitations mentioned in the explanatory report make it difficult for Roma to deny their identity. Subsequently, the unofficial estimations confront States, the whole world and especially the Roma who – notwithstanding the limitations in the explanatory report – have 'escaped' their identity by choosing another, with the fact that the Roma are far more prevalent than the census result shows.

Article 3 imposes certain obligations on States which they cannot possibly completely fulfil, especially in the case of the Roma. As will be described in the next chapter, identification as a Roma implies several disadvantages such as severe discrimination, not only by the State or local authorities, but particularly by other citizens, an area which is difficult to influence from 'above' by States.

2.5 Administrative Divisions

Not only census results, but also territorial and administrative divisions are relevant for minorities. Both Article 16 of the Framework Convention and Article 15 para. 2 (d) of the Treaty on Good Neighbourliness and

Friendly Co-operation between the Slovak Republic and the Republic of Hungary (19 March 1995) provided that the Parties shall refrain from measures which alter the proportions of the population in areas inhabited by persons belonging to national minorities.

For instance, in Slovakia,[54] where the process of public administration reform has been taking place since 1990 as part of the instigated political and social changes, the Act on Territorial and Administrative Divisions particularly affected the Hungarian minority in Southern Slovakia. In the summer of 2001 this even led to a serious government crisis when the Hungarian Coalition Party (SMK) threatened to leave the coalition if this new law was not amended. Finally, under national and international pressure the Act was amended and the SMK confirmed that the conditions for remaining in the cabinet had been 'largely implemented'.[55]

On the one hand, protection of minorities implies meaningful participation in political life on an equal basis with the majority. On the other hand, the protection of minorities also means the implementation and protection of specific minority rights. The threshold of 20 % for the minority population, which depends on an objective and accurate census and on fairly drawn administrative territorial borders, is linked to several important minority rights, such as the right to use the minority language in contacts with the authorities and to use street names in the minority language. Therefore, in Slovakia, the census results of 2002 and the positive resolution of the crisis concerning the Act on Territorial and Administrative Divisions were crucial for the implementation of some minority rights.

2.6 Conclusions

The reason for paying so much attention to the population censuses is that their results form the basis not only for internal political and social rela-

---

[54] As far as Romania and Bulgaria are concerned, changes in administrative divisions have not been reported as currently amounting to an important issue. See Romania's comment on article 16 in the Romanian State Report of 1999 and the Advisory Committee Opinion on Romania, 2001, sub. 72. In Bulgaria, according to both the Shadow Report of the Bulgarian Helsinki Committee of 1999 (p. 61) and the Bulgarian State Report of 2003 (p. 71), 'the 1999 new district administrative territorial division, does not affect in any way the rights and freedoms derived from the Framework Convention'.

[55] RFE/RL Newsline Vol. 5, No. 184, Part II, 27 September 2001.

tions, but also for the implementation of international legal obligations on the part of States and the attribution of rights and obligations on minorities. As the above example of the *Romanian Public Administration Law* shows, in some cases the 20 % threshold can be crucial. With all the practical problems, political effects and inaccurate results the censuses are a feeble basis and this must be kept in mind when taking financial and political measures and drafting laws concerning minorities.

The real figures cannot be proved, but might be completely different, especially when Roma are concerned. All the countries in Central and Eastern Europe are being pressured by the European Union to tackle Roma issues. Responses to these pressures are complicated by the absence of basic information about the numbers of these peoples. Roma often avoid identifying themselves as Roma, in order to escape prejudice (or being stigmatised). As a consequence, Roma populations are usually much larger than the figures officially registered during censuses. This leaves the magnitude of the region's 'Roma problem' unclear, and creates risks in interpreting and generalizing from the official data that are available. [56]

'International standards in practice and reality' is the leading theme in this study. The analysis of the Framework Convention has started with Article 3, an article with, at first sight, an obvious content. However, after placing this article in a practical context, the contours of a particular problem appear: the standard set by Article 3 is unrealistic.

Are the standards set by other Articles of the Framework Convention unrealistic as well? How great is the discrepancy between international law and practice? Is this gap widening and is international law becoming more and more an inspiring but unattainable ideal, or is it narrowing and is international law providing States with practical and workable guidelines and rules? In the following chapters, the inquiry into the relation between international (minority) law in theory and in practice will be pursued with an analysis of the way in which the Articles concerning non-discrimination and linguistic rights in the Framework Convention have been implemented in Slovakia, Romania and Bulgaria.

---

[56] UNDP, 2002, p. 23.

Part II
NON-DISCRIMINATION

Chapter 3
INTERNATIONAL STANDARDS AND NATIONAL PRACTICE

3.1 International (UN) Standards

The widespread and very complex phenomenon of discrimination does not only affect persons belonging to a minority group. Therefore, not only the Council of Europe Framework Convention, but every international document drafted within the framework of the United Nations dealing with human rights, such as the Universal Declaration of Human Rights of 1948 (UDHR)[57]; the International Covenant on Civil and Political Rights of 1966 (ICCPR)[58]; the International Covenant on Economic, Social and Cultural Rights of 1966 (ICESCR)[59]; the International Convention of the Rights of the Child of 1989[60], and almost every national Constitution contains a non-discrimination standard.

Article 1(1) of the International Convention on the Elimination of All Forms of Racial Discrimination of 1966 (ICERD) defines racial discrimination as follows:

> 'Any distinction, exclusion, restriction or preference based on race, color, descent, or national or ethnic origin which has the purpose or effect of nullifying or impairing the recognition, enjoyment or exercise, on an equal footing, of human rights and fundamental freedoms in the political, economic, social, cultural or any other field of public life.'

3.2 European Standards

3.2.1 The Council of Europe Framework Convention on the Protection of National Minorities

Long before the adoption of the Framework Convention, the Council of

57 Articles 1 and 2 UDHR.
58 Articles 2 (1) and 26 ICCPR.
59 Articles 2 (2) and 3 ICESCR.
60 Article 2 International Convention of the Rights of the Child.

Europe showed its concern with regard to different forms of discrimination in specific States on different occasions. As described in Chapter 1, Opinion 175 of the Council of Europe Parliamentary Assembly contained a special obligation for Slovakia to 'eliminate from its legislation all the laws or decrees adopted by previous governments which are likely to contain elements discriminating against a group of persons or an ethnic, national community living on its territory, particularly those concerning 'collective guilt' [the Beneš Decrees]'.[61] Council of Europe Parliamentary Assembly Opinion No. 176 urged Romania 'to make use of all means available to a constitutional State in order to combat racism and anti-Semitism, as well as all forms of nationalist and religious discrimination and incitement thereto'.[62] And, as far as Bulgaria is concerned, the Parliamentary Assembly highlighted in a Resolution on Bulgaria's Honouring of Obligations and Commitments 'continuing cases of police brutality, particularly towards Roma'.[63]

Gradually, with the ratification of the Framework Convention by the different States, these specific requirements laid down in the Opinions of the Parliamentary Assembly merged with the more general legal principles laid down in the Framework Convention.

According to its Explanatory Report, the aim of the Framework Convention on the Protection of National Minorities 'is to specify the legal principles which States undertake to respect in order to ensure the protection of national minorities'.[64] These legal principles are brought together in the *Framework* Convention, thus, a Convention containing 'mostly program type provisions setting out objectives which the Parties undertake to pursue. These provisions, which will not be directly applicable, leave the States concerned a measure of discretion in the implementation of the objectives which they have undertaken to achieve, thus enabling them to take particular circumstances into account.'[65] However, this large measure of discretion left to States results in the Explanatory Report underlining that the '[implementation] of the principles set out in this Framework Convention shall be done through national legislation and ap-

---

[61] COE PA Opinion No. 175 (1993).
[62] COE PA Opinion No. 176 (1993).
[63] COE PA Resolution No. 1211 (2000).
[64] Explanatory Report to the Framework Convention, sub 10.
[65] *Ibid.*, sub 13.

propriate governmental policies'.[66] Although this dependence on national legislation and governmental policies is often presented as one of the strengths of the Framework Convention ('enabling to take particular circumstances into account'), it might also appear to be its Achilles' heel especially, in the case of non-cooperative States or very complex minority problems.

The central Article on non-discrimination in the Framework Convention is Article 4.[67] Paragraph 1 reflects the 'classic'[68] approach to non-discrimination proclaiming the right of equality before the law and of equal protection of the law for persons belonging to national minorities. Paragraphs 2 and 3 are more interesting from the minorities' point of view as they make possible a – limited – possibility of positive discrimination. In Paragraph 2, States 'undertake to adopt, where necessary, adequate measures in order to promote, in all areas of economic, social, political and cultural life, full and effective equality between persons belonging to a national minority and those belonging to the majority. In this respect, they shall take due account of the specific conditions of the persons belonging to national minorities. Paragraph 3 underlines that 'the measures adopted in accordance with paragraph 2 shall not be considered to be an act of discrimination'.

According to the Explanatory Report to the Framework Convention 'adequate measures' in Article 4 Paragraph 2, means 'in conformity with the proportionality principle, in order to avoid violation of rights of others as well as discrimination against others. This principle requires, among other things, that such measures do not extend, in time or in scope, beyond what is necessary in order to achieve the aim of full and effective equality'.[69]

Also Paragraph 2 of Article 6 of the Framework Convention refers to non-discrimination and contains for States the difficult assignment 'to take appropriate measures to protect persons who may be subject to threats or acts of discrimination, hostility or violence as a result of their ethnic, cultural, linguistic or religious identity'. However, the Explanatory Report does not specify the term 'appropriate measures'.

---

[66] Explanatory Report to the Framework Convention, sub 11.

[67] See Annex I.

[68] Explanatory Report to the Framework Convention, sub 39.

[69] *Idem.*

Finally, Article 12 Paragraph 3 of the Framework Convention, in which Parties 'undertake to promote equal opportunities for access to education on all levels for persons belonging to national minorities' is relevant in the context of non-discrimination. In the next Chapter this latter issue will be discussed in relation to education for Roma children.

3.2.2 **The EU Race Directive**

In 2000, two significant developments broadened the scope of the European standard of non-discrimination: the EU Race Equality Directive and Protocol No. 12 to the ECHR.

In June 2000, the European Council of the European Union issued a directive 'Implementing the Principle of Equal Treatment Between Persons Irrespective of Racial and Ethnic Origin', the 'EU Race Equality Directive'. According to Article 2.1 of the Directive 'the principle of equal treatment shall mean that there shall be no direct or indirect discrimination based on racial or ethnic origin'. In the Directive direct discrimination is considered to occur 'when one person is treated less favourably than another is, has been, or would be treated in a comparable situation on grounds of racial or ethnic origin'.[70]

Indirect discrimination occurs, according to the Directive, 'where an apparently neutral provision, criterion, or practice would put persons of a racial or ethnic origin at a particular disadvantage compared with other persons, unless that provision, criterion or practice is objectively justified by a legitimate aim and the means of achieving that aim are appropriate and necessary'.[71]

The Directive poses high expectations on States by explicitly prohibiting direct and indirect discrimination by public and private actors in the public sphere in social security, health, and housing. Moreover, it is stated that governments that do not overturn existing discriminatory laws may violate the Directive.[72]

---

[70] Council Directive 2000/43/EC of 29 June 2000, Article 2.1.2.a.

[71] *Ibid.*, Article 2.1.2.b.

[72] *Ibid.*, Article 3.1. See also: Ina Zoon, *On the Margins, Roma and Public Services in Slovakia*, Open Society Institute, 2001, pp. 14-15; Ina Zoon, *On the Margins, Roma and Public Services in Romania, Bulgaria, and Macedonia*, Open Society Institute, 2001, pp. 17-18.

As far as the status of the EU directives for candidate Member States is concerned, they form a part of the *acquis communautaire*, the body of law which all States whishing to join the EU must adopt. Therefore Romania, Bulgaria and Slovakia are expected to incorporate the Race Directive before they joint the EU. For EU Member States the deadline for the transposition of the Race Equality Directive was in July 2003. However, 'not a single Member State has yet succeeded in transposing all provisions of the Directive into their national law'.[73]

3.2.3 **Protocol No. 12 to the ECHR**

Parallel to the adoption of the EU Race Directive, Council of Europe Protocol No. 12 to the European Convention on Human Rights and Basic Liberties (ECHR)[74] was opened for signature on 4 November 2000.[75] This Protocol broadens the scope of Article 14 ECHR: in the Preamble the Member States of the Council of Europe declare that they are 'resolved to take further steps to promote the equality of all persons through collective enforcement of a general prohibition of discrimination by means of the [ECHR]'. Further the Preamble reaffirms that 'the principle of non-discrimination does not prevent States Parties from taking measures in order to promote full and effective equality, provided that there is an objective and reasonable justification for those measures'.

Article 1 of Protocol No. 12 reads as follows:

> '(1) The enjoyment of any right set forth by law shall be secured without discrimination on any ground such as sex, race, colour, language, religion, political or other opinion, national or social origin, association with a national minority, property, birth or other status.
> (2) No one shall be discriminated against by any public authority on any ground such as those mentioned in paragraph 1'.

---

[73] Joint Statement of the European Roma Rights Center (ERRC) and the International Helsinki Federation for Human Rights (IHF) to the OSCE Conference on Discrimination, Racism and Xenophobia, Vienna, 4-5 September 2003. PC.DEL.106/03, 11 September 2003.

[74] CETS No. 177. By June 2004, this Protocol had not (yet) been ratified by Slovakia or Romania and Bulgaria had not (yet) signed it.

[75] The Protocol will enter into force three months after the date on which ten Member States of the Council of Europe have expressed their consent to be bound by the Protocol. This is not yet the case (June 2004).

Protocol No. 12 expands the anti-discrimination standard of the ECHR in several ways: 'in the enjoyment of a right specifically granted to an individual under national law; in the enjoyment of a right which may be inferred from a clear obligation of a public authority under national law, that is, where a public authority is under an obligation under national law to behave in a particular manner; by a public authority in the exercise of discretionary power (for example, granting certain subsidies); and by any other act or omission by a public authority (for example, the behaviour of law enforcement officers when controlling a riot)'.[76]

3.2.4 **Conclusion**

Although this study deals, in the first place, with the Framework Convention, other developments concerning the prohibition of discrimination within the other European instruments cannot go unnoticed; future membership of the EU and the ratification of the ECHR and the signing of Protocol No. 12 appear to be strong inducements for States to adjust their national legislation with regard to, among other things, non-discrimination.

Each in its own way, the Framework Convention, the EU Race Directive and Protocol No. 12 to the ECHR attribute to the development of the standard of non-discrimination: the Framework Convention by developing the concept of positive discrimination, the EU Race Directive by explicitly prohibiting both direct and indirect discrimination, and Protocol No. 12 by containing affirmative duties for States to prevent some forms of discrimination among private persons.

Protocol No. 12, when it enters into force, has an advantage over the Framework Convention and the Race Directive in that it is linked to the supervisory mechanism of the ECHR, which means that there is a possibility of bringing individual complaints before the European Court of Human Rights.

A negative aspect of both the Framework Convention (Article 30) and Protocol No. 12 (Article 2) is that they enable States to specify the territory or territories to which this Protocol shall apply. In fact, this might mean that minority groups who inhabit a specific region in a State, such

[76] Explanatory Report to Protocol No. 12 to the ECHR, sub 22.

as the Hungarians who live in southern Slovakia, can be excluded from the effect of the Framework Convention and Protocol No. 12.

3.3 The Relation Between International Law and National Law

Slovakia, Romania and Bulgaria are State parties to most of the Conventions and Documents which have been mentioned and are bound by their provisions as well as being obliged to transpose them into their national legislation or allow international (human rights) law to take precedence over national law.

In Slovakia, an amendment to the Constitution in 2001[77] established the precedence of international human rights law over Slovak law. In its Article 7 Paragraph 5 the Slovak Constitution proclaims that:

> 'International treaties on human rights and fundamental freedoms, international treaties whose executions does not require an act and international treaties which directly establish rights or obligations of natural persons or juridical persons and which were ratified and promulgated as required by law shall take precedence over the laws.'

In Romania Article 11(2) of the Constitution establishes the relationship between international legal regulations and Romanian domestic law by stating that: '[t]reaties ratified by Parliament in accordance with the law are part of national law'. However, this Article 11 must be interpreted in conjunction with Article 20, which is worded as follows:

> '(1) Constitutional provisions concerning citizens' rights and freedoms shall be interpreted and enforced in conformity with the Universal Declaration of

[77] Constitutional statute No. 90/2001 Coll. amending and supplementing the Constitution of the Slovak Republic No. 460/1992 Coll. as amended. Constitutional statute No. 90/2001 Coll. was adopted on 23 February 2001 by the required qualified majority within the National Council of the Slovak Republic with effect from 1 July 2001.The old text in Article 11 reads as follows: 'International treaties on human rights and basic liberties that were ratified by the Slovak Republic and promulgated in a manner determined by law take precedence over its own laws, provided that they secure a greater extent of constitutional rights and liberties'.

> Human Rights and with the covenants and other treaties to which Romania is a party.
> (2) Where inconsistencies exist between the covenants and treaties on fundamental human rights to which Romania is a party and internal laws, the international regulations shall take precedence.'

In its State Report Romania underscores that this priority which is given to international regulations is recognised only for international regulations in the sphere of human rights and that 'the solution adopted in Article 20 (...) is a modern solution, which expresses not only an attachment to international regulations but also a readiness to embrace their potential dynamism. At the same time, the correlation between international regulations and domestic law does not alter or reduce the major role which national legislation plays in proclaiming and guaranteeing human rights. That is so because the State is and remains the framework within which human rights and fundamental freedoms are realised'.[78]

In Bulgaria, according to Article 5, paragraph 4 of the Constitution, all international treaties which are ratified pursuant to the constitutional procedure and are officially published are considered to be part of the domestic legislation and take precedence over those domestic acts which contradict them.

As former socialist States, all three States emanate from a strict dualist tradition, which 'required a specific national legislative act before treaty obligations could be implemented and had to be respected by national authorities'.[79] After the reforms in Eastern Europe, in most States this strict dualist approach to international law was somewhat mitigated to make room for international human rights law. In Slovakia and Romania human rights law has acquired a position which is superior to national law. In Bulgaria, however, all international law forms an integral part of the national order, and takes precedence over contradicting domestic legislation.

---

[78] Romanian State Report, 1999, sub 3.

[79] P. Malanczuk, *Akehurst, Modern Introduction to International Law*, Seventh Revised Edition, Routeledge, London, 1997, p. 68.

3.4 THE STANDARD OF NON-DISCRIMINATION IN NATIONAL LAW

3.4.1 Minorities in the National Constitutions

The national constitutions of the majority of States which have a heterogeneous population composition contain provisions establishing the existence and the position of minority groups living in the their territories. Already in the Preamble or in the first article constitutions frequently deal with this issue. For instance, the Preamble to the Slovak Constitution[80] reads as follows:

> 'We, the Slovak nation (...) together with members of national minorities and ethnic groups living on the territory of the Slovak Republic, in the interest of lasting peaceful cooperation with other democratic States, seeking the application of the democratic form of government and the guarantees of a free life and the development of spiritual culture and economic prosperity, that is, we, citizens of the Slovak Republic, adopt through our representatives the following Constitution.'

From this construction it is clear that 'we, the Slovak nation' refers to an ethnic nation and not to a political one which could include all the population of the country. The consequence of using the principle of nationality in the Preamble to the Constitution is that this Preamble divides the citizens of Slovakia into two categories: First, individuals belonging to the Slovak nation, and second, those individuals who do not belong to the Slovak nation, thus, members of ethnic minorities. The Hungarian Coalition Party (SMK) opposed this formula and proposed another instead: 'We, the citizens of the Slovak Republic'. According to Kusý, the introduction of the principle of citizenship instead of the nationality principle in the legislation would give equal rights to all citizens of the Slovak Republic and would equally make them the subjects of civil and political rights.[81]

After some vehement debate the Constitution was amended, and the formula as proposed by the SMK was adopted. However, this discussion

---

[80] The Constitution was passed by the Slovak National Council on 1 September and signed on 3 September 1992. In 2001 the Slovak parliament adopted several amendments to the Constitution.

[81] Kusý, Miroslav, 'L'udské práva', in: Kollár, Miroslav, Meseznikov, Grigorij (eds.), Slovensko 2000, *Súhrnna správa o stave spoločnosti*, Bratislava, 2000, p. 169.

gives an impression of the political sensitivity of issues relating to Slovakia as a State in which several large (Hungarians and Roma) and some smaller minorities live alongside the Slovak majority.

The Romanian Constitution[82] has no Preamble at all. However, Article 1(1) defined Romania as 'a sovereign, independent, unitary and indivisible National State' and according to Article 4 (1): 'The State foundation is laid on the unity of the Romanian people'. According to the Democratic Alliance of Hungarians in Romania (DAHR, established in 1989) this new Constitution 'did not sufficiently take into account the existence of Romania's 16 national minorities'. The phrase was also interpreted as potentially suggesting that members of national minorities are 'inferior' citizens against whom the State may discriminate.[83] The pressure upon minorities (especially the Hungarian minority) which had to declare their loyalty to the State and to commit themselves to complying with the Romanian Constitution is also a point of concern.[84]

In fact, only the Preamble to the Bulgarian Constitution, which was adopted on 12 July 1991, contains the neutral text: 'We, the Members of the Seventh Grand National Assembly, guided by our desire to express the will of the people of Bulgaria (...)'.Unfortunately, this does not mean that minority problems are non-existent in Bulgaria.

3.4.2 **Non-discrimination in National Legislation**

In a fairly self-assured manner, the Slovak Report of 1999 underlines that Slovakia 'has a long record in the issues of securing the rights of persons belonging to national minorities. The population's current structure of nationalities, which explicitly shows the correctness of the policy of respecting the legitimate interests of national minorities on the one hand, and securing the State's role on the other, is also an outcome of historical development.'[85]

---

[82] The Romanian Constitution was amended the Law for the Revision of the Constitution of Romania, No. 429/2003, which came into force on 29 October 2003. As far the Articles 1(1), 4 (2), 6(2), and 16(1) are concerned, the text of the Romanian Constitutions of 1991 and 2003 is identical.

[83] Zhidas Daskalovski, *Different people, different destinies: Transylvanian Hungarians,* CST Transylvania, <www.rrz-uni-hamburg.de/AEGEE/CST-TRANS/e_zhidas.html>.

[84] See: Andreescu, 1999, pp. 1-2 (Comment I, Part I).

[85] Slovak State Report, 1999, p. 7.

As far as non-discrimination standards in Slovak national law are concerned, there is no special law that deals solely with non-discrimination. Provisions concerning non-discrimination are scattered over many different laws and regulations.

The first Paragraph of Article 12 of the Slovak Constitution provides that '[a]ll people are free and equal in both their dignity and rights. (...)'. Paragraph 2 provides that: '[b]asic rights and freedoms on the territory of the Slovak Republic are guaranteed to everyone regardless of (...) race, colour of skin, language, faith and religion, (...), affiliation to a nationality or ethnic group, (...). No one must be harmed or discriminated against on these grounds'(...). However, a victim of discrimination cannot press charges and seek a remedy in respect of discrimination alone, but only in connection with another statutory provision or Article of the Constitution.[86]

In other provisions of national legislation, such as Article 196 Criminal Code[87], which deals with violence against a group of inhabitants or an individual, and Article 11 of the Slovak Civil Code[88], discrimination is addressed directly or indirectly.[89] For a long time Slovak law lacked a definition of discrimination, but the new Labour Code, which entered into force on 1 April 2002,[90] prohibits discrimination, defines indirect discrimination, shifts the burden of proof in discrimination cases and enables compensation to be given to victims of discrimination.

Hrubala is rather positive with regard to current Slovak law and considers potential sanctions in Slovak law against perpetrators 'to be adequate for protecting victims against all kinds of harassment mentioned in Article 2 paragraph 3 [of the EU Race Directive]', and he adds that since the introduction of the new Labour Law 'any unwanted conduct related to racial or ethnic origin, which takes place with the purpose or effect of violating the dignity of a person and of creating an intimidating, hostile,

[86] Jan Hrubala, 'Legal analysis of national and European anti-discrimination legislation', part of a joint project entitled *Implementing European Anti-Discrimination Law*, ERRC, Interrights, Migration Policy Group, 2001, pp. 9-10.

[87] Act No. 140/1961 coll.

[88] Article 11 of the Slovak Constitution provides that 'natural persons have the right to the protection of personhood, in particular, life and health, civil honour and human dignity, as well as privacy, name and manifestations of personal nature'.

[89] See for a detailed description of national legislation on non-discrimination, Ina Zoon, 2001 Slovakia, pp. 18-20; Hrubala, 2001, pp. 8-32.

[90] The new Slovak Labour Code, Act No. 130/2001 Coll.

degrading, humiliating or offensive environment, can be considered as a unlawful act'. However, he also highlights the problem that 'public authorities sometimes refuse to recognise or underestimate the racial motivation of (...) unwanted conduct', and underlines the necessity of a definition of 'ethnic' harassment.[91]

The European Roma Rights Center is less satisfied with Slovakia's record of implementing international law concerning non-discrimination: 'Slovak law currently affords little effective protection from discrimination. The few existing legal provisions relating to discrimination are rarely, if ever invoked, rendering the rights detailed in them effectively illusory. In the absence of adequate anti-discrimination legislation, Roma are subject to discrimination in almost every aspect of their life (...).'[92]

Also the European Commission has indicated that Slovakia needs to continue to update its laws with regard to non-discrimination as part of the accession process.[93] Currently, however, efforts to adopt new legislation are paralysed by a political discussion as to whether it is better to review all existing laws or to approve a single anti-discrimination law.[94] Such single anti-discrimination law already exists in the form of the (draft) Act on Equal Treatment and Act on Establishment of the Center for Equal Treatment. These Acts contain definitions of different forms of discrimination, including direct and non-direct discrimination, harassment, and victimization. On the institutional level, the currently existing system for the protection of human rights will be amended by two new bodies: the ombudsman for the public, and the Center for Equal Treatment for the private sector. The new institutions are expected 'to give new impetus to the fight against discrimination and will cooperate with already existing structures, such as the courts, prosecutors and other specific State bodies, and will help to enforce the law more vigorously'.[95]

---

[91] Hrubala, 2001, p. 12.

[92] Written Comment by the European Roma Rights Center Concerning the Slovak Republic for Consideration by the United Nations Human Rights Committee at its 78th Session, 14 July – 8 August 2003 (hereinafter: ERRC, 2003).

[93] European Commission, 2000 Regular Report from the European Commission on Slovakia's Progress Towards Accession (8 November 2000), p. 54.

[94] Martina Pisarova, 'Anti-discrimination law on agenda again', in: *The Slovak Spectator*, 22-28 September 2003.

[95] Information on the Newly Proposed Anti-Discrimination Legislation of Slovakia, Draft as of 16 August 2001, prepared by the Center for Legal Analyses-Kalligram Foun-

According to the ERRC, 'the failure of the Slovak Parliament to even consider anti-discrimination legislation seriously calls into question the commitment of Slovak authorities to take action against discrimination, including the particularly serious harm of racial discrimination'.[96]

The Romanian Constitution declares in Article 4(2) that 'Romania is the common and indivisible homeland of all its citizens, without any discrimination on account of race, nationality, ethnic origin, language, religion, gender, opinion, political affiliation, property, or social origin'. The second Paragraph of Article 6 of the Romanian Constitution relates, rather minimally, to discrimination of minorities where it states that 'the protecting measures taken by the Romanian State for the preservation, development, and expression of identity of the persons belonging to national minorities shall conform to the principles of equality and non-discrimination in relation to the other Romanian citizens'. Finally, Article 16 adds that '[c]itizens are equal before the law and public authorities, without any privilege or discrimination'.[97] As far as non-discrimination is concerned, the Romanian State Report of 1999 does not contain any information that goes beyond a formal description of the existing Constitutional texts.

More interesting – from the perspective of anti-discrimination legislation – than the Constitution is Statutory Ordinance No.137 On Preventing and Punishing All Forms of Discrimination, adopted by the Romanian Government in August 2000.[98] This ordinance refers not only to discrimination based on race or ethnicity, but also on nationality, language, religion, social category, beliefs, sex or sexual orientation, appurtenance to a disadvantaged category or any other criterion (Article 2.1). Law 48/2002 on Prevention and Punishment of All Forms of Discrimination, however, does not include an explicit prohibition of indirect discrimination or of structural discrimination, nor does it define or sanction harassment.[99]

---

dation and the Section on Human Rights and Minorities – the Government Office of the Slovak Republic.

[96] ERRC, 2003.

[97] See also Ina Zoon, 2001, pp. 27, 79, 118.

[98] In 2002, Ordinance No. 137 was ratified as Law 48/2002 on Prevention and Punishment of All Forms of Discrimination.

[99] Romanita Iordache and Andreea Tabacu, 'Not Yet Viable: Anti-discrimination Action in Romania', in: *Roma Rights*, No. 1-2, 2003, p. 2.

Further, a provision for the reversal of the burden of proof in discrimination cases is lacking.[100]

Further, Ordinance No. 137 deals with several manifestations of discrimination: in employment and economic activity, in education, freedom of movement, choice of residence and access to public places. The Ordinance is determined to eliminate discrimination 'by means of affirmative action (...) and sanctions instituted against discriminatory behaviour (...).'[101]

Undoubtedly, by referring to all possible groups and individuals and addressing all kinds of discrimination, Ordinance No. 137 and Law 48/2002 are important legal tools in combatting discrimination. However, this new legislation has not yet demonstrated its true value in practice.[102] According to Claude Cahn of the ERRC, 'close to three years after its adoption, problems with implementation have rendered [Ordinance No.137] to date all but a dead letter'.[103]

The Bulgarian Constitution, Article 6, declares in its first Paragraph that 'all persons are born free and equal in dignity and rights'. In its second Paragraph it is added that 'all citizens shall be equal before the law', and that '[t]here shall be no privileges or restriction of rights on the grounds of race, nationality, ethnic self-identity, sex, origin, religion, education, opinion, political affiliation, personal or social status, or property status'.

For a long time, Bulgaria lacked further comprehensive anti-discrimination legislation.[104] However, on 16 September 2003, an anti-discrimination law was adopted by the Bulgarian Parliament. This new bill provides for extensive uniform protection against discrimination on a large number of grounds, including gender, race/ethnicity, religion/belief, disability, age and sexual orientation. The bill goes beyond the minimum standard of the EU Race Directive in also prohibiting racial segregation. Also the concepts of discrimination, incitement, victimisation and harass-

---

[100] *Ibid.*, pp. 2-3.

[101] Article 2.5 of Ordinance No. 137.

[102] R. Weber, *Report on the Measures to Combat Discrimination in the 13 Candidate Countries (VT/2002/47) , Country Report Romania*, May 2003, pp. 13-14.

[103] Claude Cahn, 'Roma Rights and Anti-Discrimination Law', in: *Roma Rights*, No. 1-2, 2003.

[104] See also Ina Zoon, 2001, pp. 43, 91, 133.

ment as defined under the bill are broader than the ones under the EU Race Directive and the Employment Directive.[105]

As far as minorities are concerned, the bill permits measures to ensure participation by persons belonging to ethnic minorities in education and training insofar as and as long as necessary. In terms of positive action on grounds of race or ethnicity, under the bill the authorities have 'a duty to encourage and facilitate sufficiently representative participation, in governance and decision-making by persons belonging to ethnic, religious, and linguistic minorities'. Further, 'employers have a duty, where needed, to guarantee equal treatment and equal opportunities, to encourage applications from prospective employees belonging to underrepresented ethnic groups and, where all other conditions are equal, to encourage career-building and participation for employees belonging to underrepresented ethnic groups'.[106]

The bill provides for a specialised independent Commission with broad powers to enforce anti-discrimination law, and to promote equality of opportunity on all protected grounds.[107]

In a reaction to the adoption of this new law, ERRC Executive Director Dimitrina Petrova stated: 'This law is of particular significance for Roma. It opens the door for the provision of real and significant remedies to Romani victims of the very serious harm of racial discrimination, and moves Roma rights issues to a new level in Bulgaria. The Bulgarian Parliament has provided real political leadership to the governments of other countries of the Central and Eastern European region – and indeed of Europe – by demonstrating that adopting comprehensive anti-discrimination law is both possible and desirable.'[108] However, in its Alternative Report the Bulgarian Helsinki Committee shows less optimism about this new Act: 'even after the preparation and adoption of such law it is doubtful as to whether and when effective enforcement of the anti-discrimination provisions would take place. Roma and Muslims (Turks and Pomaks) continue to be underrepresented in local governing administration and

[105] Directive 2000/78/EC.

[106] Margarita Ilieva, 'The Bulgarian Draft Anti-Discrimination Law: An Opportunity to Make Good on the Constitutional Promise of Equality in a Post-Communist Society', in: *Roma Rights*, No. 1-2, 2003.

[107] *Idem.*

[108] RFE/RL Newsline Vol. 7, No. 179, Part II, 19 September 2003.

law-enforcement institutions even in regions where they form an actual majority.'[109]

3.5 Conclusion and Overview

The implementation of International and European (EU and Council of Europe) standards concerning non-discrimination in national legislation is progressing in fits and starts. The non-discrimination provisions in the three national Constitutions are rather correct with regard to minorities (except for the Preamble of the Slovak Constitution), but not too generous in the sense of positive discrimination of minorities. For a long time, further national anti-discrimination legislation was insufficient (Romania)[110], scattered over many different laws and regulations (Slovakia), or simply non-existent (Bulgaria). New anti-discrimination legislation is of a very recent date in all States. However, it is not the standards concerning non-discrimination as laid down in the Articles 4 and 6 of the Framework Convention, but rather Protocol No. 12 to the European Convention of Human Rights (still not yet in force) and, in particular, EU Directive No. 2000/43/EC (EU Race Directive), which appear to motivate States to draft (Slovakia) and adopt (Romania and Bulgaria) national legislation concerning non-discrimination. It is remarkable that in Romania and Bulgaria, whose accession to the EU will probably not take place before 2007, the desire to already implement the *acquis communitaire*, *inter alia*, the EU Race Directive, has led to far-reaching and detailed legislation on non-discrimination.

Unfortunately, the problem of discrimination can not be solved with the adoption of national legislation only. In fact, the problem of discrimination does not lie in the sphere of the implementation of international standards in national legislation, but in the transformation of national legislation into concrete and effective measures.[111] In sum, there is a great discrepancy between, on the one hand, international and national legal standards as described in the present chapter, and reality, as experienced

[109] Bulgarian Helsinki Committee, Alternative Report, 2003, p. 10.

[110] Advisory Committee Opinion on Romania, 2001, sub 22.

[111] See, for instance, Advisory Committee Opinion on Slovakia, 2000, sub 18: 'the Advisory Committee is particularly concerned about problems related to the implementation of such legislation in practice...'

by Roma, Hungarians, Moslems, Germans and other minorities in Slovakia, Romania and Bulgaria, on the other hand. This 'reality' will be discussed in the next three Chapters.

Chapter 4 will deal with the Roma in particular. Although there are many other minorities who face discrimination as well, the complexity and intensity of the discrimination against the Roma justifies a separate Chapter on this problem. Several aspects will be discussed in the light of discrimination: education, employment, poverty, housing and healthcare. Subsequently, in Chapter 5, we will discuss the way in which the Slovak, Romanian and Bulgarian governments try to 'bridge the gap' between standards and 'reality'. Chapter 6 will describe two specific forms of discrimination: the situation of the Bulgarian Muslims and the right to use their own names, and the German and Hungarian minorities in Slovakia and the consequences of the Beneš Decrees. Chapter 7 will contain concluding remarks with regard to the implementation of the standard of non-discrimination in Slovak, Romanian and Bulgarian practice and reality.

Chapter 4
THE ROMA MINORITY IN SLOVAKIA, ROMANIA AND BULGARIA

4.1 Introduction

Not only reports by governmental organizations, such as the OSCE Report on the Situation of the Roma, and by non-governmental organizations, such as the ERRC, but everyone who travels to Slovakia, Romania and Bulgaria and visits the Roma settlements (ghettos) will arrive at the same conclusions: the above-mentioned international and national non-discrimination provisions are not reflected in practice as far as the Roma minority is concerned. The fact that the Roma in Slovakia, Romania and Bulgaria are a minority which face discrimination in almost every field of everyday life: in housing policy, health care, in education, in employment, and in public places such as restaurants, theatres, shops, trains, cannot be brushed under the carpet.

Notwithstanding these visible facts, according to the Slovak State Report of 1999, 'Interethnic relations between the citizens of the SR can be assessed as satisfactory. However, certain manifestations of intolerance are a part of life in every society. The SR is no exception'.[112] The Report does not explicitly mention the situation of the Roma minority

4.2 The Roma: Recent History

The present situation of the Roma cannot be understood without some knowledge of, especially, the recent communist past of Slovakia, Romania and Bulgaria.

Roma populations in Central and Eastern Europe have traditionally engaged in non-agrarian activities, but as the demand for traditional Roma skills declined, Roma communities increasingly became a source of cheap labour for quickly expanding, heavy industries.[113]

---

[112] Slovak State Report, 1999, p. 16.

[113] UNDP, 2002, p. 21.

During the communist period, policies towards the Roma were broadly consistent with the regimes' ideological framework. Within this framework attempts were made to 'melt' ethnic and individual distinctiveness into a homogeneous class of labourers. Working-class homogenization was expected to eradicate ethnic distinctions or at least to make their significance negligible compared to class characteristics. Since they do not own land, Roma populations were often seen as ideal subjects for social experimentation. The social engineering initiatives applied to the Roma included:

- Obligatory employment in the State and cooperative sectors;
- Administrative allocation of housing to the Roma from State funds for the socially disadvantaged, without regard to cultural patterns;
- Dispersion by settling/intermingling Roma families among majority communities;
- Enforcement of the statutory requirement that children attend school;
- Obligatory Roma participation in the health care system (immunization, periodical medical checks).[114]

The Roma under communism were better off in virtually every aspect, although this progress came at the cost of lost traditional cultural and economic patterns. According to a UNDP survey, Roma tend to view their current situation negatively in comparison to 'past memories'. During the socialist period, a significant part of the population essentially belonged to the middle class. These groups had access to goods and services. Asked in informal discussion what they miss most from the socialist period, Roma subsequently answer 'the opportunity to have a vacation with the whole family with the majority population in company tourist resorts'.[115] However, this improvement appeared to be unsustainable, as was the economic growth during the socialist period. Since socialism provided important benefits, Roma groups in a sense were tied to the socialist ideological construct, and were left particularly vulnerable by its collapse.

[114] *Ibid.*, pp. 14-15.
[115] *Ibid.*, p. 17.

4.3 The Social Context of the Roma

The phenomenon of discrimination against Roma cannot be analyzed without describing the social situation of the Roma and the interaction between Roma and the majority population.

According to several public opinion polls, the inhabitants of Slovakia generally have the most positive attitude towards the Czechs, and the most negative attitude towards the Roma. As many as 80 % of Slovak inhabitants indicated that they would be uncomfortable if Roma moved into their neighbourhood. The Roma receive negative evaluations as regards their criminal activities, the avoidance of legitimate jobs, poor hygiene, alcohol abuse, noise and trustworthiness. This negative conception of the Roma is common to the majority of Slovak inhabitants.[116]

Also in Romania the Romanians and the Hungarians (the largest minority in Romania) have a rather negative image of the Roma. When asked: 'which of the following attributes best characterize the Roma from Romania?', 16.1 % of the Romanian and 14.4 % of the Hungarians answered: 'lazy', 16.1 % and 18 % respectively, said the Roma are 'dirty', and 20.9 % of the Romanians and 16.4 % of the Hungarians considered them to be 'thieves'.[117]

What type of interactions do members of the majority have with Roma? As follows from a survey by the UNDP and ILO, the prevailing answer in Slovakia and Bulgaria was: 'Just ordinary contacts from living in the same neighbourhood'. Almost 90 % of all respondents claimed that they had daily contacts. Only in Romania is this share substantially lower: 79 %. Contacts 'intermediated by children' was the second largest response, 60 % on average for the region. Some 59 % of the respondents in Bulgaria maintain informal relationships ('have a beer together'). The frequency of Roma inter marriage with majority communities and with other Roma groups ranges from 19 % with majority communities to 73 % with other Roma groups in Bulgaria.[118]

Negative forms of interaction between Roma and the majority population are, on the one hand, the crimes commonly associated with the

---

[116] Vašečka, 1998, pp. 404-405.

[117] See: Ethnocultural Diversity Resource Center (EDRC), *Ethnobarometer, Interethnic Relations in Romania*, Cluj, 2000, p. 70.

[118] UNDP, 2002, pp. 69-70.

Roma, such as stealing crops and felling trees for firewood, and, on the other, crimes committed against the Roma.

In recent years, thefts by Roma have become a frequent occurrence in countries like Bulgaria, Romania and the Slovak Republic. Financial losses have become sufficiently serious to increasingly anger local farmers, adding an ethnic dimension to a classical petty crime issue.

According to a criminological survey conducted in Bulgaria, police statistics from 1993 to 1997 (when such data were collected) show that 'major crimes were committed by representatives of various ethnic groups with differing frequencies, and that the Roma share of committed crimes is higher than their share in the overall population.[119] However, it must be realized, as the UNDP does in its 2002 Report, that 'Roma crime is directly associated with poverty: the cost of complete compliance with the law is often starvation'.[120]

Among the factors mentioned by the UNDP which contribute to relatively high rates of Roma criminality are unfavourable economic circumstances, high unemployment rates, and the inefficiencies of the penal system. The most important new factor after 1989 is the high proportion of Roma who are addicted to drugs and gambling.[121] For a considerable part of the Roma population in the Slovak Republic, Romania and Bulgaria, petty crime is directly linked to extreme poverty. Therefore, as the UNDP suggests, 'better development opportunities, rather than improvements in penal systems, seem to be the key to reducing "Roma crimes"'.[122]

As far as crimes against the Roma are concerned, Roma themselves are, more often than other members of minorities, victims of racially motivated violence. There are numerous cases of skinheads attacking Romany young men, and also women.[123] According to a Slovak police officer the number of racially motivated crimes doubled in 2002. An explanation might be that the police pay 'more attention to crimes that used

---

[119] UNDP, 2002, p. 71, source: Crime rate in Bulgaria, Analysis for the period 1993 to 1997. Criminological survey, IMIR's archives, Sofia.

[120] *Idem.*

[121] *Ibid.*, p. 70-72.

[122] *Ibid.*, p. 70-72.

[123] See, for instance, the documentation by Romani CRISS (Roma Centre for Social Intervention and Studies), *Human Rights department Discrimination and Violence Cases*, January-October 2001; ERRC, *Time of the Skinheads*, 1997.

to be neglected and to the activities of extremist groups that were formerly treated with indifference'.[124]

Still another form of discrimination of Romani involves the behaviour of the police during investigations into racially motivated attacks against them. There are still many cases in which Roma are involved which are denied or not taken seriously by the police.[125] In general it can be said that the police's discriminatory behaviour in cases concerning Roma consists of:

- the denial of a criminal act after a racial attack against a Roma person;
- the denial of any racial dimension in an attack against a Roma person: the police assert that attacks against the Roma do not have a racial dimension because the Roma are not a separate race, but instead belong to one Indo-European race, along with the Slovaks (or Hungarians). Many victims of racially motivated violence have met with similar arguments;[126]
- misrepresentation of the claims after a racial attack against the Roma;
- the denial of public violence in general against the Roma.[127] Illustrative is a case reported by Amnesty International in its Annual Report (2003) of a conflict in Poprad, central Slovakia, between a bartender and a Rom which resulted in 15 young men attacking Romany homes and the injury of one Rom. According to Amnesty International, 'after arriving late, the police denied the incident was racially motivated and subsequently launched an investigation against a human rights lawyer who had criticized their behaviour'.[128]

Equally serious, however, is the occurrence of racially motivated violence against the Roma by the police themselves in Slovakia[129], Ro-

---

[124] RFE/RL Newsline Vol. 7, No. 75, Part II, 18 April 2003.

[125] ERRC, *State of Impunity, Human Rights Abuse of Roma in Romania*, 2001, Section 3, pp. 20-50. <www.errc.org/publications/reports/index.shtml>. See also Advisory Committe, Opinion on Slovakia, 2001, sub 28 and 29.

[126] Vašečka, 1998, p. 406.

[127] *Idem.*

[128] RFE/RL Newsline Vol. 7, No. 100, Part II, 29 May 2003.

[129] See for several cases of police raids in Romani communities: ERRC, *Time of the Skinheads*, 1997, pp. 36-53.

mania,[130] and Bulgaria[131] . For instance, in its Annual Report (2003) Amnesty International states that there are numerous reports of police torture and ill-treatment of detainees in Romania. Many of the victims of torture and ill-treatment are ethnic Roma the report says.[132] Not surprisingly, this form of violence is denied by the governments of Slovakia, Romania and Bulgaria respectively.

Several measures have been taken by the governments (see Chapter 5) and by citizens to better monitor and prevent racially motivated attacks. For instance, in Slovakia a hotline against racism was introduced for victims of racially motivated attacks. According to two lawyers who took the initiative for this hotline, many people do not know whom to contact, do not trust the police, or the police refuse to help them. Besides, only a small number of racially motivated attacks are reported to the police and almost no activities by the Neo-Nazis.[133]

As already said, discrimination is a very complex phenomenon, and the difficult social situation of the Roma is both the cause as well as the consequence of discrimination. In fact, this is only one of the vicious circles in which Roma find themselves. The following sections will describe several forms of discrimination against the Roma minorities in Slovakia, Romania, and Bulgaria.

4.4 Education

Roma criminality, as described in the above section, is often caused by poverty.[134] Poverty is linked to unemployment which is often caused by a lack of education. In Part III, the complex issue of minority language education (Article 14 of the Framework Convention) will be extensively dealt with. In this context, the teaching of (and in) the Roma language

---

[130] See for several cases of police raids in Romani communities: ERRC, *Sudden Rage at Dawn, Violence Against Roma in Romania*, 1996, pp. 11-21.

[131] See for several cases of police raids in Romani communities: Bulgarian Helsinki Committee, Alternative Report, 2003, pp. 12-13.

[132] RFE/RL Newsline Vol. 7, No. 100, Part II, 29 May 2003. Also see: ERRC, *State of Impunity,* 2001, pp. 40-50.

[133] RFE/ RL Newsline Vol. 5, No. 184, Part II, 27 September 2001.

[134] UNDP, 2002, pp. 70-72.

and the linguistic rights of the Hungarian minority in Slovakia and Romania will be discussed.

The present section will deal exclusively with the problem of discrimination of Roma in access to education (Article 12 Framework Convention). The scope of this problem justifies separate attention in this Part II on non-discrimination.

4.4.1. **Equal Opportunities for Access to Education (Article 12(3) Framework Convention)**

Article 12.3 of the Framework Convention states that 'the Parties undertake to promote equal opportunities for access to education at all levels for persons belonging to national minorities'.

The exclusion of Roma manifests itself in every sphere of social life, but exclusion from schooling has a more far-reaching and harmful effect. Discrimination in access to education occurs in different ways.

First, there is *de facto* segregation of schools and in schools. The following quote from Radio Free Europe, shows where the despair of the Roma children in Bulgaria with regard to their education opportunities might lead to:

> 'A group of 29 Romany children from Sofia's Fakultete ghetto announced on 21 May [2003] that they will sue the Education Ministry and the Sofia city administration for not providing them with adequate school education and equal opportunities. The attorney representing the group, said 'the ministry and the city administration have violated the children's rights by setting up segregated schools', and that she is prepared to take the case to the European Court of Human Rights if the Bulgarian courts fail to issue an acceptable ruling.'[135]

Schools in exclusively Roma neighbourhoods, the so-called neighbourhood schools, are reminiscent of the communist period. In 1998, there were around 100 such schools in Bulgaria. However, in order to improve the integration of the Roma children in Bulgarian society a rather successful 'desegregation program' was initiated by several Roma NGOs and adopted by the government. In Romania, quite remarkably, Roma children attend the same schools as Romanian-speaking or Hungar-

[135] RFE/RL Newsline Vol. 7, No. 96, Part II, 22 May 2003.

ian-speaking children. There are situations in which Roma children are grouped in separate classes. Where this is so, according to the Romanian Government, 'the decision of the head of the school simply reflects the fact that the children study in their mother tongue'.[136] In Slovakia, 'Roma schools' are increasingly tolerated by the public authorities. Most of the pupils attending these schools are of Romani origin. 'Some of these schools have been established by administrative decision; others have developed gradually as non-Roma parents transfer their children from schools with a high or growing percentage of Romani children.'[137] These schools are often poorly maintained, overcrowded, and the teachers lack standard educational qualifications. In 2001, the elimination of segregated classes for Roma did 'not figure in current government plans', and racial segregation in schools was even denied by the government.[138]

Another form of discrimination and segregation is the practice of placing Roma children in 'special schools' for the mentally retarded and for juvenile delinquents.[139] In all Central European countries Roma children outnumber non-Roma in schools for mentally retarded children, and in most cases there are no justified health-related grounds for this. In Bulgaria, according to some statistics, a third of the pupils in these schools are of Roma origin.[140] In the Slovak Republic, there are approximately 380 special schools for mentally and physically disabled children attended by roughly 31,000 students. A majority of Roma students from segregated villages in the Slovak Republic attend such schools. In Romania[141], according to official data there are 246 special schools, and the number of children with disabilities registered in those schools was 48,237.[142]

Finally, there is a large group of Roma children who, for various reasons, do not attend school at all. According to UNDP data, Roma children are heavily over represented among school-age children who do not

---

[136] Romanian Comment, 2002, sub 58.

[137] Monitoring the EU Accession Process: Minority Protection in Slovakia, Open Society Institute, 2001, p. 446 (hereinafter: OSI AP Report on Slovakia, 2001).

[138] *Ibid.*, p. 447.

[139] Monitoring the EU Accession Process: Minority Protection in Bulgaria, Open Society Institute, 2002, p. 92 (hereinafter: OSI AP Report on Bulgaria, 2002).

[140] Bulgarian State Report, 2003, p. 66. See for several projects pp. 66-68.

[141] ERRC, *State of Impunity,* 2001, pp.106-110.

[142] UNDP, 2002, p. 55.

attend school. In Bulgaria, Roma drop-outs are estimated to be between 22,000 and 66,000. Data from a representative survey conducted for the needs of the Social Assessment of Childcare in Bulgaria show that 8 % of surveyed households have a school-aged child or children not attending school. The highest drop-out rate is among Roma (32 %), followed by Bulgarians (8 %) and Turks (6 %). Field research conducted by the Institute for Minority Studies in Bulgaria shows that, out of 100 Roma children entering school, only five (three boys and two girls) have the opportunity to pursue a secondary education, and of these, only one has an opportunity to receive a higher education. [143]

During its visit to Romania the Advisory Committee of the Council of Europe identified as one 'particularly unacceptable' cause of absenteeism the lack of food. 'It is clear,[...] that Roma children are proportionally far more affected than others by school absenteeism associated with their parents' inability to pay for their daily meal.'[144] Subsequently the Advisory Committee proposed that the Committee of Ministers should recommended that the Romanian authorities 'tackle this problem as a matter of urgency'.[145]

The high drop-out rate of Roma children is also a serious problem in Slovakia. As far as the education of Romany children is concerned, the 1999 Slovak Report to the Council of Europe stated, very optimistically, that:

> 'the education of Romany students is carried out in normal primary school classes. Students with specific educational needs can, beginning from the 1998/99 school year, attend 'specialized classes' in the first and second year of primary school, which focus on the specific educational needs of pupils with an emphasis on the development of their communication skills and reinforcement of their knowledge of the State language. The State Pedagogical Institute in Bratislava became the expert co-ordinator of the education of this group of pupils.'[146]

---

[143] *Ibid.*, p. 54.

[144] Advisory Committee Opinion on Romania, 2001, sub 57.

[145] Proposal for Conclusions and Recommendations by the Committee of Ministers, concerning Article 12, in: Advisory Committee Opinion on Romania, 2001. However, the Committee of Ministers did not follow this proposal, see: CM Resolution on Romania, 2002.

[146] Slovak State Report, 1999, p. 28.

However, in practice, very few Romani children attend kindergarten and Romani pupils in the elementary schools demonstrate much less progress than do the children in the majority population. Few Romani children attend secondary schools and the number of Romani university students is statistically negligible.

Results of psychological tests have shown that children from Romani settlements are discriminated against because of their environment and subsequently they are often ranked within a lower intelligence range. According to Michal Vašečka, this is caused by 'the underdeveloped environment in Romani settlements, and by insufficient education and lack of preparation for life within the family'.[147] Therefore, the Slovak Report identifies as one of the goals of the education of Romany children and students 'the gradual modification of values within Romany families so that education becomes an accepted value and precondition for resolving social, cultural and economic problems, with support from the Roma themselves'.[148]

Quite differently, the UNDP concludes on the basis of surveys that there are two systemic reasons for exclusion in education: poverty and the perpetuation of the ghetto culture. Discrimination is often an effect rather than a cause, and unless the systemic causes are dealt with, Roma children will continue to have negligible educational opportunities. Poor families cannot provide children with clothes and books – the basic items necessary for school. Poverty also limits access to education by requiring that Roma children be engaged in income generating activities, or by helping to raise younger siblings.[149]

A successful way to avoid future exclusion from education appears to be pre-school education for Roma children. According to the UNDP,

> 'poor knowledge of majority languages, as well as social differences between school and their local communities, are major barriers to Roma children's failure to attend school. Pre-school attendance can help to bridge these social differences. (...) If Roma children are included in the education system from

[147] Michal Vašečka, 'The Roma', in: Slovakia 1998-1999, Meseznikov, Grigorij, Ivantyšyn, Nicholson (ed.), *A Global Report on the State of Society*, Bratislava, 1999, p. 408. See further, Dostál, 2000, pp. 185-186.

[148] Slovak State Report, 1999, p. 27.

[149] UNDP, 2002, pp. 61-62.

the very beginning, they have better chances of avoiding the spiral of poverty, unemployment, and marginalisation.'[150]

For instance, for several years in Plovdiv, Bulgaria, summer pre-school courses for bilingual children have been organized by a local Roma NGO. Each pre-school group had a professional teacher and an assistant teacher from the Roma community. The results were impressive. Within four months the children had acquired the necessary proficiency in the Bulgarian language and an important knowledge of society 'outside the neighbourhood'.When school began the Roma children were already well integrated with the rest of the children. Subsequent monitoring showed that the drop-out rate was negligible. Subsequently, the Bulgarian Parliament amended the Public Education Act in September 2002, making pre-school education obligatory and financed by the State budget.[151]

According to the Romanian Comment, the reasons why Roma children drop out of compulsory schooling are economic and not institutional. As part of the Romanian Government's Strategy for improving the situation of the Roma minority (see below), several measures have been taken such as the 'Start for Schools' project and other programs 'to develop the capacity of Roma communities to withdraw their children from dangerous forms of work and integrate them in the national education system'.[152]

Notwithstanding numerous efforts and some successful projects, the scope and complexity of the problem remains overwhelming. For instance, a report on Bulgaria describes numerous efforts to provide Roma children and their teachers with textbooks and instruction materials in order to help the Roma children to overcome their major education obstacles.[153] In 1994, the Ministry of Education established 180 preparatory pre-school groups to provide special preparation for Roma children to attend Bulgarian language education.[154] Notwithstanding these efforts, between 1992 and 2001 the illiteracy rate among Roma in Bulgaria rose

150 UNDP, 2002, p. 62. Compare the 'Skola dokoran' (School Openwide) Foundation project in Slovakia, which focuses on co-operation between nursery schools and families to eliminate the fear of school that some children from the Romany community have and which is being tested at nursery schools in Slovakia. Monitoring Committee, Doc. No. 8496, 6 September 1999, sub 135.

151 UNDP, 2002, p. 61.

152 Romanian Comment, 2002, sub 58.

153 Maria Spirova, *Roma of Bulgaria*, CEDIME-SE, pp. 27-29.

154 *Idem.*

from 11.2 % to 14.9 %, and the share of Roma being awarded a university degree decreased from 0.3 % in 1992 to 0.16 % in 2001.[155] Apparently, the 'numerous efforts' have not been enough to overcome the complex problems with regard to education of the Roma: the practice of *de facto* segregation of schools and in schools, the practice of placing Roma children in special schools for mentally retarded children, the high drop-out rates among Roma children, poverty, and (in some cases) a lack of motivation for education within the family. With enough political will, States and respective governments can change their policies and practices with regard to the Roma, but even then some of these problems will remain unsolved. Inevitably, part of the co-operation and changes, such as motivating children to attend school, must come from the Roma themselves.

4.5 Unemployment

Unemployment levels are difficult to assess for several reasons. First, exact Roma population numbers are not known. Second, unemployment registries usually do not maintain ethnically segregated statistics. Third, the concept of 'unemployment' may have different interpretations for different people. Respondents often understand 'employment' as having a 'steady job'- in other words a stable wage or self-employment. But according to the standard ILO definition, an unemployed person is one who is willing, able and actively seeking work.[156]

According to UNDP, 'the complexities of employment opportunities are often oversimplified both by Roma and by different actors involved in Roma employment issues. The real problem is in determining where inadequate skills end and ethnic discrimination begins'.[157] The most serious problems underlying Romani unemployment include a low level of training, a lack of job opportunities, a lack of a good work ethic and a disinterest among employers to employ such workers. Many Roma also show an indifference to be employed within community-development works.[158]

[155] OSI AP Report on Bulgaria, 2002, p. 92.
[156] UNDP, 2002, p. 31.
[157] *Ibid.*, p. 34.
[158] Vašečka, 1998, p. 412.

According to UNDP, the issue of employability is also often approached by focusing on traditional skills as sources of potential competitive advantages for Roma workers: 'But are these skills marketable today and could they serve as a basis for sustainable employment? The answer is generally "no". Traditional forms of Roma employment (e.g., smiths, spindle makers, horse traders) are no longer viable in industrialized Central and Eastern European societies.'[159] Therefore, UNDP suggests that 'instead of emphasizing exotic but outmoded handicrafts, the flip side of traditional Roma occupations should be promoted: their flexibility and service-oriented character. The real advantage of traditional Roma skills may lie not in the skills themselves but in the entrepreneurship that underpins them.'[160]

The rate of Romani unemployment is very high. Roma unemployment is often even reported to reach 95 to 100 %. These assumptions, however, do not take into consideration involvement in the informal sector, which is often not perceived as 'employment'. By taking into account involvement in the informal sector, the UNDP claims to provide a realistic reassessment of the magnitude and duration of unemployment which leads to unemployment rates which are far below the levels that are often reported. Roma households, however, are still heavily dependent on social assistance and moneylenders.[161]

According to UNDP, social assistance should go hand in hand with efforts to increase social aspirations (especially among the young), and must somehow be linked to productivity for those able to work.[162] However, the social welfare systems in Slovakia, Romania and Bulgaria are based on passive measures (e.g., unemployment compensation) that create negative work incentives and perpetuate dependency cultures. Roma

---

[159] The survey data produced by the UNDP/ILO study support this analysis. The three responses to the question: what traditional Roma activities practised in your close community could be a source of income today?, that received the greatest support are music (60 %), commerce (56 %), and handicrafts (43 %). The expectation that music can be a source of competitive advantage is lowest in Bulgaria and Romania (supported respectively by 48 % and 50 % of the respondents). Handicrafts are seen as an area of potential advantage mostly in Bulgaria (73 %, which places this option as the first in the country). All other options receive negligible support. The problem is the lack of sufficient demand for these skills in the current economic environment. UNDP, 2002, p. 37.

[160] *Idem.*

[161] *Ibid.*, pp. 37-38.

[162] *Ibid.*, p. 41.

participation in formal social welfare systems is asymmetrical: active regarding benefits, but less so regarding contributions.[163]

This might have implications affecting both majority and minority populations. 'The minority can fall into a "vicious circle" of marginalisation: weak incentives to leave the social safety net' and 'income-generating populations become increasingly concerned about the uses of their social security tax contributions. Such economic frictions between Roma communities and income-generating non-Roma populations are often behind allegations that "employed" non-Roma populations "raise Roma children". This issue goes far beyond social welfare: it is a key cause of ethnic intolerance and Roma exclusion'.[164]

Since they do not have access to other financial opportunities many Roma borrow money from moneylenders at monthly interest rates of 100 % or more, and repay these loans under death threats. Faced with real threats to the lives of family members, people will do everything possible to pay the money back. Moneylenders sometimes act as criminal organizations and are a major factor encouraging criminality in Roma communities[165]. According to the UNDP, providing lending opportunities linked to sustainable, legitimate, income-generating activities will reduce the economic underpinning of a significant part of Roma criminality. It is not a coincidence that local moneylenders in many communities are undermining development efforts undertaken by many donors. [166]

4.6 Housing Conditions and Health

Unemployment leads to poverty and poverty may lead to insufficient housing conditions and health problems.

Where Roma live near cities, their housing conditions tend to lean toward de facto ghettoization. Three post-communist trends have significantly exacerbated the already ghettoized situation of the Roma. First of all, Roma are now precluded from joined new patterns of migration toward potential employment through the use of location-specific residence

[163] *Ibid.*, pp. 42-43.
[164] *Idem.*
[165] *Ibid.*, p. 50.
[166] *Ibid.*, pp. 50-51.

permits. Secondly, mythic beliefs about Roma and housing ('Roma destroy their flats') lead to discriminatory practices by local housing authorities. Finally, Roma are expelled from their homes or live under the threat of expulsion by local and regional authorities.[167]

One such 'ghetto' which received international publicity is the housing project called Lunik IX, on the eastern edge of Kosiče, Slovakia. Lunik IX used to be one of the worst Roma ghettos in Slovakia, when some years ago all Roma from Kosice where forced to move to Lunik IX. Recently the living conditions in Lunik IX have improved considerably due to the efforts and organizational skills of one person. The rubbish piles have disappeared, there is a school for the youngest children, a bakery and even a small 'police' force of young Roma men. There were plans to start a biological farm and to open a health care Center, but it appeared to be very difficult to find a doctor prepared to work there. This latter fact, though, is denied by the Slovak Government. According to its Comment, 'the Ministry of Health Care has not registered any case of discrimination of the Roma minority in State Health Care facilities (...) and no complaints by Roma citizens have been received either'. The government further adds 'that the Roma population is provided with specific prophylactic epidemiological and hygienic measures in Roma settlements free of charge and compared with other populations of Slovakia this service is above the standard level'.[168] Notwithstanding the lack of a doctor in its medical center, due to many improvements Lunik IX has now become a 'model' Roma settlement (ghetto) which can be shown to foreigners interested in the situation of the Roma. However, Lunik IX is only one of 617 Roma settlements in Eastern Slovakia.

The link between insufficient housing conditions and serious health problems cannot be denied. As follows from several UNDP Reports, health conditions in Romani settlements in Slovakia, Romania and Bulgaria are alarming because of poor hygiene, and increased epidemics threaten many settlements. Since 1989 the incidence of bronchitis has increased and in some settlements tuberculosis has begun to spread. Some Romani children suffer from contagious and parasitic diseases, which no longer occur in the majority population.[169] Insufficient nutrition and

---

[167] ERRC, 1997, pp. 57-58.
[168] Slovak Comment, 2001, sub 3.
[169] UNDP, 2002, pp. 64-65.

health care for children[170] result in Roma children being a special at risk group in terms of health. Infant mortality data are scarce due to the lack of consistent monitoring by ethnic groups. Still, various, albeit fragmentary, data show large discrepancies between majority and Roma populations. In Romania, Roma child mortality rates are 3 to 4 times higher than those for the majority population or other ethnic groups. In the Slovak Republic, these figures were 8 % and 18 %, respectively. The situation in Bulgaria is even worse: in 1989, the infant mortality rate for Roma children was 240 per 1000, compared to the national average of 40.[171]

Other major problems affecting the health conditions of the Romani population include the following: inadequate hygienic conditions within dwellings; absence of drinking water and adequate drainage; lack of regular rubbish collection; absence of toilets; pregnancy among young girls; and poor health care for pregnant woman.

Limited access to health services is another cause of the poor health status of the Roma. Ina Zoon analyzed the 'hidden impediments' to social services in, *inter alia*, Slovakia, Romania, and Bulgaria.[172] She noted that access to health care for certain social groups - like Roma - is often denied on administrative grounds.[173] In the context of health care for women and discrimination it must also be mentioned that according to a shocking report by the Center for Reproductive Rights, *Body and Soul, Forced Sterilization and Other Assaults on Roma Reproductive Freedom in Slovakia*, Romani women in Slovakia are regularly coerced by doctors and nurses to have themselves sterilized. This report concludes that the rights of Romani women in Slovakia

> 'to informed consent to sterilization, accurate and comprehensive health information, non-discriminatory health services, and unimpeded access to their medical records have been blatantly violated. Romani women endure severe discrimination that is exacerbated by the intersection of their gender and racial identities.'[174]

---

170 Vašečka, 1998, p. 413.

171 UNDP, 2002, pp. 65-66.

172 See, for a detailed overview: Ina Zoon, 2001, pp. 77-100; Ina Zoon, 2001 Slovakia, pp. 49-76.

173 See: Ina Zoon, 2001.

174 Center for Reproductive Rights and Poradňa pre občianske a ľudské práva, in consultation with Ina Zoon, *Body and Soul, Forced Sterilization and Other Assaults on Roma Reproductive Freedom in Slovakia*, 2003, p. 119. Also a report presented by the ERRC,

The scale on which these practices exist in many – publicly funded – hospitals in Slovakia suggests that there is a specific underlying policy. However, government officials have, so far, failed to condemn and put an end to these practices. The Slovak Government and hospital administrators dismiss evidence of discriminatory treatment as either inconsequential or untrue, and some measures, such as segregation in maternity wards and discriminatory standards of care, are defended as being necessary for medical and social reasons.[175] However, not only the Slovak authorities consider the reproduction of Roma as something which is negative. In its *National Report on Human Development: Slovakia 1998*, the UNDP warns that 'considering the annual increase of the Romani population (approx. 2.3 %), the Romani problem will gradually become one of the most serious social, cultural and civilization problems of Slovakia and that this will have tremendous influence on sustainable human development'.[176]

It goes without saying that, even if only a part of the allegations of the reports mentioned is true, this constitutes severe violations by Slovakia of the most fundamental human rights of the Romany women.

4.7 Conclusion: Migration, Rebellion, or Political Participation?

The Roma are a completely marginalized group, with very high unemployment, a high infant mortality rate, and without a future. The causes of the poor situation of Roma in Slovakia, Romania and Bulgaria are very complex. The core problem, although denied by the authorities, is discrimination of Roma by other citizens in practically every field of daily life. Discrimination and, as one of its consequences, insufficient education/qualifications are the main causes of high unemployment among Roma which leads to extreme poverty. This poverty is reflected in finan-

---

the International Helsinki Committee and the Slovak Helsinki Committee claims the existence of forced sterilization of Romany women. According to Clause Cahn of the ERRC, 'some doctors view Romany women as inferior patients and thus insufficiently explain the consequences [of sterilization]'. RFE/RL News line Vol. 7, No. 71, Part II, 14 April 2003.

[175] *Body and Soul*, 2003, pp. 17-18.

[176] Kusý, 1998, p. 99.

cial problems and dependency on moneylenders, petty crime, terrible housing conditions, and serious health problems.

One of the consequences of the difficult living conditions of the Roma is the migration of Roma to Western Europe. In 2000, Belgium received 1,372 Slovak Roma asylum seekers. In the first half of 1998, 1,256 Slovak Roma requested asylum in Great Britain. In June 1999 more than 1000 Slovak Roma requested asylum in Finland. According to UNHCR, the Roma formed the most significant part of the asylum case-load in Finland in 2000, resulting in widespread attention by the media and decision-making bodies. The July amendments to the Aliens Act were largely aimed at preventing ethnic Roma asylum seekers with 'manifestly unfounded' claims from remaining in Finland through a long, drawn-out procedure. Finland continued to deny asylum to ethnic Roma from Eastern Europe, stating that they came from 'safe' countries and that many were fleeing social and economic hardship.[177] Also Slovak Government officials were said to challenge the stated motivations of Roma individuals seeking asylum.[178] According to Vincent Danihel the Romani exodus to Finland was connected to the financially lucrative asylum benefits offered by the Finnish government. The Finnish government denied the right to asylum to all of the Romani applicants and introduced visa obligations for Slovak citizens fearing another wave of Slovak Roma.[179]

After record numbers of Slovak Roma had applied for asylum in Belgium, Denmark, Finland, Ireland, Luxembourg, Norway, and the United Kingdom, these countries imposed temporary visa requirements on Slovak citizens in 2000. Belgium tried to encourage some 1,500 rejected Slovak asylum seekers to repatriate by offering them free flights and a small reintegration sum.[180]

Few Slovak Roma obtain asylum in Western Europe, and most are returned on safe country of origin or safe third country grounds.[181] Therefore, many Roma flee from Slovakia to the Czech Republic. According to some estimates, as many as 20,000 Slovak Roma have moved to the

[177] <http://209.225.33.28/world/countryrpt/europe/finland.htm>.

[178] Advisory Committee Opinion on Slovakia, 2000, sub 27.

[179] Vašečka, 1998, p. 407.

[180] Although there are exceptions: for instance, in 2003 Belgium granted asylum to a Romany family who had been brutally assaulted by skinheads in Slovakia. RFE/RL Newsline Vol. 7, No. 72, Part II, 15 April 2003.

[181] <http://209.225.33.28/world/countryrpt/europe/slovak_republic.htm>.

Czech Republic due to cuts in social benefits in Slovakia and widespread usury, which reportedly leads to some Roma going abroad to flee creditors.[182] Several high-level political representatives have stated that a repeat of the mass exodus of Slovak Roma represents a serious threat to Slovak efforts to integrate into the European Union. Furthermore, the exodus has aroused emotional and negative public responses and has worsened relations between the Roma and the majority population.[183]

One could imagine that another possible reaction of the Roma to their very difficult living conditions would be to protest or even rebel against the government. However, except for one recent case of rebellion and striking in Plovdiv in 2002 when the electricity was cut off, Roma as a group do not form a serious political threat to governments. Although Roma are well organized in many non-governmental organizations, these organizations, unfortunately, tend to fight each other instead of forming one voice against the government. As possible explanations for this situation the following have been suggested: the fact that Roma are organized in clans and families; that they do not have a common goal; that they lack a common religion; that they have a nomadic lifestyle and mentality; that they have very little education (many Roma are illiterate) and have a low political conscience.

It is further mentioned among the factors contributing to this poor situation and to a downward spiral the fact that the Roma are underrepresented at all levels of government.[184] However, the answers to the question 'Who best defends your interests in your community?' reveal major tensions in Roma attitudes concerning the representation of their interests. Despite being underrepresented at various levels of government, most respondents expect support from State institutions, particularly social assistance agencies and local government bodies. The responses to this question also suggest that, despite low levels of trust in informal leaders, Roma still expect these leaders, rather than Roma NGOs or Roma political parties, to defend their interests.[185]

Roma elites in Slovakia, Romania, Bulgaria are generally characterized by political fragmentation and the absence of common political strat-

---

[182] Roman Kristof of the Czech government's Council for Romany Affairs. RFE/RL Newsline Vol. 7, No. 79, Part II, 25 April 2003.

[183] Vašečka, 1998, pp. 407-408.

[184] Kusý, 1998, p. 98-99.

[185] UNDP, 2002, p. 73-78.

egies. This may be one of the reasons why Roma usually vote for other (majority) political parties in national elections. But after having captured Roma votes in elections, these parties often forget about Roma concerns. Minimum electoral thresholds for entering parliament are another common problem. Given the number of Roma in Slovakia and their demographic characteristics (i.e. the high proportion of children under 18 and their low literacy rate), it appears almost impossible for even a single Roma party to cross the 5 % threshold for parliamentary representation. Since Roma voters constitute a relatively small share of the electorate, even strong Roma support for a single national Roma party would not guarantee that party the votes needed for parliamentary representation.

For instance, in Slovakia at the beginning of September 1999, representatives of 14 Roma political parties established the Coalition Council of Roma Political Parties. In October 2000, 14 Roma political parties and 37 Roma NGOs signed an agreement on a joint Strategy for the 2002 parliamentary elections. The agreement stated that all Roma political parties would team up behind the ROI, the oldest and most consolidated Roma political party. Joint action was not achieved in practice, however, and two Roma political parties ran independently in the October 2002 parliamentary elections. Both failed, receiving respectively 8,420 votes (0.29 %) and 6,234 votes (0.21 %). As a result there were no Roma representatives in the National Council of the Slovak Republic.[186]

As far as the Roma are concerned, rapporteurs Magnusson and Sinka arrive at the more general and sad conclusion that 'the Roma question is not unique to Slovakia, but is ultimately a problem for Europe as a whole, although each State must seek solutions applicable to its own realities. Despite any goodwill on behalf of the authorities, it requires a change of mentalities and long-term reforms (...).'[187]

According to Kusý

> 'granting the Roma the right to vote will not help improve their situation unless it is accompanied by the elimination of racial discrimination in access to employment and to education. It is the role of the State to guarantee equal opportunity and to create realistic chances for the implementation of the human rights of the Roma, including economic, social and cultural rights.'[188]

---

[186] UNDP, 2002, Michael Vašecka, p. 78, Box 17.

[187] Monitoring Committee, Doc. No. 8496, 6 September 1999, sub 141.

[188] Kusý, 1998, p. 104.

The next chapter will discuss several measures and plans which the governments of Slovakia, Romania, and Bulgaria have developed to combat discrimination and to improve the situation of the Roma minorities.

Chapter 5
NATIONAL MEASURES CONCERNING THE ROMA

5.1 Introduction

The difficult situation of the Roma population in Slovakia, Romania and Bulgaria could not, and did not, remain unnoticed by different Roma and Human Rights NGOs and, most importantly, by the governments of these States and the European Union. The adoption of a plan or program to improve the situation of the Roma became a priority in the Accession Partnerships of Bulgaria, the Czech Republic, Hungary, Romania and Slovakia.

As a consequence, in these States programs (plans, strategies) were drafted, mostly initiated by the Roma NGOs, to enable the practical implementation of international and national human rights and minority standards. These programs were adopted by the respective governments. Since 2001 the Open Society Institute (OSI) has published, on a yearly basis, EU Accession Monitoring Program (OSI AP) reports on minority protection in the ten candidate States of Central/Eastern Europe[189]. These reports do not only examine the legislative and institutional framework for minority protection in these States, but also make an assessment of the government efforts to address the problems of the minorities and, more specifically, of the different Roma programs.

5.2 Slovakia: Strategy for the Solution of the Problems of the Roma National Minority and the Set of Measures for Its Implementation (Strategy for Roma)

5.2.1 **Background**

Since 1991, the government of Slovakia has initiated and accepted three

[189] See: <www.eumap.org>.

conceptual programs regarding the Roma.[190] The first two have not been implemented. A third plan, from 1997, was well elaborated and workable, but 'political manoeuvring undermined its implementation. While the [Mečiar] government supported the plan in the law, it had no intention of implementing it'.[191]

The government determined as one of its priorities, a plan to tackle the Roma question. In its Program Declaration, it stated that: 'According to the Constitution of the Slovak Republic it will not tolerate any forms of racial or nationality intolerance. No citizen of the Slovak Republic can have disadvantages due to their belonging to a national minority or ethnic group. The government will support all forms of education leading to a mutual respect of nationality, and in this area it counts with the co-operation of NGOs'.[192] Further, the Government stated that it will 'support concrete programs for the integration of the Roma minority into the life of the society and for solutions of this issue it will also form the necessary organizational structures'.[193]

The year 1998 did not bring the expected union of Romani political and social leaders to help solve Romani issues in the Slovak Republic.[194] However, at the end of 1998 the new government created the new Office of Commissioner of the Slovak Government regarding the solutions to the problems of the Romani minority at the Office of the Government.[195] Shortly afterwards this Office started working on a new plan to solve Roma issues and in 1999 and 2000 a two-stage *Strategy for Roma* was developed.[196]

---

190 1991: Guidelines of Governmental Policy Regarding the Roma (Resolution No. 153/2001); 1996: Program Regarding the Approach towards the Citizens with Special Needs (Resolution No. 130/1996); 1997: Conceptual Plans of the Government of the Slovak Republic Regarding the Solutions to the Roma Problems (Resolution No. 796/1997). The patronizing attitude of the Slovak government towards the Roma minority is apparent in these documents. In particular, see: European Roma Rights Center (ECCR),1997, pp. 69-70.

191 Vašečka, 1998, p. 399.

192 Monitoring Committee, Doc. No. 8496, sub 134.

193 *Idem.*

194 Vašečka, 1998, p. 395.

195 Vincent Danihel, who is from the Roma community, was appointed to the post of governmental Commissioner.

196 'Strategy of the Government of the Slovak Republic for the Solutions of the Problems of the Roma National Minority and the Set of Measures for Its Implementation-Stage I', Government Resolution No. 821, 27 September 1999 and 'Elaboration of the

The Strategy is aimed at 'creating conditions of the Roma national minority problem resolution in areas where the situation is critical – unemployment, housing, health status, social sector and the school system, or where there are any grounds for improvement – human rights, rights of persons belonging to national minorities, cooperation with NGOs and regional development'.[197] Stage II of the Strategy focuses on the implementation of these objectives through concrete measures.

In general, the present version of the Strategy has been severely criticized. According to the EU Accession Monitoring Report of 2002, it

> 'reflects insufficient research and planning, and implementation has consisted principally of short-term projects in a few priority areas; these projects do not add up to a coherent long-term policy. Funding from the State budget has also been insufficient. Moreover, Strategy implementation has offered few opportunities to Roma to participate as decision-makers and managers in developing solutions to the problems their communities face'[198]

Next to this, the implementation of the measures proposed in the Strategy is hampered by the weakness of the supervisory mechanism: the Plenipotentiary for Roma Issues, officially responsible for coordinating and reporting on the fulfillment of the Strategy, can do little more than request implementation reports from the ministries involved. As a consequence, little information is available on the use and effect of national and international funding allocated to support the implementation of the Strategy, with the risk of misallocation of these funds.[199]

In April 2003, however, the Slovak cabinet approved priorities for 2003 aimed at improving the integration of the Roma in line with the Strategy for integration up to 2010. The document stipulates 'that both education and infrastructure improvement among Romany settlements are to be considered priorities this year [2003]'. Further, some $ 13 million was allocated for this purpose.[200]

Government Strategy for Addressing Problems of the Romani National Minority into a Package of Concrete Measures for year 2000 – Stage II', Government Resolution No. 294/2000, 3 May 2000. For some general comments on the 'Strategy' see: Advisory Committee Opinion on Slovakia, 2000, sub 23 and 24.

[197] Strategy for Roma, Stage I, 1999, p. 15.

[198] Monitoring the EU Accession Process: Minority Protection in Slovakia, Open Society Institute (hereinafter: OSI AP Report on Slovakia), 2002, p. 530.

[199] OSI AP Report on Slovakia, 2001, p. 432; 2002, pp. 550-551.

[200] RFE/RL Newsline Vol. 7, No. 79, Part II, 25 April 2003.

5.2.2 The Strategy for Roma and Discrimination

As far as discrimination is concerned, the Strategy acknowledges that Roma have experienced discrimination in the past and aims to prevent future discrimination by public administration authorities.[201] However, as the 2002 EU Accession Monitoring Report points out, the Strategy assigns partial responsibility for the fact that Roma are discriminated against to Roma themselves: 'some aspects of life of a certain part of this minority cause social distance in the majority society, which is then unjustly applied to the whole minority'.[202]

The Strategy outlines several measures to combat discriminatory practices by providing human rights training (with special attention to the Roma minority) to members of professional groups such as the police, prison guards and court officials, and local authorities.[203] In practice, human rights training for professional groups and public awareness activities were proposed and organized, and successful results were reported.[204]

In the 2001 Report, the OSI had already warned that the Strategy does not sufficiently focus on the need to combat violence and discrimination against Roma, *de facto* segregation in some cities and towns, and the overrepresentation of Roma in schools for retarded children.[205] Further, the Strategy was criticized both in the Report of 2001 and that of 2002, for not identifying any specific discriminatory practices and not proposing any concrete measures to combat them.[206]

Therefore, the OSI recommends adopting, *inter alia*, comprehensive anti-discrimination legislation in line with the EU Race Equality and Employment Directive[207] (which, so far, has been lacking); adopting guide-

---

[201] Strategy for Roma, Stage I, 1999, pp. 15-16.

[202] Strategy for Roma, State I, 1999, p. 15. OSI AP Report on Slovakia, 2002, p. 553.

[203] Strategy for Roma, Stage II, 2000, pp. 6-8. OSI AP Report on Slovakia, 2002, p. 553.

[204] OSI AP Report on Slovakia, 2002, pp. 553-554.

[205] However, 'the Strategy acknowledges that State efforts to support minorty education for Roma have been insufficient and States that, depending on the need and interest of the Roma community, it will promote Romanes as a supplementary language of instruction. It proposes to do this through the implementation of pilot initiatives such as the employment of Roma assistants. However, it does not propose to establish schools or classes providing Romani language education'. OSI AP Report on Slovakia, 2002, 576-577.

[206] OSI AP Report on Slovakia, 2001, pp. 431-432; 2002, pp. 583-584.

[207] Council Directive 2000/43/EC of 29 June 2000 (OJ L 180, 19/07/2000).

lines and training programs for public officials and social workers in the implementation of anti-discrimination provisions, with a view to increasing institutional capacity to ensure equal access to pubic goods and services in practice; developing training programs to prepare Roma for employment in public administration; revising the Strategy to incorporate measures to settle the ownership of the land on which Roma settlements are located; and, consideration to be given to the development of a policy to promote integration into majority communities rather than the reinforcement of existing patterns of segregation.[208]

5.3 Romania: Strategy of the Government of Romania for Improving the Condition of Roma (Government Strategy)

5.3.1 **Background**

Since 1989, after the death of Ceaucescu, a great deal of positive changes have taken place in Romania. The living conditions of the Roma minority, however, have not improved. In fact, as Gunnar Jansson reported in 1997, the Roma still 'constitute a sub-proletariat ravaged by unemployment and destitution and confined in veritable ghettos. Such insecurity obviously engenders a high rate of delinquency which in turn prompts racist reactions'.[209] In 1997, therefore, the Assembly of the Council of Europe 'earnestly requested' the Romanian authorities to 'promote a campaign against racism, xenophobia and intolerance and take all appropriate measures for the social integration of the Rom population'.[210]

Maybe as a result of this earnest request, the Advisory Committee on the Framework Convention, in its Opinion on Romania of 2001, was able to 'welcome the improvements recorded in recent years in the inter-community relations in particular between the Hungarian minority and other parts of the population of Romania'.[211] However, there was one important

---

[208] OSI AP Report on Slovakia, 2002, pp. 585-586.

[209] Monitoring Committee Doc. No. 7795, 11 April 1997, Honouring of Obligations and Commitments by Romania, (rapporteur: Jansson).

[210] COE PA Resolution 1123 (1997), on the Honouring of Obligations and Commitments by Romania.

[211] Advisory Committee Opinion on Romania, 2001.

remark concerning Romania's State report (of 24 June 1999): the information it contained essentially referred to existing legislation and said little about the way in which Romania implements the Framework Convention in practice.

Since little initiative could be expected from the government, Roma organizations in Romania have initiated the drafting of a *Strategy for Improving the Condition of the Roma*. In 2001, this draft was adopted by the Romanian government.[212] A positive consequence of this 'history' of the Strategy is that it includes both the government perspective (considering poverty to be the cause of the difficult situation of the Roma) and the Roma perspective (seeing discrimination as its cause) and that this Strategy can count on the support of the Roma community and the political will of the Government.

However, the fact that there is an understanding concerning the Government Strategy at a higher level, does not mean that there is an understanding at the lower level of, for instance, mayors. The example of Piatra Neamt is notorious. The mayor of this town proclaimed that if the Roma living in the center of Piatra Neamt would not raise the money needed to refurbish the apartment blocks, they would be forced to live in a ghetto (a former chicken farm surrounded by barbed wire and guarded by gendarmes with dogs) near Piatra Neamt.[213] The association of Romanian Mayors supported the idea of forcing Roma to live outside the city. As is apparent from this example, there is a further need for commitment and the building of understanding concerning the Government Strategy and minority rights in general.

5.3.2 **The Government Strategy**

The Government Strategy of 2001 is aimed at improving the condition of the Roma through the implementation of political, social and legal minority standards in practice, thus, at a level which is as close as possible to

[212] The Ministry of Public Information is the principal government body responsible for the elaboration and implementation of the Strategy in the field of public information and inter-ethnic relations. The Ministry's Department for Inter-Ethnic Relations is responsible for minority issues in general, including Roma issues.

[213] John O'Mahony, 'In the ghetto', *Guardian Unlimited*, 3 November 2001. RFE/RL Newsline Vol. 5, No. 211, Part II, 6 November 2001. Romani CRISS, *Piatra Neamt Case, documenting report* by D. Gergely and M. Mortean.

the Roma. This follows, *inter alia*, from the general objectives of the Government Strategy, which are: delegating political objectives and responsibilities concerning the Roma, currently assumed by the Government, to the central and local public authorities; supporting the formation and promotion of an intellectual Roma elite; counteracting stereotypes and discrimination and encouraging change in public opinion concerning Roma; stimulating Roma participation in several fields, based on their involvement in various assistance and community development projects.[214]

The Government Strategy contains broad directives in its chapter on Lines of Action and in the Master Plan of Action it provides a list of 123 more specific activities and projects concerning both the prevention of discrimination and the promotion of minority rights. Most of these activities and projects contain specific deadlines for their completion, but in most cases these deadlines have not been met. Further, due to a lack of specificity in assigning tasks to the different ministries responsibilities are shifting between different departments and the release of resources allocated for implementation is being delayed. Nevertheless, the general impression of the OSI is that the Romanian 'Government has demonstrated a commitment to assessing itself in regard to Government Strategy implementation, which will be increasingly important as the pace of implementation improves'.[215]

As far as the implementation of the whole Strategy is concerned, it has, so far, concentrated on the establishment of Roma expert bureaux with highly qualified Roma in every county in Romania. Further, mixed ministerial commissions for Roma have been established and specific programs have started in order to improve the education of Roma students.[216] Finally, with the appointment, in July 2002, of the National Council for Combating Discrimination the *structural* measures of the Government Strategy were largely implemented, according to the EU Accession Report of the OSI on Romania.[217]

However, measures that would tangibly improve the conditions in Roma communities have not yet been realized. According to the OSI, the number of projects which the Government has carried out to implement

---

[214] Government Strategy, 2001, Chapter III.

[215] OSI AP Report on Romania, 2002, pp. 488-489.

[216] Interview with Florin Moisa, Resource Center for Roma Communities (RCRC), Cluj, 22 November 2001.

[217] OSI AP Report on Romania, 2002, pp. 478-479.

the practical provisions of the Government Strategy remains very low.[218] In an interview, when answering a question concerning the implementation of the Strategy, the Romanian Secretary of State for Minority Issues from the Ministry of Public Information admitted that Romania has not implemented anything. Further, he said that the Roma Government Strategy is ambitious, not very detailed, and has deadlines which has already expired the moment the Government Strategy was adopted. And, above all, he underlined that there is no money to implement all the measures mentioned in the Government Strategy, though there is the political will to do so.[219] It is a fact that no estimation was made of the costs at the time of drafting the Government Strategy (105 million Euro).

In May 2003 the Romanian Government launched a program called Partnership for Aiding Roma – 2003. This program allocates $1.78 million for local government bodies to devise programs aimed at improving the situation of the Roma by creating jobs, renovating houses and the acquisition of agricultural land by Roma.[220]

In order further to improve the implementation of the Government Strategy, the OSI recommends, *inter alia*, re-estimating the costs of implementation and allocating Government Strategy funds under the State budget for 2003-2004; setting up a Ministerial Commission on Roma in each ministry and establishing and enforcing specific deadlines and targets; reanalysing the anti-discrimination legislation in order to bring it into compliance with the European Union Race Directive; providing training for lawyers, attorneys and judges regarding the new anti-discrimination legislation, including professionals from the Roma community; and continuing to carry out measures to raise public awareness as to discrimination and possibilities for recourse. Among the recommendations for Roma organizations are: to ensure open communication between Roma communities and those responsible for Government Strategy implementation at the local and national level; to support the local Experts for Roma within the County Bureaux for Roma through local working groups; and to make use of the National Council for Combating Discrimination (NCCD) in order to file complaints concerning discrimination.[221]

---

[218] *Ibid.*, p. 478.

[219] Interview with Georgi Ivanov, Secretary of State, 20 November 2001.

[220] RFE/RL Newsline Vol. 7, No. 90, Part II, 14 May 2003.

[221] OSI AP Report on Romania, 2002, pp. 524-526.

5.3.3 **Discrimination**

As far as discrimination is concerned, the Government Strategy identifies the elimination of discrimination as one of the most important factors in improving the condition of the Roma. Several measures[222] are set out to combat discrimination, such as: establishing the NCCD and including Roma representatives in this structure. So far, no Roma member has been appointed.[223] The NCCD will be the monitoring and enforcement body of Law 48/2002 on the Elimination of All Forms of Discrimination.[224] This law is probably the most powerful tool against discrimination. It includes a broad definition of discrimination on the grounds of ethnicity, race, and sex, and stipulates equality in a wide range of areas such as economic activity, public health services and education. In order to present the new anti-discrimination legislation to the vulnerable minority (Roma) groups information campaigns were organized by NGOs and by the European Initiative for Democracy and Human Rights. As a result of the campaign 4,000 Roma community members learned about the legislation and at least 200 Roma now know its content in detail and understand the role of the NCCD and other institutions defending human rights.[225]

Nevertheless, this law has been criticized in the EU Accession Report for not meeting the standards prescribed in the EU Race Equality Directive. The law fails, *inter alia*, to adequately define indirect discrimination, referring only to 'active' and 'passive' discrimination. Further, there are no provisions regarding harassment or intimidation, and the burden of proof cannot be reversed in discrimination claims.[226]

As one of the important strengths of the Government Strategy, the OSI mentions the degree to which it provides for Roma participation at all levels of Government. The establishment of local structures, with Roma representation, to implement the Government Strategy makes it possible to know and meet the needs of individual Roma communities. Moreover, there is no shortage of Roma professionals: affirmative action measures have resulted in approximately 800 young Roma studying at different

---

[222] Government Strategy, 2001, Chapter VII, Section J. See also: OSI AP Report on Romania, 2002, pp. 498-500.

[223] OSI AP Report on Romania, 2002, p. 499.

[224] Government Ordinance 137/2000.

[225] OSI AP Report on Romania, 2002, p. 500.

[226] *Ibid.*, p. 499.

universities.[227] According to the OSI, the Roma Expert offices in every county 'have the potential to institutionalize Roma representation in local governance, and to create a powerful network of Roma civil servants'.[228] According to the EU Admission Monitoring Report of 2002, other promising results in the fight against discrimination have been achieved in the field of healthcare. Access to healthcare has improved through the introduction of health mediators, who are to act as a representatives of the community and facilitate communication with medical staff.[229]

However, according to the OSI, the overall implementation of substantive anti-discrimination projects remains very low.[230] A special point of concern is the fact that the Government Strategy fails to explicitly mention racially motivated violence, and in particular police brutality and the use of excessive force against the Roma, which both domestic and international observers[231] have identified as a serious problem, but which is denied by the government.[232]

5.4 Bulgaria: Framework Program for Equal Integration of Roma in Bulgarian Society

5.4.1 **Background**

After 1989, the 'Program for Resolution of Problems of Roma in the Republic of Bulgaria' was the ambitious title of a program that explicitly

[227] *Ibid.*, p. 524.

[228] *Ibid.*, p. 523.

[229] *Ibid.*, p. 510.

[230] *Ibid.*, pp. 480-481.

[231] In its resolution concerning Romania, the Committee of Ministers of the Council of Europe concluded: 'Despite the determination of the authorities to speed up the social integration of the Roma, real problems remain, notably as regards acts of discrimination in a wide range of societal settings and wide socio-economic differences between a large number of Roma and the remaining population as well as their treatment by some law-enforcement officials', CM Resolution on Romania, 2002.

[232] See, for instance, U.S. State Department Report on Human Rights Practices in Romania in 2002, RFE/RL Newsline Vol. 7, No. 63, Part II, 2 April 2003. See for the reaction of the Romanian Government: RFE/RL Newsline Vol. 7, No. 64, Part II, 3 April 2003. Further: OSI AP Report on Romania, 2002, pp. 480, 513-515. For examples of racially motivated violence by private and public actors see the documentation of organizations such as Romani CRISS in Bucharest and the ECCR in Budapest.

addressed the situation of the Roma. In this program Roma were approached as a socially disadvantaged group, rather than an ethnic group facing discrimination. The measures proposed in this program totally disregarded the prevention of discrimination and their content was very general in nature. This Program did not realize even the beginning of its implementation.[233]

So far, the Bulgarian Government has drafted two policy documents with regard to minorities: the Framework Program for Equal Integration of Roma in Bulgarian Society (Framework Program)[234], endorsed by the Bulgarian Government on April 22,1999, and a section on 'Integration of Minorities' in a comprehensive government program entitled 'People are the Wealth of Bulgaria'[235], adopted in October 2001. This latter document recognizes some continuity with the Framework Program, but it deals with a more limited number of issues. The exact relation between these two documents remains unclear.[236]

The difference between the two documents starts with their drafting process: Although the Government 'scaled back'[237] the version of the Framework Program finally adopted in 1999, originally a team of Roma and NGO experts were involved in its drafting and had a considerable input in the draft text. The draft addressed the most serious problems affecting the Roma community and, as a consequence, this program was accepted with enthusiasm by the Roma community and abroad. The Integration Program, however, was 'the result of a purely political process and was adopted without being discussed publicly. It is narrower in scope and weaker in measures proposed than the Framework Program'.[238] As a consequence, the Integration Program is not as well known to the public and the Roma communities as the Framework Program. The Roma leaders who are aware of the Integration Program disagree with its content and consider it to be too general and too vague.[239]

---

[233] OSI AP Report on Bulgaria, 2002, p. 77.

[234]<www.bghelsinki.org.>. See, for a list of projects related to the Framework Program, the Bulgarian State Report, 2003, pp. 30-33.

[235] <www.government.bg/English/Government/Program/>.

[236] OSI AP Report on Bulgaria, 2002, pp. 74-75.

[237] One of the reasons was that the government did not want to admit the existence of racially motivated assaults by public officals. *Ibid.*, p. 77.

[238] OSI AP Report on Bulgaria, 2002, p. 72.

[239] *Ibid.*, p. 84.

5.4.2 The Bulgarian Programs and Discrimination

Although racial discrimination is recognized as a serious problem by the Government as well as by different sectors of civil society, the existing anti-discrimination provisions in the Constitution and a number of laws have never been enforced. Even this fact was not denied by the Government: in its Program of 2001, the Government Stated that 'anti-discrimination legislation and the mechanisms for its implementation, are not effective enough'.[240]

The Framework Program includes measures both to prevent discrimination and to promote minority rights. In the Framework Program the 'elimination of discrimination against Roma' is 'one of the main political priorities of the Bulgarian State'[241] To achieve this objective, the Program sets out measures in the following fields: Anti-discrimination legislation; employment and economic development; healthcare and sanitation; housing and neighbourhood regulation; education; protection of Roma culture; national media; elimination of discrimination against Roma women. The Integration of Minorities Program gives less attention to anti-discrimination measures, but rather to the promotion of minority identity.

However, according to the OSI, in both programs the promotion of minority rights remains underdeveloped: Mother-tongue education is theoretically available but no classes have been organized; Roma representation in public and political life is very low, and structures that would increase representation have not been developed. Further, the Framework Program does not adequately address discrimination in healthcare: due to high levels of unemployment and their exclusion from the welfare system, many Roma do not have medical insurance and consequently have no access to healthcare.[242] Also the criminal justice system is not free from discrimination. According to a recent survey by the Bulgarian Helsinki Committee, 'the probability of being represented by a lawyer during trail decreases between four and six percent if the defen-

---

[240] Bulgarian State Report, 2003, pp. 25 and 30; OSI AP Report on Bulgaria, 2001, p. 84; *Ibid.*, 2002, p. 88.

[241] Framework Program, Part I.

[242] OSI AP Report on Bulgaria, 2002, pp. 74, 104-107.

dant is not an ethnic Bulgarian'.[243] Earlier surveys already showed that 'minorities are more likely to be physically abused during detention, less likely to be represented by a lawyer, more likely to be charged with serious crimes and more likely to be sentenced to effective imprisonment'.[244] Neither program deals with the problem of discrimination within the criminal justice system.

Another serious problem, for a long time denied by the authorities, but finally admitted in the Bulgarian State Report submitted to the Council of Europe in 2003[245], is the use of racially motivated violence by the police. Different surveys show that Roma 'are more likely than the other defendants to be physically abused during arrest and inside the police station'.[246] The draft version of the Framework Program recognized the existence of racially motivated discrimination by law enforcement officials and included specific measures, such as the establishment of committees to review complaints against law enforcement officers. In the final version of the Framework Program every reference to such discrimination by the police was deleted by the Government. Neither the Integration Program nor any other Governmental Program deals specifically with this issue, although several projects – seminars and training – have been realized since November 2001 dealing with human rights and police work.[247]

The main problem with both programs is that their objectives are not being implemented. In the case of the Framework Program, the Bulgarian Government has not, three years after its adoption, even started with this implementation. According to the OSI, with the Integration of Minorities Program it has even retreated from some of its objectives. Therefore,

[243] Access to Legal Defense in the Criminal Justice System of Bulgaria. See: <www.bghelsinki.org>.

[244] OSI AP Report on Bulgaria, 2002, 107-108.

[245] Bulgarian State Report, 2003, pp.37, 41-43.

[246] Bulgarian Helsinki Committee, 'Human Rights in Bulgaria in 2001', in: *Obektiv*, Special Issue, March 2002, see: <www.bghelsinki.org>. Several cases before the European Court of Human Rights, have been filed against Bulgaria by victims of police misconduct: *Assenov and Others* v. *Bulgaria*, EurCourtHR, Appl. No. 24760/94, Judgment of 28 October 1998; *Velikova* v. *Bulgaria*, EurCourtHR, Appl. No. 41488/98, Judgment of 18 May 2000; *Anguelova* v. *Bulgaria*, EurCourtHR, Appl. No. 38361/97, Judgment of 13 June 2002. Also see Rooker, M., *The International Supervision of Protection of Romany People in Europe*, Nijmegen, 2002, pp. 172-176, 178-180.

[247] OSI AP Report on Bulgaria, 2002, pp. 108-112.

there is an urgent need to clarify the relation between the two programs.[248] Further, there is no effective mechanism for program administration, and there have been few Government-sponsored projects to realize the necessary commitments. Support and funding for different projects take place mainly through NGOs and international organizations.

The following school desegregation program may serve as an example. As is also admitted by the government in the Bulgarian State Report of 2003, 'there is a system which places Roma children under virtual segregation', in fact, a practice of 'racism in classrooms'.[249] According to the Framework Program, the key to the equalization of educational opportunities for Roma is desegregation, which calls for the development of a 'long-term Strategy towards full abolition of segregated schools in Roma neighbourhoods', ensuring the free access of Roma children to 'normal' schools and prohibiting the enrolment of Roma in segregated classes. Further, the Program envisages pre-school education in Bulgarian for Roma children who speak Bulgarian as a second language, the dismissal of unqualified teachers, the recruitment of Roma 'teacher assistants' and material and logistical support. In practice, the desegregation program works as follows:

School busses (logistical support) bring children from their 'ghettos'[250] to 'normal' schools, where they are provided with breakfast (many Roma children are undernourished) and clothes (material support). Every school has additional classes for the Roma children and mentors paying special attention to these children (the teacher assistants). The desegregation program has, so far, been applied in seven cities (Vidin, Pleven, Montana, Stara Zagora, Sliven, Sophia, Khaskovo) and involves more than 1500 children. The desegregation program cannot be applied in settlements with 100 % Roma population without a non-Roma settlement in the vicinity. However, the establishment of real Roma schools in these Roma ghettos is also not realistic because there are no Roma teachers and the political will for such schools is lacking.[251]

---

[248] *Ibid.*, p. 74.

[249] Bulgarian State Report, 2003, p. 26.

[250] Segregation of Roma in the educational system is a heritage of the communist period when rapid urbanisation led to the establishment of Roma ghettos in almost every large city. Schools were established in the midst of these ghettos. Altogether 70% of Roma children are enrolled in such schools. OSI AP Report on Bulgaria, 2002, p. 92-93.

[251] Interview with the director of the Human Rights Project, Sophia, 27 November 2001.

According to the Bulgarian Human Rights Project, the desegregation system is a way to fight discrimination since it enables a break to be made in the vicious circle of discrimination and underdevelopment as a consequence of a lack of education. Studying and education in a multicultural environment give Roma children an opportunity to develop contacts and relations with non-Roma children. Mutual knowledge and understanding of each other's background will improve the social integration[252] of the Roma and is a precondition for the employment of the Roma.[253]

So far, the Program's desegregation plans have been sponsored, realized, organized and implemented by NGOs and the Open Society Foundation. Although the desegregation approach to the Roma is considered to be a success[254] by both the Roma concerned as well as Roma NGOs, the Bulgarian State still does not finance it from its own budget. The Bulgarian Government's Action Plan for Implementation of the Framework Program for Equal Integration of Roma in Bulgarian Society through 2004, does not envisage 'funds for the desegregation of Romani education – one of the priorities of the Framework Program for Equal Integration of Roma in Bulgarian Society. Nor does the Action Plan envisage any funds for transportation of Romani children from segregated schools into mainstream schools.'[255]

In order to improve the protection of the Roma minority, the OSI recommends, *inter alia*, that the Bulgarian Government reconfirms its commitment to implement the Framework Program at the highest governmental level; clarifies the relation between the two programs; supplements the programs with concrete measures in areas such as the criminal justice system, protection from racially motivated violence and health-

[252] On 8 April 2003, the Day of the Roma, Prime Minister Simeon Saxecoburggotski received representatives of the Romany minority and discussed issues related to the integration of the Roma, such as their economic and social problems and the issue of segregation in schools. RFE/RL Newsline Vol. 7, No. 68, Part II, 9 April 2003.

[253] Interview with the director of the Human Rights Project, Sophia, 27 November 2001.

[254] However, the Bulgarian Helsinki Committee noted in its Alternative Report: 'The implementation of the Framework Program for the Integration of Roma into the Bulgarian Society, an important part of which is desegregation of education for Roma, proves to be going clumsily and unsuccessfully'. Bulgarian Helsinki Committee, Alternative Report, 2003, p. 10.

[255] *Roma Rights*, No. 4, 2003.

care; and allocates funds for implementation. The OSI recommended to the European Union, *inter alia*, that it makes the Framework Program and its implementation the yardstick for monitoring (and financing) the Government's efforts to ensure human rights and minority protection.[256]

5.5 Concluding Remarks on the Different Roma Programs

In their positive aspects the three programs differ considerably. In Slovakia, although the overall implementation was very low, the measures to fight discrimination and to raise public awareness were successful. In Bulgaria, a positive aspect of the program is that it was adopted with the support of a broad range of civil society organizations and the Roma community.[257] Further, in its approach to non-discrimination the Bulgarian desegregation program is unique (though not uncontested). The most positive things that could be said about the Romanian program are the following: although carrying the burden of a terrible history and of an almost bankrupt State, the Romanian government has shown in its program and in its implementation in the field of education and healthcare a certain commitment and a political will to combat discrimination.

Although there are considerable differences between the Roma programs of Slovakia, Romania and Bulgaria, these programs have some negative points in common. First, there is no budget to implement the measures of the different programs. In the case of Slovakia this is partly due to the quality of the program – insufficient research and program planning –, in the case of Bulgaria the lack of funding probably hides a lack of political will to implement the program. In the case of Romania the estimation of implementation costs, and of the State's budget, were too optimistic.

Second, racially motivated violence by public officials (the police) has been documented by different NGOs and in cases before the European

[256] OSI AP Report on Bulgaria, 2002, pp. 120-121. Actually, by its decision No. 693, the Council of Ministers approved the Bulgarian Government's Action Plan for Implementation of the Framework Program for Equal Integration of Roma in Bulgarian Society through 2004. The Action Plan is welcomed as the Bulgarian government's first such initiative in the course of four years since the adoption of the Framework Program in 1999. See: *Roma Rights*, No. 4, 2003.

[257] *Ibid.*, p. 120.

Court of Human Rights, but mostly denied by the government in question. Consequently, the different programs to combat violence against minorities, especially the Roma, do not contain measures to counter this form of racial discrimination. Bulgaria, however, recently admitted that 'some Roma have suffered brutal treatment on the part of policemen in a number of towns and villages' and several human rights seminars and training programs have been organized for police officers.[258]

Third, the anti-discrimination legislation in all three States is not in compliance with the EU Race Directive. Last but not least, the overall implementation of the programs by the three governments is insufficient: the Bulgarian program has raised great expectations but it has 'so far come to nothing'.[259] The OSI even concludes that the 'implementation of the Framework Program so far is a model case of a failed attempt to bring about improvements in the area of minority protection'.[260] In Romania the level of implementation is 'very low'.[261] In Slovakia the program does not deal with the different problems in any depth and implementation is 'still at an early stage'.[262]

The future of the three Roma programs depends in the first place on political will and support. There is a difference in political will and support for the Roma programs between Slovakia and Bulgaria, on the one hand, and Romania on the other. But even in Romania, this support is more at the governmental level than at the local level. According to UNDP 'the only way to generate the necessary political support for national and international legislation concerning minority protection among majority communities is to make both majority and Roma communities to perceive their joint interests'. For instance, 'high Roma birth rates could be both a problem and an opportunity for aging European societies. The same applies to other aspects of Roma culture, such as the ability to enjoy life, to be grateful for even modest improvements (a trait that is vanishing in consumer societies), the highest respect for freedom and independence, for flexibility and adaptation, and for internal mobility. In the current setting, all these attributes are latent assets – provided they are understood in

[258] Bulgarian State Report, 2003, p. 41.
[259] OSI AP Report on Bulgaria, 2002, p. 119.
[260] *Ibid.*, p. 120.
[261] OSI AP Report on Romania, 2002, p. 478.
[262] OSI AP Report on Slovakia, 2002, p. 583.

a clear development perspective. It is only within such a perspective that current obstacles can be transformed into benefits.'[263]

[263] UNDP, 2002, p. 77.

Chapter 6
THE MUSLIMS IN BULGARIA

6.1 INTRODUCTION

Discrimination of the Roma in Slovakia, Romania and Bulgaria is discrimination in its most primitive form. However, this does not mean that other minorities do not face discrimination at all. The Hungarians and Germans in Slovakia and Romania and the Turks (and Muslims) in Bulgaria are also groups with deep roots in this region and with a long history of interethnic tension and discrimination. However, there is one important difference with the Roma: unlike the Hungarians, Germans and Turks in this region, the Roma have historically never occupied the role of the oppressor.

Chapters 6 and 7 will deal with two specific forms of discrimination: in Chapter 6 the Muslim minority in Bulgaria will be discussed with regard to the right to use their Turkish names; Chapter 7 will deal with the Hungarian and German minorities in Slovakia in the light of the Beneš Decrees.

6.2 MUSLIMS IN BULGARIA

Muslims in Bulgaria include Turks[264], Bulgarian Muslims (Pomaks)[265], Muslim Roma, and Muslim Tatars. According to the last population census, the Muslims in Bulgaria amount to 13 % of the population (1,110,295 Muslims in Bulgaria, out of a total population of 8,487,317). Almost 80 % of the Turks live in North-eastern and South-eastern Bulgaria, 90 % of the Bulgarian Muslims (Pomaks) live in the Rhodope Mountains on the Bulgarian-Greek border. A small number of Pomaks live around the town of Lovech in Northers Bulgaria. Muslim Roma live

[264] The Turks constitute between 9.4 and 9.8 % of the Bulgarian population. More specifically on the Turks, see Marianna Lenkova, *Turks of Bulgaria*, CEDIME-SE, pp. 19 ff.

[265] On the relations between Turks and Pomaks, *ibid.*, p. 24. Also see on the Pomaks: Bulgarian Helsinki Committee, Alternative Report, 2003, pp. 2-5.

in Plovdiv, Pazardzhik, Peshtera (Southern Bulgaria) and Shoumen, Silistra and Dobrich (Northern Bulgaria). The Muslim Tatars live in North-eastern Bulgaria around the town of Shoumen.[266]

6.3 Historical Background

The present situation of the Muslims in Bulgaria can only be understood when placed in the perspective of their situation in the past. The roots of the Muslim minority in Bulgaria can be traced back to the 14th century. Between 1878 (Bulgaria's liberation from Ottoman rule) and the Communist takeover in 1944, the Muslims of Bulgaria (ethnic Turks, Bulgarian Muslims and Muslim Roma) were treated in a relatively benevolent way and enjoyed some rights with respect to their religion. After the Communist takeover the new regime targeted Islam in particular as a religion that had retarded the development of the Bulgarian people and civilization during the five centuries of Ottoman rule. It was also stated that Islam prevented believers from adopting a new modern and 'progressive' socialist identity.[267] Anti-Islamic propaganda and sentiments became strong with the rise of Bulgarian Communist nationalism. Especially the name-changing campaign has been considered to be a black page in Bulgaria's history.

The policy of forced name-changes already started in the 1950s with the renaming of the Muslim Roma, followed in July 1971 by a campaign to rename the Bulgarian Muslims. However, the most flagrant violation of minority rights started in 1984 with a campaign in which the ethnic Turks were forced to change their Muslim names into Bulgarian ones. Armed forces and militia units, as well as all Communist party local activists were involved in this campaign. Those who refused to change their names were met by violence. Police with dogs surrounded some villages together with tanks and troops in order to force the population to accept their new identity cards with their new Slavic names. Between 100 and 5,000 people were killed during this campaign.[268] Thousands of people were imprisoned or detained in concentration camps. Muslim cemeteries

[266] Maria Koinova, *Muslims of Bulgaria*, CEDIME-SE, p. 2.
[267] *Ibid.*, pp. 11-12, 44-45.
[268] *Ibid.*, p. 11.

were desecrated, the hospital files of persons with Turkish names were destroyed, and speaking Turkish in public places was strictly prohibited. Compulsory lists of 'Bulgarian' first names were introduced for parents to choose the name of their newborn babies.[269]

Furthermore, religious festivities like *Ramadan* and *Kurban Bayram* (Festival of Sacrifice) were banned. Circumcision, traditional clothing and Muslim burial rituals were prohibited. Instead new social rituals had to be adopted. According to these rituals, Muslim and Christians had to be buried in common cemeteries. Many of the existing mosques were destroyed and turned into museums. The Koran was neither published in the country, nor imported from abroad.[270]

In May 1989 the authorities suppressed demonstrations by ethnic Turks in Northern Bulgaria and opened the borders with Turkey, allowing everybody who wanted to emigrate to do so. The result was a mass exodus of 330,000 Turks, half of whom remained in Turkey, while the other half returned discontented with their treatment there. This exodus of people from the country created ethnic tension between Christian and Muslims and hastened the political developments that led to the downfall of the Zhivkov regime on 10 November 1989.

In December 1989 the new Communist Government issued a decision which allowed the Muslims of Bulgaria to restore their names and their right to profess their religion openly.[271] In the new Constitution (Article 29) a right was even included stating that 'no one shall be subjected to torture or to cruel, inhuman, or degrading treatment, or to forced assimilation'

Notwithstanding these restoration measures, the name-changing campaign had already left deep marks: a field study conducted in 1990 showed that nearly 45 % of men and women preferred their Turkish name while 6.5 % of the men and 24 % of the women preferred their Bulgarian name. A large number, nearly 40 %, used various types of hybrids between their Bulgarian and their Turkish name.[272] In practice there are still

[269] Bulgarian State Report, 2003, p. 9.

[270] Maria Koinova, *Muslims of Bulgaria*, CEDIME-SE, pp. 12, 45.

[271] *Law on Names of Bulgarian Citizens* (Official Gazette No. 20 of 9 March 1990), *Law on Amendments to the Law on Bulgarian Citizens' Names* (State Gazette No. 9, 23 November 1990); See further the laws as described in the Bulgarian State Report, 2003, pp. 10, 57-58; Maria Koinova, *Muslims of Bulgaria*, CEDIME-SE, pp. 13, 14, 46.

[272] Maria Koinova, *Muslims of Bulgaria*, CEDIME-SE, p. 26.

cases of discrimination against Muslims who have retained their Turkish name.

6.4 The Present Situation

In general, Muslims in Bulgaria have been enjoying many rights since 1989. Article 6 of the Constitution lays down the principles of equality and non-discrimination, but these principles are not consequently implemented. For instance, Article 11 states that 'political parties may not be founded on an ethnic, racial or religious basis'. Enforcement of this provision has led to the disqualification of several minority parties from participating in elections. This Article has been criticized both domestically and internationally due to its discriminatory and restrictive character.[273]

Further, the Constitution of 1991 proclaims freedom of religion and separation between church and State. It defines the Christian Orthodox Church as 'the traditional religion of the Republic of Bulgaria' suggesting a preference for this religion in contrast to others. The Constitution contains a number of prohibitions. First, there is a prohibition on the use of religious communities and institutions for political purposes and the formation of parties along ethnic and religious lines. Second, freedom of conscience is restricted on five grounds (national security, public order, public health, good morals and the rights and freedoms of others).[274]

In practice, Muslims have few problems in practicing Islam: the State no longer interferes in the election of the Chief Mufti of the Muslims in Bulgaria[275], the Koran is available, and Muslims have more houses of worship per capita than the Orthodox Christians. Since 1989 many new mosques have been built (with money provided by the Muslim community); however, of the previous 82 mosques in Sophia only a few were re-

---

[273] See the famous case of *Boris Stankov and the United Macedonian Organization Ilinden* v. *Bulgaria*, application nos. 29221/95 and 29225/95, EurCourtHR, Judgment of 2 October 2001. Recently, the organizations representing the ethnic Macedonian minority in Bulgaria signed a protocol to form an umbrella organization. This organization is to represent the minority, which has some 5,000 members. RFE/RL Newsline Vol. 7, No. 66, Part II, 7 April 2003.

[274] Maria Koinova, *Muslims of Bulgaria*, CEDIME-SE, p. 36.

[275] See the case of *Hasan and Chaush* v. *Bulgaria*, EurCourtHR, Appl. No. 30985/96, Judgment of 26 October 2000. In this case the Court decided that there had been State interference with the internal organization of the Muslim community.

opened.[276] Muslims have three private high schools and one school for higher Islamic theology which have been opened and are regulated by the Muslim community itself. They have their own printed media as well as political representation in Parliament. So much for the positive developments.

One way in which the State interferes in the affairs of the Muslim community in Bulgaria is through delaying the restitution of *vakif* property. This is land and real estate, owned by the Muslim community, which were confiscated during the Communist rule in the 1940s. The restitution of *vakif* property is very important for the ability of the Muslim community to finance itself and not to rely on subsidies from the State.[277]

Further, social relations between Muslims and the majority are still problematic. Bulgarians often view Turks, Bulgarian Muslims and Roma as people who cannot be trusted and who are hostile to them, because of the name-changing campaign[278], even though this is not substantiated by the Turks themselves.[279] Sociological surveys show that in 1994 72.3 % of the Bulgarians viewed Turks as religious fundamentalists who live among themselves in a conservative, closed society. More than 80 % would not marry a Turk. In Bulgarian eyes only Roma have a worse image than Turks. On the other hand, Turks see Bulgarians as intelligent, with a good insight, cultural, but tend to say that interpersonal relations, family relations etc. among Turks are much more sophisticated than among Bulgarians. [280]

Out of all the Muslim ethnic groups, Bulgarian Muslims have the worse image in the press. Turks are still a subject of contradictory coverage, stressing the negative. The media's attitude towards the Roma is very negative. It is based much more on the Roma ethnic and social status than on their religious affiliation.[281]

---

[276] Interview with Mustafa Hadji, Chairman of the Supreme Muslim Council, Sophia, 30 November 2002.

[277] Maria Koinova, *Muslims of Bulgaria*, CEDIME-SE, pp. 24, 33.

[278] 'Most Bulgarians passivley supported the Communist authorities in their activities to change the names of the Turks. The Turks were associated with "the five ages of Turkish Yoke". Thus, most Bulgarians were silent, due to lack of information and freedom of expression in the totalitarian society'. See: Marianna Lenkova, *Turks of Bulgaria*, CEDIME-SE, p. 22.

[279] Maria Koinova, *Muslims of Bulgaria*, CEDIME-SE, p. 28.

[280] Marianna Lenkova, *Turks of Bulgaria*, CEDIME-SE, p. 23.

[281] Maria Koinova, *Muslims of Bulgaria*, CEDIME-SE, pp. 29, 47.

Discrimination of the Muslims in Bulgaria occurs particularly in the military and at the workplace. During compulsory military service, most Muslims are placed in construction units where they perform commercial or maintenance work. According to Yanakiev

> 'there are two interrelated factors that produce problems in integration of minority groups in the military. The first one is the territorial method of recruitment and service of the conscripts, and the second one is related to the comparatively lower education level of conscripts fro, ethnic minority groups. As a result, the ethnic composition of the Services and the units is not well balanced. Conscripts from ethnic groups are mainly concentrated in the infantry, in mechanized and guard units of the Army. In addition, they are the majority in some units, while in most of the units of the Navy and the Air Force there are few conscripts of Turkish and Roma minority groups.'[282]

Discrimination at the workplace is especially strong against the Roma due to their low training and education and against those Muslims who have retained their Muslim names.[283] Supervisory jobs are usually given to ethnic Bulgarians. Unemployment among the Muslims is high, sometimes amounting to twice the country's average.[284] Ethnic Turks, Pomaks and Roma are usually the first to be laid off.[285]

6.5 Conclusion

Compared to the very harsh times the Bulgarian Muslims have lived through during the Communist regime, their present situation is less problematic. However, the potential for ethnic tension and discrimination remains great. The social position of the Turkish minority in Bulgaria is only slightly better that the situation of the Roma. In the context of this chapter on non-discrimination especially the name-changing campaign,

---

[282] Yantsislav Yanakiev, *Integration of Ethnic Groups in the Military the Case of Bulgaria*, Paper presented during a workshop on 'Military and Society' held in Prague, 15-19 November 2002, organized by the Working Group on Military and Society of the Geneva Centre for the Democratic Control of Armed Force, p. 8.

[283] OSI AP Report on Bulgaria, 2002, pp. 98, 100.

[284] Bulgarian State Report, 2003, p. 26; Interview with Mustafa Hadji, Chairman of the Supreme Muslim Council, Sophia, 30 November 2002.

[285] Bulgarian Helsinki Committee, Alternative Report, 2003, pp. 9-10. Maria Koinova, *Muslims of Bulgaria*, CEDIME-SE, p. 33-34.

as a specific form of discrimination, and its effects on inter-ethnic relations must be underlined. The name-changing campaign has disturbed and even destroyed inter-ethnic relations for a long time. Although the Government has restored the right to use Turkish names, in practice there are still cases of discrimination in the employment of persons using their Turkish names, and many people have chosen, for pragmatic reasons, no longer to use their Turkish names. This situation shows that a discrepancy between international standards (Article 11 of the Framework Convention which states that persons from minority groups 'have the right to use his or her surname (patronym) and first names in the minority language and the right to official recognition of them') and practice may persist for a long time after the government has changed its official policy concerning discrimination into a policy which complies with international standards. Originally, the name-changing campaign probably took advantage of negative sentiments among the Bulgarian population after five centuries under the 'Ottoman yoke'. However, these sentiments were stirred up and abused by the campaign, and subsequently it appears to be difficult to extinguish the resulting prejudices and resentment among the various ethnic groups.

Chapter 7
THE BENEŠ DECREES

7.1 Introduction

The reason for dealing with the so-called Beneš Decrees in the context of Part II of this study on non-discrimination, is that they constitute a form of discrimination against minorities which violates international standards concerning non-discrimination. However, the Beneš Decrees are specific in the sense that they were inherited from a previous regime and have managed to disturb inter-ethnic (and international) relations, for several decades. Moreover, the issue of the Beneš Decrees seems to have inherited the character of a litmus test for both the Slovak and the Czech Republic before joining the EU.

7.2 Historical Background

In 1918, the newly founded Czechoslovak Republic emerged out of the Austro-Hungarian Dual Monarchy. Hungary lost 71.5 % of its territory, and 63.6 % of its population. The Trianon Treaty of June 4, 1920, forced three and a half million Hungarians to live, without their consent, in Czechoslovakia, the Kingdom of Serbs, Croats and Slovenians and Romania. A systematic oppression of the minorities condemned to live in the (former) Czechoslovak Republic began in 1918. The Czechoslovak government confiscated land from German and Hungarian owners, without compensation, for distribution among Czech and Slovak colonists in pure German or Hungarian regions. More than 2,000 Slovak and Moravian colonies were created in the Hungarian inhabited frontier zone in Slovakia alone.[286]

For their part, the Sudeten Germans, with a population of 3.5 million and representing the largest minority group in Czechoslovakia, sought to

[286] Human Rights for Minorities in Central Europe – Vancouver Society, *Study Paper on the Beneš Decrees*, Conference on the Beneš Decrees, 28 November – 1 December 2001, Komárno/Révkomárom, Slovak Republic.

establish contact with the Slovak Populist Party, as well as with the Hungarian and Polish minorities, by forming an autonomic bloc against the Czechs.[287]

The radicalization of the internal political situation in Czechoslovakia worried the founders of the country, the British and French governments, and a mediator was sent to Prague to arrive at a negotiated settlement of the minority problem. This led to the convocation of the four-power Munich conference at the request of the Czechoslovak government, culminating in the Munich agreement of 29 September 1938, and the cession of the Sudeten German districts to Germany[288]. These political events forced President Edward Beneš (1935-1938) from office. On 5 October 1938, Beneš resigned from office, and several days later escaped by air to Britain.[289] In 1940, the British recognized Beneš' group as a provisional Czechoslovak government in exile with Beneš as president.

After the outbreak of hostilities between Germany and the Soviet Union, Moscow gave diplomatic recognition to the political agents of Beneš in London, and concluded a treaty with them on mutual aid against Germany. The Soviet Union recognized the pre-Munich Czechoslovak boundaries and, later in 1942, the Munich agreement was declared null and void by the British and French, both signatories to the 1938 agreement. Beneš began to scheme his political future based on Russian assistance and, against the advice of the British government, the Beneš group went from London to Moscow, and from there they followed the Soviet army pursuing German forces westwards. On 5 April 1945, in Košice, Beneš proclaimed the agenda of the newly appointed government. This, so-called, Košice government program reflected Beneš' ambitions to prevent a second 'Munich' by finding a definitive solution for the minority problem in Czechoslovakia, especially for the German and Hungarian minorities.[290]

---

[287] Z. Zeman and A. Klimek, *The life of Edvard Benes 1884-1948*, Clarendon Press, Oxford, 1997, pp. 123-124.

[288] Vancouver Society, 2001.

[289] Zeman and Klimek, 1997, p. 143.

[290] V. Arndt, Der Zweite Präsident Edvard Beneš, Helmuth-Block-Verlag, Magdeburg, 1992, pp. 84-85; E. Bakker, *Minority Conflicts in Slovakia and Hungary?*, Ridderkerk, 1997, pp. 48-50.

7.3 The Beneš Decrees

The 'definitive solution to the minority question' in the Košice government program contained elements of oppression, persecution and the expulsion of the non-Czech, non-Slovak, non-Slavic, and non-allied population of the restored Czechoslovakia.[291] Subsequently a series of orders were issued, the Beneš Decrees, which branded the German and Hungarian minorities in Czechoslovakia with 'collective guilt'.[292]

On August 2, 1945, Beneš issued Constitutional Decree 33/1945 Sb., under which persons of German and Hungarian nationality lost their Czechoslovak citizenship, unless they could show that during the time when the republic was threatened they had officially registered themselves as Czechs or Slovaks, had remained faithful to the Republic, had themselves suffered at the hands of the fascists or had taken an active part in the resistance movement. After the removal of citizenship, the official expulsion of Germans from Czechoslovakia began, approved by the Allies at the Potsdam Conference. According to information from the Sudeten German Council, 250,000 Germans died during the transferral. Czech historians say that of the total number of expelled Germans, 18,889 people died as a direct result of the expulsion. It is certain that among these victims were people who were not active Nazis but Germans who had not transgressed any Czechoslovak laws.

Decree 71/1945 Sb. introduced labour obligations for those peoples stripped of their Czechoslovak citizenship. More than 40,000 Hungarians from Slovakia were brought to the Czech lands to work. The aim was to weaken the Hungarian minority of half a million in Southern Slovakia, which had been occupied by Hungary in 1938 as an ally of Germany.[293]

Under Decree 108/1945 Sb., all movable and immovable property belonging to persons of German and Hungarian nationality was confiscated without compensation. Inhabitants of Hungarian nationality had to give up their nationality in order to retain their property and gain some of their civil rights.[294]

---

[291] Vancouver Society, 2001.

[292] See, for a detailed description of all Decrees: Center for Legal Analyses-Kalligram Foundation, Memorandum on the Beneš Decrees, <www.cla.sk.>.

[293] Zeman and Klimek, pp. 246-247.

[294] 'Profile of the Beneš Decrees', <http:/www.ctknews.com/archiv/docdene1.html>.

7.4 Present Situation

At present the Sudeten Germans are still requesting the abolition of those Beneš Decrees (a total of 143) that deprived the Sudeten Germans of their rights. They ask for compensation only in some extreme cases where about 1000 people were tortured and forced to work in the uranium mines in Jachymov.[295]

In 1999 the Council of Europe Parliamentary Assembly had already urged upon the Czech Republic to rescind these Decrees.[296] A breakthrough came in June 2003, however, 'in a unique moment of the EU referendum's aftermath', when the Czech government issued a statement to the effect that 'neither World War II nor the events and deeds of the period that followed it are acceptable from the perspective of the present'. Deputy Prime Minister Petr Mares even added that he wants to assess possible compensation for members of the German minority still living in the Czech Republic for injustices against them in the past. The Austrian and German governments and the European Commissioner for Enlargement, Guenter Verheugen, welcomed this Czech statement and believed that 'the past will increasingly make room for a future within the EU'.[297]

The position of the Slovak government is that it will not discuss the Beneš Decrees, despite negotiations with the EU. According to many authors the Beneš Decrees are incompatible with human rights and a country in which they are still valid cannot join the EU. This latter argument seems, however, to have lost its power after the accession of Slovakia to the EU has now become certain, while the Beneš Decrees are still in force.

According to Foreign Minister Eduard Kukan and his deputy, Jan Figel, the decrees are a 'sensitive question' that must first be tackled by historians before it can be taken up by politicians. It must be noted in this context that the participation of the Hungarian Coalition Party in Dzurinda's Cabinet was accepted by some coalition members only on condition that the 1945 Decrees were not revised during the coalition's term in office (until 2002).[298] The positive developments in the Czech

[295] <http:/www.geocities.com/eerstnl/news/sudetengermans.html>.
[296] <http://www.hhtf.org/monitor/904slo.htm>.
[297] RFE/RL Newsline Vol. 7, Nos. 116 and 117, Part II, 20 and 23 June 2003.
[298] <http://www.slovakia.org/news/0001-1.htm>.

Republic with regard to the Beneš Decrees, however, might have an influence on the opinion of the Slovak government as well, and might finally lead to a solution to this lingering form of discrimination.

7.5 Conclusion

The Beneš Decrees are a sensitive problem from a historical and political point of view. However, it cannot be denied that, from the point of view of human rights, the Beneš Decrees, as long as they remain in force in Slovakia, do not only constitute an embarrassing form of discrimination, but are also illogical for a State which has ratified the Framework Convention, the European Convention on Human Rights and most of its Protocols and which is a member of the European Union. Therefore, Slovakia's stubborn refusal to rescind the Beneš Decrees, notwithstanding strong international pressure, and the fact that Slovakia has not (yet) ratified Protocol No. 12 to the European Convention on Human Rights which deals with non-discrimination, must be taken seriously because they indicate that among some Slovak politicians and people a human rights perspective on discriminatory practices like the Beneš Decrees is not obvious. Notwithstanding the world wide developments in the field of human rights, historical and political rhetoric seem to prevail in the issue of the Beneš Decrees not only to the detriment of the victims, but also to the detriment of Slovakia's credibility as a member of the Council of Europe and the EU.

Chapter 8
CONCLUSIONS CONCERNING NON-DISCRIMINATION

Except for the Beneš Decrees which are, notwithstanding national and international protest, still in force, most provisions in Slovak, Romanian and Bulgarian legislation concerning non-discrimination are in conformity with international law. However, what really counts in the case of discrimination is the implementation of the non-discrimination provisions in practice.[299]

Whereas most minorities in Slovakia, Romania and Bulgaria are confronted with discrimination, its extent and intensity vary considerably according to the minority concerned. While, on the one hand, (hidden) discrimination of the Hungarian and Muslim minorities mainly results in a relatively higher unemployment rate, discrimination against the Roma in all three States is much more visible (even for tourists) and goes much deeper affecting almost every aspect of the daily life of the Roma.[300]

Generally speaking, the Roma are still not seen and treated as a 'minority' in the way other minorities are. For instance, as far as education is concerned, there is one major difference in the situation of the Roma minority and the other minorities. As was observed in a report by the Council of Europe: 'in the field of education, it seems that there is no discrimination of Roma as far as the organization of the educational system is concerned. This system allows education for all pupils, including pupils belonging to the national minorities in the Slovak Republic. However, the question is whether there are any realistic opportunities for Roma children to attend school.'[301] Thus, *de facto* there is segregation through a disproportionally high rate of Roma children in special schools, in neighbourhood schools and through the high drop-out rate among Roma children.

The impression of a difference in treatment between the Roma and other minorities is strengthened by a statement by Guenter Verheugen,

---

[299] Advisory Committee Opinion on Slovakia, 2000, sub 18.
[300] *Ibid.*, sub 56.
[301] Monitoring Committee, Doc. No. 8496, 6 September 1999, sub 136.

the EU's Commissioner for enlargement, said that EU candidates must adopt 'credible strategies' to deal with 'the thorny and disturbing problem' of integrating Romany populations into mainstream European life. 'It would be an illusion to believe that social and cultural discrimination against the Roma can be eliminated before membership,' Verheugen commented, saying that 'it will take decades to achieve that'. However, 'we do expect all applicant countries to devise and put into practice credible strategies for the better integration of Roma, and they must do this before accession'.[302] Whereas the protection of minority rights, which means, for instance, the establishment of minority schools and the teaching of, or in, their language, is one of the requirements for accession to the EU, the requirement as far as the Roma are concerned appears to be a different one: integration.

Mutual distrust and prejudices between the Roma population and the ethnic Slovaks, Romanians and Bulgarians make cohabitation and cooperation between these groups extremely problematic. Also the ongoing unsuccessful exodus of the Roma to Western countries, although government officials deny that this has anything to do with the discrimination they face, says something about the way in which the Roma perceive their future. Although Slovakia, Romania and Bulgaria are not the only States which have to deal with the problem of integrating Romany populations, these are the countries with – unofficially – the largest Roma population living in very harsh conditions. These States do not have to solve all these problems on their own – there are all kinds international support programs – and as mentioned above, the EU does not even require that all these problems are solved before membership. However, the discrimination of the Roma often takes place at grass-roots level, in the attitude of citizens,[303] and there is a serious and difficult task for local governments, municipalities, and the media to change this attitude and to fight discrimination. The role of international standards in this process is one of inspiration rather than concrete solutions and measures.

The purpose of this research is to find out whether international legal standards concerning minority protection are implemented not only in the national legal systems, but also in reality. As far as non-discrimination is

[302] RFE/RL Newsline Vol. 5, No. 168, Part II, 5 September 2001.

[303] The Opinion refers to this as 'a certain lack of a spirit of tolerance and of intercultural dialogue', see, Advisory Committe Opinion on Slovakia, 2000, sub 25.

concerned, the international standards and European Standards as formulated in the Framework Convention, the EU Race Directive, Article 14 EHCR and Protocol No. 12 to the ECHR are clear. As noted in section 3.6, the impact of the Framework Convention on national anti-discrimation legislation is lower than that of the EU Race Directive and Protocol No. 12: all new anti-discrimination legislation, thus Romanian Ordinance No. 137 and Law 48/2002, the Bulgarian law of 16 September 2003 and the Slovak draft Act on Equal Treatment and the Act on the Establishment of the Center for Equal Treatment were 'inspired' by the latter two documents. This does not mean, however, that these new laws comply in all their aspects with these documents: the Romanian law is in some aspects more limited than the EU Race Directive, while the protection offered by the Bulgarian law is more far-reaching. The fate of the new Slovak law is still uncertain. But, to what extent do these new laws comply with the anti-discrimination standards laid down in the Framework Convention? Before answering this question, it must again be underlined, that the requirements as formulated in the Framework Convention are almost without clear obligations: in Article 4 Paragraph 2, the Parties 'undertake to adopt, where necessary, adequate measures (...) to promote (...) full and effective equality (...)'.

On the one hand, it could be concluded that all three States have fulfilled their obligations following from this Article in the Framework Convention; all three have undertaken to adopt specific measures. In the case of Slovakia, this adoption has not (yet) succeeded. In the case of Romania and Bulgaria, new legislation has been adopted.

On the other hand, the core question is the following: are these measures adequate to promote full and effective equality? As far as Bulgaria is concerned, its new law contains very broad affirmative action provisions, which certainly can promote full and effective equality. The Bulgarian law, however, is of very recent date, and its value has not yet been proved in practice. The Romanian anti-discrimination law is also intended to promote full and effective equality. However, three years after its adoption, problems with implementation are said to have rendered it 'not yet viable'[304] and even a 'dead letter'.[305] Apparently, (so far) the law

[304] Romanita Iordache and Andreea Tabacu, 'Not Yet Viable: Anti-discrimination Action in Romania', in: *Roma Rights*, No. 1-2, 2003.

[305] Claude Cahn, 'Roma Rights and Anti-Discrimination Law', in: *Roma Rights*, No. 1-2, 2003, p. 2.

has not been adequate to deal with the obstacles which hamper the promotion of full and effective equality.

What of the different programs (strategies, plans) of the three States which aim to improve the situation of the Roma; do they fulfill the States' obligations from the Framework Convention? The positive aspects of the different programs are overshadowed by financial problems and a lack of political will. But, above all, the overall conclusions concerning the three programs is that their implementation by the three governments is insufficient: in Slovakia implementation is 'still at an early stage'[306]; in Romania the level of implementation is 'very low'.[307] The title of a field report on Romania is that 'two years after the adoption of the Government Strategy' [there is] 'no visible change'[308]; the Bulgarian program has raised great expectations but it has 'so far come to nothing'.[309]

In sum, for the different Roma programs the same conclusion can be drawn: they are not adequate to deal with the obstacles which hamper the promotion of full and effective equality. UNDP mentions two major factors which hamper the effectiveness of the Roma programs: The first is 'the lack of an internally consistent conception of what to do and how to do it. The different plans in Slovakia, Romania and Bulgaria concerning the Roma are ambitious attempts to formulate such internal policy. However, they are characterized by too optimistic goals and deadlines, and above all, they are confronted with an enormous lack of financial resources to implement all these programs.' A second and related factor, mentioned by the UNDP, has been 'inadequate administrative and policymaking capacity in those agencies that would have to execute a strategy based on the human development approach to Roma issues.'[310] Symptoms of this inadequacy are i) the tendency to use the whole system of minority protection in a window dressing policy, ii) a policy to look good abroad, iii) corruption ('an old reflex'), iv) and ethno business: money from special funds for minority issues is spent by minority repre-

---

306 OSI AP Report on Slovakia, 2002, p. 583.

307 OSI AP Report on Romania, 2002, p. 478.

308 Tara Bedard, 'Romanian Roma: Two years After the Adoption of the Government Strategy, No visible Change', in: *Roma Rights*, No. 1-2, 2003.

309 OSI AP Report on Bulgaria, 2002, p. 119.

310 UNDP, 2002, p. 77.

sentatives which are unqualified and not monitored while spending the money.'[311]

The two factors mentioned by the UNDP reflect another problem: the scope of the discrepancy between standards and reality, especially in the case of the Roma minorities. Perceived from everyday practice the international and national non-discrimination standards seem unrealistically distant and almost unattainable. The only way to bridge this gap, without lowering the standards, is to improve and intensify the implementation mechanisms and measures, especially with regard to the Roma minority.[312] These implementation measures can take different forms, ranging from (passive) abstention from more negative image building and prejudices concerning the Roma in the media[313] to active financial support for desegregation programs (Bulgaria). However, whatever form this implementation takes, there are two important factors which should not be forgotten: first, the involvement of and consultation with the Roma themselves in programs or decisions concerning their situation is very likely to improve the effectiveness of the implementation measures.[314] Second, there is a need to convince national and local authorities of the use, necessity and inevitability of fighting discrimination and, consequently, of the implementation measures. The EU Ambassador to Romania Jonathan Scheele pointed out on a visit to Transylvania that 'Romania's legislation on the rights of national minorities reflects European standards', and he added, very diplomatically, that 'there might be some problems with the implementation of the legislation'. He said the integration of the Romany minority in Romania is dependent on a 'process of a change in mentalities', which 'will take time and must be taken seriously'.[315]

---

[311] Interview with Istvan Horvàth, Research Center for Interethnic Relations, Cluj, 22 November 2001.

[312] See the lists of recommendations in almost every report on the Roma.

[313] Marianna Lenkova, 'Black & White v/s Diversity, The Image of the Roma in the Balkan Media', *Greek Helsinki Monitor*, <www.greekhelsinki.gr/english/articles/montpellier-marianna.html>.

[314] See 'the consensus principle' in the Romanian Roma Strategy. For a practical example see the work of Spolu International Foundation: *Breaking the Vicious Circle, Lessons Learned from Experience in Social Inclusion of Roma Communities Through Participation*, Sofia, 2000, <www.spolu.nl>.

[315] RFE/RL Newsline Vol. 7, No. 97, Part II, 23 May 2003.

Drafting a Convention in the form of a Framework Convention is very attractive for States, especially when delicate issues like the protection of minorities is concerned. It seems very easy to comply with the Framework Convention: the vagueness of the wording of some of the provisions of the Framework Convention gives the impression that even the slightest effort to 'undertake' or 'encourage' or 'endeavour' something in favour of minority protection is sufficient to fulfil treaty obligations. However, at the same time one might have the impression that the standards of the Framework Convention can never be completely fulfilled because of their vagueness: the Framework Convention does not explain what is meant by 'adequate' or 'effective' measures. The challenge to complying with the Framework Convention lies in the fact that it seeks to awaken, within a framework of vague minimum standards, States' own conscience and States' own sense of responsibility with regard to the situation of their minorities. As far as the standard of non-discrimination in the Framework Convention is concerned: the real purpose is not in promoting, but in actually attaining full and effective equality.

Part III
LINGUISTIC RIGHTS

Introduction to Part III

Part III will discuss the protection of cultural identity, and more specifically, the protection of linguistic rights of minorities as laid down in the Framework Convention. In Part I, the case of the Roma, forming a minority in all three States in question, enabled a comparison to be made between the legal and practical situation of these three States. Somewhat differently, the cases used in Part III will rather illustrate specific problems with regard to the practical implementation of linguistic rights in the different States. A comparison will be made only where the problems and minorities demonstrate some overlapping. The reason for this approach is that, first, not all linguistic rights are equally problematic in all three States, and, second, that the minority groups in question (the Hungarians in Slovakia and Romania) do not constitute a minority in Bulgaria. An exception will be made with regard to the Roma and their rights under Article 14 (2) Framework Convention , the rights 'to be taught the minority language or for receiving instruction in this language'. As in Part I, the implementation of these rights of the Roma will be assessed in the light of reality in all three States.

Chapter 9 will discuss the international standards with regard to the protection of cultural identity in general and, more specifically, the protection of linguistic rights. Although the main focus of this part of the study is on the implementation of some specific standards as contained in the Framework Convention, other international documents, such as the International Covenant of Civil and Political Rights and the European Charter of Regional or Minority Languages, will be taken into account where necessary.

As said, the practical value of linguistic rights will particularly be considered in relation to the Hungarian minorities in Slovakia and Romania. In order better to understand the present situation and the specific problems pertaining to these minorities, Chapter 10 will provide some background information on the Hungarian Minorities in Slovakia and Romania, respectively, and will discuss two important issues which relate to these minorities: Hungarian autonomy and the Hungarian Status Law.

Chapter 11 will deal with several public aspects of the use of minority languages (Articles 10-11 Framework Convention) The practical implementation of these rights will be discussed in relation to the situation of the Hungarian minority in Slovakia.

The educational rights of the Framework Convention (Articles 12-14) will be dealt with separately in Chapter 12. The practical relevance of these international standards will be assessed in the light of the situation of the Hungarian minority in Slovakia and Romania and the Roma minorities in Slovakia, Romania and Bulgaria. Chapter 13 will contain concluding observations on Part III, linguistic rights.

Chapter 9
INTERNATIONAL STANDARDS CONCERNING THE LINGUISTIC RIGHTS OF MINORITIES

9.1 The Protection of Cultural Identity: the UN framework

The protection of minorities implies not only protection against discrimination, but also the protection of their cultural identity. The essential elements of the identity of persons belonging to a national minority are generally considered to be their religion, language, traditions and cultural heritage.[316] In international law, the protection of cultural identity is referred to in several documents, such as Article 27 of the Universal Declaration of Human Rights, dealing with 'participation in cultural life of community', and Article 15 of the International Convention on Economic, Social and Cultural Rights (ICESCR) dealing with 'culture and science'.

Relating more specifically to minorities, although not legally binding, the UN Declaration on the Rights of Persons Belonging to National or Ethnic, Religious and Linguistic Minorities[317] states in Article 1 that 'States shall protect the existence and the national or ethnic, cultural, religious and linguistic identity of minorities within their respective territories and shall encourage conditions for the promotion of that identity'. With regard to language the Declaration says in Article 4 Paragraph 4, that 'States should take appropriate measures so that, wherever possible, persons belonging to minorities have adequate opportunities to learn their mother tongue or to have instruction in their mother tongue'.

However, the most important article with regard to the protection of the cultural identity of minorities at the UN level is Article 27 of the International Covenant on Civil and Political Rights (ICCPR). According to this Article, '[i]n those States in which ethnic, religious or linguistic minorities exist, persons belonging to such minorities shall not be denied the

[316] Article 5 Framework Convention.
[317] Adopted by UN Assembly Resolution 47/135, 18 December 1992.

rights, in community with other members of their group, to enjoy their own culture, to profess and practice their own religion, to use their own language'.

The distinction between non-discrimination and the protection of minority rights has been made clear by the UN Human Rights Committee as follows:

> 'the entitlement [under articles 2 (1) and 26] to enjoy the rights under the Covenant without discrimination applies to all individuals within the territory or under the jurisdiction of the State whether or not those persons belong to a minority. (...) Some States parties who claim that they do not discriminate on grounds of ethnicity, language or religion, wrongly contend, on that basis alone, that they have no minorities.[318] (...) The terms used in article 27 [ICCPR] indicate that the persons designed to be protected are those who belong to a group and who share in common a culture, a religion and/or a language. Those terms also indicate that the individuals designed to be protected need not be citizens of the State party.'

With regard to the exercise of the cultural rights protected under Article 27 ICCPR, the UN Human Rights Committee provides the possibility of taking positive measures, observing that

> 'culture manifests itself in many forms, including a particular way of life associated with the use of land resources' (...) and that 'the enjoyment of those rights may require positive legal measures of protection and measures to ensure the effective participation of members of minority communities in decisions which affect them'.[319]

Slovakia, Romania and Bulgaria have ratified the ICCPR[320] and ICESCR[321] without making any major reservations and, consequently, are

[318] France, for instance, claims that: 'In the light of article 2 of the Constitution of the French Republic, the French Government declares that article 27 is not applicable so far as the Republic is concerned.' United Nations Treaty Collection, Declarations and Reservations.

[319] UN Human Rights Committee, General comment No. 23 (50) on Article 27 /Minority rights, UN Doc. CCPR/C/21/Rev.1/Add.5, 6 April 1994, sub 7.

[320] The ICCPR entered into force in Slovakia on 1 January 1993, in Romania and Bulgaria on 23 March 1976. All three States have ratified Optional Protocol No. 1 to the ICCPR.

[321] The ICESCR entered into force in Slovakia on 28 May 1993, in Romania and Bulgaria on 3 January 1976.

bound by the obligations following from these documents. In a certain sense, Article 27 ICCPR serves as a safety-net provision for many minorities[322]: where the implementation of other international documents dealing more specifically with minority or indigenous peoples' rights depends on political will, financial resources, and on State reports, the rights under Article 27 are protected by an individual claims procedure before the Human Rights Committee.[323]

9.2 The European Convention on Human Rights

Unlike the ICCPR, the European Convention on Human Rights (ECHR) does not contain an article on minority rights. However, Article 14 (the general non-discrimination article) might lead, when invoked in relation to other articles, like Article 8 (the right to respect for private and family life, home and correspondence), Article 9 (freedom of expression), Article 10 (freedom of thought, conscience and religion), Article 2 First Protocol (right to education) to a case concerning the cultural identity of minorities. For instance, in the Belgian Linguistic Case, a case was brought before the European Court of Human Rights under Article 14 and Article 2 of the First Protocol (parental right to ensure (...) education and teaching in conformity with their own religions and philosophical convictions). In this case the Court found a violation due to the fact that there was an absence of French language schools in a Dutch monolingual region of Belgium, which implied discrimination on the ground of language.[324]

Further, with regard to linguistic rights, the European Convention on Human Rights states in its Article 5 (2): 'Everyone who is arrested shall be informed promptly, in a language which he understands, of the reasons for his arrest and of any charge against him'. Article 6 (3): 'Everyone charged with a criminal offence has the following minimum rights: a) to be informed promptly, in a language which he understands and in detail, of the nature and cause of the accusation against him; (...) e) to have the

[322] As of 10 October 2003, the ICCPR had been ratified by 150 States.

[323] See the extensive case-law of the HRC on Article 27.

[324] Case Relating to Certain Aspects of the Laws on the Use of Languages in Education in Belgium (Merits), EurCourtHR, Judgment of 23 July 1968, Series A, No. 6.

free assistance of an interpreter if he cannot understand or speak the language used in court.' This right is available to all persons, irrespective of whether they belong to minorities or not. This right does not, however, in any circumstances, confer on accused persons the right to use the language of their choice in court proceedings.

9.3 The Framework Convention

In the solemn style which characterizes all Preambles, the Preamble to the Framework Convention underlines that 'the creation of a climate of tolerance and dialogue is necessary to enable cultural diversity to be a source and a factor, not a division, but of enrichment for each society'. Indeed, most substantial provisions of the Framework Convention refer, in one way or another, to the protection, preservation and development of minority culture:

In Article 5, Paragraph 1, Parties undertake to promote the necessary conditions to maintain and develop the culture and identity (religion, language, traditions, and cultural heritage) of persons belonging to minorities. Paragraph 2 contains a prohibition of assimilation. Article 6 'encourages a spirit of tolerance and intercultural dialogue'. Article 7 deals with the 'freedom of association, freedom of expression, and freedom of thought, conscience and religion'. Article 8 contains the rights to manifest one's religion or belief and to establish religious institutions, organizations and associations.

Articles 9 to 11 deal with several public aspects of the linguistic rights of minorities: Article 9 deals with the right to access to the media, which includes 'the right to freedom to hold an opinion and to receive and impart information and ideas in the minority language'. The first Paragraph of Article 10 contains the right of minorities 'to use freely and without interference his or her minority language, in private and public, orally and in writing'. According to the Explanatory Report to the Framework Convention, this right is extremely important as 'the use of the minority language represents one of the principal means by which such persons can assert and preserve their identity'.[325] The second Paragraph refers to the use of the minority language in relations with the administrative authori-

[325] Explanatory Report to the Framework Convention, sub 63.

ties. This provision has been worded very flexibly leaving Parties a wide degree of discretion, which is a recognition of the 'possible financial, administrative (...) and technical difficulties associated with the use of minority languages in relations (...) [with] administrative authorities'.[326] The third Paragraph refers to the use of the minority language in criminal proceedings. These Articles do not go beyond safeguarding that which is laid down in Articles 5 and 6 of the ECHR.[327]

The first and second Paragraph of Article 11 deal with the right to have a name and to use language signs, inscriptions and other information of a private nature in the minority language. The third Paragraph deals with the right to 'display traditional local names, street names and other topographical indications intended for the public' in the minority language.

Articles 12-14 contain several educational rights: Article 12, Paragraph 3, deals with equal access to education, and Paragraph 2 with 'adequate opportunities for teacher training and access to textbooks'. Article 13 contains the rights of minorities 'to set up (at their own costs) and to manage their own private [schools]'. The Explanatory Report adds that the schools 'may be subject to the same forms of supervision as other [schools], particularly with regard to teaching standards' and that 'it is important that any qualifications awarded are officially recognised'.[328]

Finally, Article 14, first Paragraph, mentions the right of persons belonging to a national minority to learn the minority language. Like the above-mentioned right to use a minority language in public (Article 10, Paragraph 1), the present right also concerns 'one of the principal means by which [a minority] can assert and preserve its identity'. And the Explanatory Report adds that '[t]here can be no exceptions to this'. Nevertheless, the right to learn the minority language 'does not imply positive action, notably of a financial nature, on the part of the State'.[329] Paragraph 2 formulated very flexibly concerns teaching and instruction in a minority language: the Parties 'shall endeavour to ensure, as far as possible and within the framework of the education systems, that persons belonging to these minorities have adequate opportunities for being taught the minorities' language or for receiving instruction in this language'.

---

[326] *Ibid.*, sub 64.

[327] *Ibid.*, sub 67.

[328] Explanatory Report to the Framework Convention, sub 72.

[329] *Ibid.*, sub 74.

In Chapters 10 and 11, the different provisions of the Framework Convention which concern linguistic rights, thus Articles 10 to 11 and Articles 12 to 14, respectively, will be discussed in the light of their implementation in national legislation and in the light of their practical value for the minorities concerned.

9.4 The European Charter of Regional or Minority Languages

More so than the Framework Convention and much more so than Article 27 ICCPR and the ECHR, the European Charter of Regional or Minority Languages (hereinafter: Languages Charter) deals exclusively with minority languages. This document, which was also drafted within the framework of the Council of Europe, was signed by Slovakia on 20 February 2001, and ratified on 20 July 2001. Romania signed the Charter on 17 July 1995, but has not yet ratified it. Bulgaria has not signed this Charter. In this study, the Languages Charter will be discussed, where relevant, in relation to Slovakia.

One of the ideas underlying the Languages Charter is that 'the protection of the historical regional or minority languages of Europe, some of which are in danger of eventual extinction, contributes to the maintenance and development of Europe's cultural wealth and traditions'. Further, the Charter stresses 'the value of interculturalism and multilingualism'.[330]

The Languages Charter defines 'regional or minority languages' as 'languages that are: traditionally used within a given territory of a State by nationals of that State who form a group numerically smaller than the rest of the State's population; and different from the official language(s) of that State; it does not include either dialects of the official language(s) of the State or the languages of migrants'.[331]

The Charter defines 'non-territorial languages' as 'languages used by nationals of the State which differ from the language or languages used by the rest of the State's population but which, although traditionally used within the territory of the State, cannot be identified with a particu-

[330] Preamble Languages Charter.
[331] Article 1 Languages Charter.

lar area thereof[332]. An example of a non-territorial language is the Roma language.

The Charter lists in Article 7 several objectives and principles on which the Parties are expected 'to base their policies, legislation and practice'. Such principles are, for instance, 'the recognition of the regional or minority languages as an expression of cultural wealth'; 'the need for resolute action to promote regional or minority languages in order to safeguard them'; 'the provision of appropriate forms and means for the teaching and study of regional or minority languages at all appropriate stages'.

Article 8 of the Languages Charter provides that the Parties undertake, 'within the territory in which such languages are used, according to the situation of each of these languages, and without prejudice to the teaching of the official language(s) of the State', to make (partly) available in the relevant regional or minority languages: pre-school education, primary education, secondary education, technical and vocational education; university and other higher education.

Article 10 deals with the use of regional or minority languages by Administrative authorities and in public services.

Articles 15 to 17 describe the system of Periodical reports which shall be presented to the Secretary General of the Council of Europe. The reports shall be examined by a committee of experts which shall be composed of one member per Party, appointed by the Committee of Ministers 'from a list of individuals of the highest integrity and recognised competence in the matters dealt with in the Charter'.

9.5 Conclusion

The international documents mentioned in this Chapter deal, to an increasing extent, with minority languages. More so than the provisions concerning non-discrimination as described in Part II of this study, the provisions concerning linguistic rights in the Framework Convention leave a margin of discretion to States in the implementation of these rights. Possible financial, administrative and technical difficulties associated with the use of minority languages in relations with public authori-

[332] *Idem.*

ties and with the instruction of or in minority languages are explicitly taken into account. Also the Languages Charter is flexibly formulated, but contains more details concerning objectives and principles on which the Parties are expected to base their policies, legislation and practice.

Taken together, the Framework Convention and the Languages Charter constitute a broad scale of standards concerning the linguistic rights of minorities from which States, as far as the Languages Charter is concerned, can choose whatever fits best with regard to their financial, administrative or political circumstances.

However, flexibility for States means non-uniformity and dependence on national regulations for minorities. National legislation with regard to linguistic rights and the practical use of these standards concerning linguistic rights for individuals belonging to a minority group will be analyzed in Chapters 11 to 13 on the basis of the situation of mainly the Hungarian minorities in Slovakia and Romania. However, before starting with this analysis, Chapter 10 will provide some background information on the position of these Hungarian minorities.

Chapter 10
THE HERITAGE OF TRIANON

10.1 INTRODUCTION

Slovakia and Romania do not only share the Roma as a minority, but also the Hungarians. The recent history of the Hungarian minorities in Slovakia and Romania starts in 1920 with the Peace Treaty of Trianon.[333] On the one hand, Hungary became fully independent from Austria, on the other, it lost a substantial part of its territory, inhabited by Hungarians and by different minority groups, to Czechoslovakia, Yugoslavia and Romania. The way in which the Hungarians treated their minorities at the time they were part of the Austrian-Hungarian Empire was later reflected by the way the Hungarian minorities were (and still are) treated by the new States which emerged after the Treaty of Trianon.

The heritage of Trianon is twofold: in the first place there is a latent fear by the governments of Romania and Slovakia of nationalism and irredentist tendencies of the Hungarian minorities. Another consequence of the existence of large Hungarian minorities in, especially, Romania and Slovakia is the ambition of the subsequent Hungarian governments to protect the Hungarian minorities living in neighbouring States.[334] Recently, this ambition has resulted in the adoption in Hungary of the *Hungarian Status Law* which has led to international tension and discussion. Sections 10.4 and 10.5 will deal with these two issues which Slovakia and Romania have in common with regard to their Hungarian minority. First, however, the next two sections will provide some background information on, respectively, the Hungarians in Slovakia and Romania.

---

[333] The Treaty of Trianon was signed on June 4, 1920 at the Grand Trianon Palace at Versailles, France, between the United States of America, the British Empire, France, Italy and Japan, Belgium, China, Cuba, Greece, Nicaragua, Panama, Poland, Portugal, Roumania, the Serb-Croat-Slovene State, Siam, Czechoslovakia (the Allied and Associated Powers) and Hungary. Section VI (Articles 54-60) of the Treaty of Trianon deals with the protection of minorities, but only with the protection of minorities living within the new borders of Hungary.

[334] G. de Keersmaeker, 'Hongarije en de Hongaarse minderheden in Slowakije en Roemenië', in: *NoordZuid Cahier*, December 1997.

10.2 THE HUNGARIAN MINORITY IN SLOVAKIA

The Hungarian minority in Slovakia constitutes approximately 10 % of the Slovak population. They live in settlements along Slovakia's southern border with Hungary. Until 1919 when the Austro-Hungarian Empire was divided and Czechoslovakia was created, the Hungarians dominated this area both politically and culturally. Now the roles are reversed.

Since 1989, nationalist sentiments have been growing in Slovakia. One of the characteristic features of the Mečiar regime was a confrontational approach to the Hungarian minority. Both the government's policy after 1994 and the fact that the Hungarian Government did take an active interest in the well-being of Hungarians living abroad, did not strengthen Slovak-Hungarian mutual solidarity and confidence, but rather nurtured feelings of suspicion and prejudice.

The 1998 and 2002 parliamentary elections brought about a crucial change in the status of the Hungarian minority: the Hungarian Coalition Party (SMK) became part of the ruling coalition, and its participation in decisions concerning the development of Slovakia increased significantly.[335] The Slovak Report of 1999 even mentions that 'the relations between persons of Hungarian ethnic origin and citizens of Slovak origin in the ethnically mixed areas of southern Slovakia are friendly, non-confrontational and stabilized as a result of long-term co-existence'.[336] And, according to the Advisory Committee 'there has been a significant improvement in attitudes towards the Hungarian minority (...) especially in regions where Hungarians constitute a relatively high proportion of the population and where there is constant interaction between the majority and the said minority'.[337]

However, there is a gap between the perceptions of ethnic Hungarians and Slovaks. Hungarians perceive their status much more critically. While 63 % of ethnic Hungarians assessed the conditions of the Hungarian minority as being less favourable, only 5 % of ethnic Slovaks shared this view. The conviction that Hungarians and Slovaks have equal condi-

---

[335] Zora Bútorová, Ol'ga Gyárfášová, and Marián Velšic, 'Public Opinion', in: Meseznikov, Grigorij, Ivantyšyn, Nicholson (eds.), *Slovakia 1998-1999, A Global Report on the State of Society*, Bratislava, 1999, p. 157. Slovak elections 2002: <www.radio.cz/en/article/32675/limit>.

[336] Slovak State Report, 1999, p. 16.

[337] Advisory Committee Opinion on Slovakia, 2001, sub 25.

tions for their development prevailed among Slovaks (58 %), but not among Hungarians (33 %). A quarter of the Slovaks (26 %) even interpreted the status of the Hungarians as being privileged, in contrast with only 1 % of the Hungarians.[338]

A tolerant and consensus-seeking approach is considered to be typical of Slovaks living in ethnically mixed regions, as opposed to purely Slovak districts where a 'significant segment [of the Slovaks] view the Hungarians either as intruders or Magyarized Slovaks, who endanger the Slovak national identity'.[339] The attitudes of Slovaks towards the Hungarian minority are also influenced by a set of socio-demographic factors. Ethnic Slovaks with secondary and higher education, as well as inhabitants of medium-sized and larger cites, tend to be less suspicious and less confrontational. However, the strongest factor remains political affiliation.[340]

Hungarians, on their part, are strongly aware that they live in their ancient homeland, and accept 'as a reality the fact that their historical and native land is now in a country that shows enmity towards the community'. Further, although they are socially and politically well organized they do not really support the Slovak State or participate in it.[341]

It is not primarily their economic situation, but rather political and cultural issues that are the main points of concern for the Hungarian minority in Slovakia. They fear the social and cultural dominance of Slovaks especially in the area of language, such as the right to use Hungarian names; the right to put up bilingual street signs; the right to use Hungarian in contacts with the authorities; and the right to education in their mother tongue. Further, as will be seen below, there is a call for autonomy within Slovakia among some of the Hungarians. They do not want to secede, but autonomy with respect to language, education and cultural issues. A third major issue in relations between the Hungarian

---

338 Zora Bútorová, Ol'ga Gyárfášová, and Marián Velšic, 'Public Opinion', 1999, p. 158.

339 Miklos Duray, *Hungarians Nation in Slovakia*: <www.slovakia.org/society-hungary.htm>.

340 Zora Bútorová, Ol'ga Gyárfášová, and Marián Velšic, 'Public Opinion', 1999, p. 159.

341 Miklos Duray, *Hungarians Nation in Slovakia*: <www.slovakia.org/society-hungary.htm>.

and German minority on the one hand, and the Slovak Government on the other, are the Beneš Decrees of 1945, as discussed in Chapter 7.[342]

10.3 The Hungarian Minority in Romania

In Romania the Communist regime under both dictators Gheorghe Gheorghiu-Dej (1944-1965) and Ceaucescu (1965-1989) was among the harshest and most repressive in Central and Eastern Europe and affected the Romanian people as a whole, not only the minorities. In 1989, the Council of Europe vigorously condemned

> 'the activities of the *Securitate* and the systematisation plan devised by President Ceaucescu, under which almost half of the 13,000 or so Romanian villages are to be destroyed and whose Implementation has already commenced in the Bucharest area.'

However, the Council of Europe also recognized that the human rights violations were more specifically directed against minorities, especially the Hungarian and Roma minorities. The Jewish and German minorities gradually left the country. In fact, the German minority was sold to West Germany by Ceaucescu for between 4,000 and 10,000 DM per person, depending on age and qualifications. Between 1967 and 1989 some 200,000 ethnic Germans left Romania in this way.[343]

According to the Council of Europe, contrary to all its international obligations, the Romanian Communist regime blatantly disregarded the rights conferred on its 'cohabitating nationalities' in terms of freedom of expression, freedom of the press, freedom to engage in political activities, cultural freedom, freedom of religion and freedom of circulation, and it expressed its admiration for the courage and resolution of the Romanian dissidents. Consequently, members of the Hungarian minority were increasingly opting to flee to Hungary.[344]

---

[342] <www.slovakia.org/society-hungary2.htm>.

[343] Tony Judt, 'Romania: Bottom of the Heap', *New York Review of Books*, Vol. 48, No. 17, Nov. 1, 2001.

[344] COE PA Recommendation No. 1114 (1989), on the situation of minorities in Romania.

After the revolution of 1989, the Hungarians asserted their rights and, since 1996, have been represented in Parliament by their own political party (Democratic Alliance of Hungarians in Romania (DAHR)). At present, the Hungarians in Romania (their number is estimated between 1.4 million[345] and 2 million[346]) are in fact made up of three groups: a group of approximately 9,500 Hungarians who settled in Berceni, today a part of Bucharest; the Csangos (between 60,000 and 70,000 people)[347] which are a non-homogenous group of Roman Catholics forming an enclave near the border with Moldavia near Iaşi. This ethnic group is a relic from the Middle Ages that has survived in Moldavia, in the eastern part of the Romanian Carpathians. Csangos speak an early form of Hungarian and are associated with ancient traditions, and a great diversity of folk art and culture[348]; the largest group of about 1 million Hungarians live in Transylvania.

10.3.1 **Hungarians in Transylvania**

The largest group of Hungarians in Romania live in Transylvania where they make up 20 % of the population. After the Communist take-over, the so-called 'nationalization process' in 1948 made it possible to deprive the Hungarian population of its financial basis, institutions, and school system, and to reduce to a minimum the opportunities for Transylvania's Hungarian Churches to function. While the laws formally ensured the free use of the native language, from the 1960s onwards, the Hungarian language was gradually driven out of public life.[349]

Nevertheless, the Hungarian minority in Romania managed to preserve their language as well as their ethnic and cultural identity.[350] In 1989 the Democratic Alliance of Hungarians in Romania (DAHR) was established. This party represents the interests of the Hungarians in Ro-

---

[345] See Annex II.

[346] Number mentioned by the Unrepresented Nations and Peoples Organisation, <www.unpo.org>.

[347] This number is mentioned in COE PA Recommendation No. 1521 (2001), on the Csango minority culture in Romania.

[348] *Idem.*

[349] For general information about Hungarians in Romania: <www.minority2000.net/Gr-75/t84gb.htm>.

[350] More specifically on this identity see: Cathy O'Grady, Zoltán Kántor, Daniela Tarnovschi, *Hungarians of Romania*, CEDIME-SE, pp. 21-29.

mania in the Romanian parliament and participated in the ruling coalition from 1996 to 2000.[351]

The interethnic relations between Romanians and Hungarians are fairly stable, although mutual perception and stereotypes differ. Romanians perceive Hungarians as: hard-working, united, civilized and vain, while they see themselves as: decent, hospitable, hard-working and honest. Hungarians perceive Romanians as: united, religious and hypocritical, while they consider themselves as: hardworking, trustworthy, civilized and divided.[352] The everyday interaction between the two groups is correct but not very warm, especially from the side of the Romanians: almost 21 % of the Romanians avoid Hungarians and 67.3 % do not greet their Hungarian neighbours. On the other hand, 15.2 % of the Hungarians avoid the Romanians, and 'only' 28.1 % do not greet their Romanian neighbours.[353]

In general, it can be concluded that the situation of the Hungarians in Romania has improved in comparison with the situation before 1989. The interethnic relations between the Hungarians and Romanians do not demonstrate a great deal of cordiality, but at least Hungarians are not openly discriminated against. For most Hungarians in Romania it is important to have their own political party and (cultural) institutions, which, to a large extent, have been re-established after 1989, and to be able to speak Hungarian also in relations with public officials. This, however, is especially important for elderly Hungarians who have problems with expressing themselves in the Romanian language. So far, the problems of the Hungarians in Romania mainly focus on two issues: Teaching in and of the Hungarian language (mother tongue education is also an issue for the Csango and some other, smaller minorities, such as the Croats and Ukrainians), and the question of autonomy for the Hungarians in Transylvania.

10.4 Hungarian Autonomy in Slovakia and Romania

With regard to the participation of persons belonging to national minorities in cultural, social and economic life and in public affairs, Article 15

[351] *Ibid.*, p. 30.

[352] Ethnocultural Diversity Resource Center (EDRC), *Ethnobarometer, Interethnic Relations in Romania*, Cluj, 2000, pp. 68-69.

[353] *Ibid.*, pp. 37-38.

of the Framework Convention states that '[t]he Parties shall create the [necessary] conditions'. In Slovakia, Article 30 (1) of the Constitution reads as follows: 'Citizens have the right to participate in the administration of public affairs either directly or through the free election of their representatives.' According to Act No. 424/1991 Coll. on Association in Political Parties and Political Movements, section 1 (1) states: 'Citizens have the right to associate in political parties and political movements. The exercise of this right serves citizens for their participation in political life, especially in the forming of legislative bodies and local self-government bodies.' The Act on Local Self-Government was adopted by the government in August 2000. This Act concerning regional self-government enlarges and establishes the local self-government.[354]

According to the Slovak Report of 1999, 'all citizens of the SR, including persons belonging the national minorities, are guaranteed the right to actively participate in the country's political life by the Constitution. For national minorities, this right is also secured through their active work in political parties based on the ethnic principle'.[355]

However, some minorities aim at more than political participation. For instance, the Hungarians living in Slovakia envisage three options for their future: 1) territorial autonomy, either with the Hungarian majority, or a balanced ethnic composition, with self-governing special status regions; 2) institutional autonomy with an adequate legal framework; 3) the consistent application of the principle of subsidiarity in the spirit of the European Charter of Local Self-Government.[356] Slovakia ratified the latter Charter on 20 July 2001.

As far as the decentralization of the State is concerned, this was one of the set priorities of the new government in 1998. Reform in this area was aimed, on the one hand, at increasing the powers of the local self-government authorities and, on the other, at introducing regional self-government.[357] Where the protection of minorities implies meaningful participation in political life on an equal basis with the majority, Slovakia has created, by introducing regional and local governments, the

[354] Kusý, 2000, p. 170.

[355] Slovak State Report, 1999, p. 39.

[356] Miklos Duray, *Hungarian Nation in Slovakia*, see: <www.slovakia.org/society-hungary.htm>.

[357] Monitoring Committee, Doc. No. 8496, 6 September 1999, sub 133.

possibilities for (smaller) minorities to participate in Slovakia's political life and to become involved in decision-making which affects them.[358]

Autonomy, however, whether territorial or institutional, is for most States 'many bridges too far'. In Romania, for instance, the issue of Hungarian autonomy emerges, especially, in election campaigns and is presented as irredentism in the propaganda of Romanian right-wing extremists. However, the idea of the re-emergence of a Hungarian Autonomous Region – such a region existed in the 1950s – also makes 'ordinary' Romanians nervous and suspicious. For instance, a recent agreement between the Romanian Government and the Hungarian Democratic Federation of Romania (UDMR) concerning the redrawing of Romania's economic zones was seen by ethnic Romanians and the Orthodox Church as an 'act of defiance' towards non-Hungarians.[359] Politicians from other political parties rejected these plans as contradicting the 'European spirit', and declared it to be 'out of the question' to set up any structures based on ethnic criteria.[360] Another recent example of this tension between the Hungarians and Romanians on the issue of autonomy occurred when ethnic Hungarians established the National Council of Hungarians in Transylvania which called for territorial and cultural autonomy for ethnic Hungarians living in Romania. Subsequently, Prime Minister Nastase asked the Prosecutor-General's office 'while fully observing the rights to free association' to investigate these calls for territorial autonomy.[361]

In sum, ambitions concerning autonomy of the Hungarian minorities in Slovakia and Romania reach beyond both the patience of States and the provisions of the Framework Convention. The scope of the Framework Convention is confined by the principle of territorial integrity: Article 21 Framework Convention states that '[n]othing in the present Framework Convention shall be interpreted as implying a right to engage in any activity or perform any act contrary to (...) territorial integrity and political independence of States'.

---

[358] For Romania, see the new Local Government and Local Self-Government Regulation Act in force since 25 May 2001which includes all the rules governing the rights of persons belonging to national minorities as laid down in the Government Order amending Act No. 69/1991.

[359] RFE/RL Newsline Vol. 7, No. 70, Part II, 11 April 2003.

[360] RFE/RL Newsline Vol. 7, No. 71, Part II, 14 April 2003.

[361] RFE/RL Newsline Vol. 7, No. 81, Part II, 29 April 2003.

This Framework Convention is the result of a political process and has been concluded by States, not by minorities. For the international community, a *Framework* Convention, thus a construction which leaves a large margin of discretion to States, is the attainable maximum in a thorny and threatening issue such as rights for national minorities. Within States, local and regional self-government constitutes the acceptable maximum. These factors make an autonomous status for the Hungarian minorities in Slovakia and Romania very unlikely.

10.5 The Hungarian Status Law

By adopting the law on the 'ethnic Hungarians living in neighbouring countries' ('Hungarian Status Law') which entered into force on 1 January 2002,[362] Hungary aims 'to comply with its responsibilities for Hungarians living abroad' and 'to ensure that Hungarians living in neighbouring countries form part of the Hungarian nation as a whole and to promote and preserve their well-being and awareness of national identity within their home country'.[363]

This law might be seen as an example of an extreme form of protecting the (Hungarian) cultural identity of minorities. Under the law, preferential treatment in the field of social security, health, transportation and education benefits[364] is granted to almost 4 million citizens of Hungarian (Magyar) "nationality" living in the following neighbouring countries: Croatia, Serbia and Montenegro, Romania, Slovenia, Slovakia and Ukraine. Hungarians living in Austria are excluded from the scope of the law. Further, it gives ethnic Hungarians the right to work in Hungary for three months each year.[365] Persons who wish to receive those benefits need to apply for a certificate proving their Hungarian origin, which will be issued by a Hungarian authority and will be based on recommendations by ethnic Hungarian organizations in those countries.[366]

[362] Act LXII of 2001 on Hungarians living in neighbouring countries, adopted by Parliament on 19 June 2001.

[363] Preamble of Act LXII of 2001 on Hungarians living in neighbouring countries.

[364] Articles 4-14 of Act LXII of 2001 on Hungarians living in neighbouring countries.

[365] Article 15 and 16 Act LXII of 2001 on Hungarians living in neighbouring countries.

[366] See, Articles 19-26, 'Rules of Procedure of Application for Benefits and Assistance', Act LXII of 2001 on Hungarians living in neighbouring countries.

The Hungarian Status Law is a cause of great concern for the governments of those countries with Hungarian minorities, such as Romania and Slovakia, and to international organizations such as the Council of Europe. It was even said that this law has 'damaged Hungary's international reputation'.[367]

According to Hungarian government officials, the law intends to prevent mass immigration by some 3 million ethnic Hungarians once Hungary joins the EU.[368] Foreign Minister Janos Martonyi defended this law in an interview saying that the law has been 'wrongly evaluated', as is often the case with 'documents of historic significance', and added that 'the prosperity and the preservation of the distinct identity of minorities in our region serves the development of the region as a whole' and will therefore contribute to 'the development of good neighbourly relations'.[369] In 2003, some amendments to this law were submitted to the Hungarian Parliament for approval. In the amended version of the law, educational benefits will be extended to members of any ethnic group who study the Hungarian language, culture, or history. Further, the employment benefits granted to ethnic Hungarians are to be rescinded by the Hungarian government.

The reactions to the Status Law and on the amendments by the neighbouring States, such as Slovakia and Romania, vary considerably.

Initially, in 2001, Slovak Prime Minister Dzurinda said that he did not believe the issue itself will have a lasting impact on relations between Hungary and Slovakia. Both countries, he explained, are 'already halfway' on the road to the EU, and the Status Law will not apply to Hungarian minorities living in EU countries. Dzurinda said the preservation of the ethnic identity of Hungarians in Slovakia is guaranteed by the European Charter on Minority Languages, which the Slovak parliament has ratified.[370] However, since then the Slovak attitude became has hardened: in 2003, Slovak Premier Dzurinda called the amendments 'wholly unacceptable' and said that Slovakia will 'take appropriate measures to prevent the implementation of the law in Slovakia due to the legislation's remaining "extraterritorial and discriminatory" aspects, and because the

[367] RFE/RL Newsline Vol. 5, No. 179, Part II, 20 September 2001.
[368] RFE/RL Newsline Vol. 5, No. 179, Part II, 20 June 2001.
[369] RFE/RL Newsline Vol. 5, No. 199, Part II, 22 June 2001.
[370] RFE/RL Newsline Vol. 5, No. 160, Part II, 23 August 2001.

Status Law is "in violation of international legislation"'. He said that he will continue to oppose the law.[371]

Romania's reaction to the Status Law is more co-operative: in Romania over 400,000 members of the Hungarian minority (which is 27.89 % of Romania's ethnic Hungarians) applied for Hungarian ID cards.[372] In 2003, Romania and Hungary signed a bilateral agreement on the implementation of the Status Law. 'Romanian Prime Minister Nastase described the agreement as another Abattle for Europe that we have won together". The agreement stipulates that the ID cards must not carry the insignia of Greater Hungary, must not resemble passports, and must only be issued in Hungary. Financial aid for the purpose of preserving Hungarian culture is to be granted only to institutions, not to individuals.'[373]

Also on the international level, the Status Law could not go unnoticed and uncriticised: In 2001, according to a motion by some members of the Parliamentary Assembly of the Council of Europe, 'the law establishes the principle of discrimination between the Hungarian minority living in the respective countries and the majority population as well as the extra-territoriality principle for its implementation which may generate new tensions between these populations and favour regional instability'. Further, they considered this law to be incompatible with Protocol No. 12 to the ECHR, Article 21 of the Framework Convention and Article 13 of the European Union Treaty. Finally, they called upon the Hungarian authorities to suspend the implementation of the law and to put into practice the existing European conventions and documents regarding human rights and national minorities.[374]

However, in 2003, in a Resolution on this subject the Parliamentary Assembly stated in more diplomatic terms:

> 'in principle, [it] welcomes assistance given by kin-states to their kin-minorities in other States in order to help these kin-minorities to preserve their cultural, linguistic and ethnic identity. However, the Assembly wishes to stress that such kin-states must be careful that the form and substance of the assis-

---

[371] RFE/RL Newsline Vol. 7, No. 98, Part II, 27 May 2003; No. 115, Part II, 19 June 2003.

[372] RFE/RL News line Vol. 7, No. 181, Part II, 23 September 2003.

[373] RFE/RL News line Vol. 7, No. 182, Part II, 24 September 2003.

[374] COE PA Motion, Doc. No. 9153, 28 June 2001.

> tance given are also accepted by the States of which the members of the kin-minorities are citizens (...)'.[375]

Further, the Assembly considered that:

> 'responsibility for minority protection lies primarily with the home States. (..)The emergence of new and original forms of minority protection, particularly by their kin-states, constitutes a positive trend in so far as they can contribute to the realisation of this goal within the framework of international co-operation.'[376]

Further, the Assembly warned that:

> 'States should abstain from taking unilateral measures, which would risk compromising the climate of co-operation with other States.[377] But it 'notes with satisfaction that on 23 June 2003, the Parliament of Hungary amended the law in question on several points, thus responding in part to the critical comments that have been made'.[378]

Finally, the Parliamentary Assembly urged Hungary to find ways to make further amendments to the Hungarian Law on Hungarians Living in Neighbouring Countries and called on all governments concerned to enter into or to continue substantial negotiations.[379] Also the European Commission has warned that the Status Law may not be applied outside Hungary without the agreement of the relevant governments.[380]

In sum, it took Hungary some time and an enormous diplomatic effort to convince its neighbouring States of the use and necessity as well as the harmless intentions of the Status Law. And still, it is only in its amended version and subject to the condition of continuing negotiations with the States concerned, that (some) neighbouring States and international organizations seem to temper some of their suspicions with regard to the Status Law.

---

[375] COE PA Resolution No. 1335 (2003), on the Preferential Treatment of National Minorities by the Kin-state: the Case of the Hungarian Law on Hungarians Living in Neighbouring Countries of 19 June 2001, sub 1.

[376] *Ibid.*, sub 2.

[377] *Ibid.*, sub 8.

[378] *Ibid.*, sub 13.

[379] *Ibid.*, sub 14.

[380] RFE/RL Newsline Vol. 7, No. 85, Part II, 6 May 2003; No. 101, Part II, 30 May 2003.

10.6 Conclusion

Slovakia and Romania do not only share a large Hungarian minority on their territory, but they also share some problems relating to these minorities. The two issues described in this Chapter, the call for autonomy and the Hungarian Status Law, give an impression of the (possible) strength of the Hungarians as minorities in Romania and Slovakia. Unlike the Roma, they are backed by a kin-state, Hungary, and this seems to make them less vulnerable in political, economic and cultural terms. Especially the recent Hungarian Status Law has this effect. However, the vicinity of a kin-state has not always been a guarantee either, as the (post-Trianon) history of these minorities in Slovakia and Romania has shown. The Hungarian minorities were important victims of the harsh communist regimes in Slovakia and, especially, Romania, and Hungary was not in a position to prevent this.

Although the Hungarians share the call for autonomy and the effect of the Hungarian Status Law, there are also differences in their ambitions and demands. On the one hand, the Hungarians in Slovakia are concerned about the social and cultural dominance of Slovaks especially in the area of language, such as the right to use Hungarian names; the right to put up bilingual street signs; the right to use Hungarian in contacts with the authorities; and the right to education in their mother tongue.[381] Their call for autonomy envisages autonomy with respect to language, education and cultural issues.

On the other hand, for most Hungarians in Romania it is important to have their own political party and (cultural) institutions and, especially for elderly Hungarians who have problems in expressing themselves in the Romanian language, it is important to be able to speak Hungarian also in relations with public officials. However, the main issue for the Hungarians in Romania (and also for the Csangos and some other, smaller minorities, such as the Croats and Ukrainians), is teaching in and of the mother tongue.

[381] Compared with Slovakia (see: Advisory Committee Opinion on Slovakia, 2000, sub 36) these issues do not constitute major problems in Romania (see Advisory Committee Opinion on Romania, 2001, sub 49 and 50).

Chapter 11
THE USE OF MINORITY LANGUAGES IN PUBLIC; THE CASE OF SLOVAKIA

11.1 Introduction

How do States use the margins of discretion left in the Framework Convention? Articles 9 to 11 of the Framework Convention all deal, in flexible wording, with the use of minority languages or minority names in a public setting: thus in a public place, outdoors, in the media, in relations with public authorities, in court proceedings. This Chapter will discuss these rights, their implementation in the national legislation and their practical effect, in relation to one particular minority in Slovakia: the Hungarians. As described in Chapter 9, this minority is not primarily concerned with their economic situation, but rather with political and cultural issues. They fear the social and cultural dominance of Slovaks especially in the area of language, such as the right to use Hungarian names; the right to put up bilingual street signs; the right to use Hungarian in contacts with the authorities; and the right to education in their mother tongue.

11.2 Act on the State Language of the Slovak Republic

According to Article 6 of the Constitution, '(1) Slovak is the State language on the territory of the Slovak Republic, and (2) the use of other languages in dealings with the authorities will be regulated by law'. However, surprisingly, Article 34 of the Slovak Constitution gives a promising legal basis to the position of minority languages in Slovak national law. This Article of the Constitution provides that:

> '(1) The comprehensive development of citizens representing national minorities or ethnic groups in the Slovak Republic is guaranteed, particularly the right to develop their own culture, together with other members of the minority or ethnic group, the right to disseminate and receive information in their mother tongue, the right to associate in national minority associations,

> and the right to set up and maintain educational and cultural institutions. Details will be set out in a law.
> (2) In addition to the right to master the State language, citizens belonging to national minorities or ethnic groups also have, under conditions defined by law, a guaranteed a) right to education in their own language, b) right to use their language in dealings with the authorities, c) right to participate in the solution of affairs concerning national minorities and ethnic groups. (...)'

One of the legacies of Mečiar's Government is the Act on the State Language of the Slovak Republic, which was approved by Parliament on 15 November 1995. This law took effect on 1 January 1996.[382] In accordance with Article 6 of the Slovak Constitution this Act repeats the fact that 'the State language on the territory of the Slovak Republic is the Slovak language',[383] and that 'the State language has a priority over other languages applied on the whole territory of the Slovak Republic'. Although this law 'does not regulate the usage of national minority languages and ethnic groups', and 'usage of those languages is arranged by separate laws',[384] this law certainly restricts the use of minority languages.[385]

According to the Commentary on the Act on the State Language of the Slovak Republic,

> 'the main purpose of this Act consists in the creation of a solid legal framework for the use of the Slovak Language with the aim to ensure the smooth operation of both State administration organs and municipal self-governing bodies on the whole territory of Slovakia. The necessary prerequisite of such functioning of State and society and their integrity is the existence and adequate status of the State language as a general communication means providing all citizens with freedom and equality in their rights. It is entirely self-evident that countries in which the population includes also national minorities have to make sure that the legal norms on a language do not infringe upon the legitimate linguistic rights of persons belonging to national minori-

[382] Act No. 270/1995 Coll., on the State Language of the Slovak Republic.

[383] Article 6, Section 1, of the Slovak Constitution.

[384] E.g. Act No. 141/1961 Coll., on Penal Judicial Proceedings; Act No. 81/1966 Coll., on Periodical Press and on Other Information Mass media; Act No. 29/1984 Coll., on the System of Elementary and High Schools (The School Law); Act No. 254/1991Coll., on Slovak Television; Act No. 255/1991 Coll., on Slovak Radio Broadcasting; Act No. 191/1994 Coll., on Denomination of Municipalities in the Language of the Minorities.

[385] See Article 1 sub 1, 2, and 4 Act No. 270/1995 Coll.

> ties. The Act on the State Language of the Slovak Republic fully respects those legitimate linguistic rights and therefore it is in compliance with the international commitments of Slovakia in this field.'[386]

According to Heinz Tichy from the Internationales Zentrum für Nationalismus- und Minderheitenforschung in Vienna, 'to establish a "State Language" by law might be a form of taking care of the development of this Language. Yet in general, establishing a "State Language" results from a competition of Languages. Establishing a "State Language" directly or indirectly concerns the position of the other Languages' use in a State.'

Tichy concludes that the Slovak Republic is

> 'entirely free to establish one or more "official language(s)"or, even, one or more "State language(s)" as long as the aforementioned positions of the minority Languages in particular the rights of the members of ("national") minorities are respected. As such establishing inevitably concerns the latter positions, in case of need this has to be done uno actu with the necessary adaptation or clarification in the sphere of language in particular minority rights.'[387]

Notwithstanding this comment, the adoption of the new Act on the State Language was criticized both domestically and internationally. According to a decision by the Constitutional Court of the Slovak Republic, at least a part of the law contradicted the Constitution and the National Commission for European Integration approved a Resolution asking Vice-Premier Josef Kalman to elaborate the meaning of the law on minority Languages when used in an official context. In spite of a verbal assurance by the government, no actual steps were taken to clarify the law.[388]

The then OSCE High Commissioner on National Minorities Max van der Stoel sent a letter of concern to the then Slovak Minister for Foreign Affairs, Juraj Schenk, urging the Slovak authorities to prepare new legislation on this subject in order to fill the legal vacuum. 'To my mind, it

---

[386] Commentary on the Act on the State Language of the Slovak Republic, National Council of the Slovak Republic, 1995, pp. 1-2.

[387] COE PA Committee on Legal Affairs and Human Rights, Consideration on the Act of the Slovak Republic on its State Language in the Light of the Standards of the Council of Europe by Dr. Heinz Tichy, AS/Jur (1996)7, 1996, pp. 4 and 9.

[388] Michal Vašečka,1999, p. 410.

would also be wrong to conclude that mere accession to the European Charter for Regional or Minority Languages would fill this vacuum; domestic legislation on the basis of provisions of the Charter would in any case be necessary.'[389] Further, the European Roma Rights Center in Budapest arrived at the conclusion that 'with this new law the Slovak authorities have effectively abandoned their commitment to the right to the use of minority languages in official settings. If this is so, Roma will remain linguistically excluded in Slovakia and Romanes will continue to be regarded as a quaint pidgin, unworthy of any status beyond colloquial speech'.[390]

Finally, the Advisory Committee of the Framework Convention concluded in its Opinion of 2000 that 'it needs to be ascertained to what degree the State Language Law affects minority Languages. The Advisory Committee finds that, in this essential question, the State Language Law is lacking clarity.' Such as 'ambiguous legal situation is unsatisfactory from the point of view of legal certainty and (...) may give rise to negative consequences for persons belonging to national minorities. Further, the Advisory Committee considered it 'essential that this issue be addressed through proposals for amending the State Language Law if necessary, with a view to ensuring that the rights of persons belonging to minorities are protected in a clear and comprehensive manner both in law and practice'.[391]

However, the Advisory Committee also had to recognize that the implementation of the State Language Law 'has not, to date, had a widespread negative impact on minority languages and that, according to the Government, no sanctions have been imposed for non-compliance or violations of the said law'.[392]

Against the background of the tension between the Act on the State Language of the Slovak Republic and Article 34 of the Constitution the following question arises: what is the position of languages other than the 'State language' in Slovakian legislation and practice? This question will be discussed with regard to Articles 10 and 11 Framework Convention.

---

[389] Letter of 26 February 1996, REF.HC/96, 23 April 1996 and letter of 13 August 1996, REF.HC/96, 25 October 1996.

[390] ERRC, 1997, pp. 55-56.

[391] Advisory Committee Opinion on Slovakia, 2000, sub 34 and 35.

[392] *Ibid.*, sub 33.

11.3 The Use of One's Mother Tongue in Dealings With the Authorities (Article 10 (1) and (2) Framework Convention)

Article 10 of the Framework Convention refers to the right to use one's mother tongue in dealings with the authorities. Its first Paragraph deals with the right 'to use freely and without interference his or her minority language, in private and in public, orally and in writing'. According to Paragraph 2 '(...) the Parties shall endeavour to ensure, as far as possible, the conditions which would make it possible to use the minority language in relations between those persons and the administrative authorities'. The third Paragraph deals with the use of minority languages in criminal proceedings.

Subject to conditions defined by law, the right to use one's language in dealings with the authorities is guaranteed in Article 34 (2) sub b of the Slovak Constitution of 1992. The most recent and most comprehensive document on the use of minority languages in dealings with the authorities is the Law on the Use of Languages of National Minorities[393] of 1999.

Its Preamble states that 'recognizing and appreciating the importance of mother tongues of citizens of the Slovak Republic belonging to national minorities as an expression of the cultural wealth of the State... ', but also 'that the Slovak language is the State language in the Slovak Republic, and that it is desirable to regulate the use of the languages of Slovak citizens belonging to national minorities'.

The drafting of the Law on the Use of Languages of National Minorities had 'the purpose to regulate, in conjunction with other specific laws, rules on the use of minority languages also in official communication',[394] and it was a long and difficult process. Its adoption had been delayed and postponed by the Mečiar government since 1995; a policy which received a great deal of criticism from the international community.[395] However, the next government included the adoption of a law on the use of minority languages among its priorities. It was also considered to be one of the

393 Act No. 184/1999 Coll.
394 Section 1 of Act No. 184/1999.
395 Kusý, 2000, p. 170.

conditions for the Slovak Republic to join accession discussions with the European Union.[396]

The opposition, but also some members of the coalition parties, were against the adoption of the new law arguing that it was unnecessary since there were already several laws (the numbers varied between 26 and 36) on the use of minority languages. Another point of disagreement was the scope of the new law, namely whether it would only cover the use of minority languages in official communications or the use of these languages also in other fields, in particular education. Finally, there was the question of the percentage of the minority population required in a locality for the law to be applicable (namely 10 % or 20 %).[397]

In its Opinion on Slovakia of 2000 the Advisory Committee concluded that the Law on the Use National Minority Languages does not explicitly address the issue of its relation with the State Language Law. The Committee, however, recommended that Slovakia informs the public and officials concerned that the Law on the Use of Languages of National Minorities, as *lex specialis*, should take precedence.[398] In its reaction the Slovak Government stated that it 'cannot identify itself with the (...) pertinent proposal (...) on the priority use of minority Languages towards the official language', and declared that 'Slovakia will handle this issue in compliance with the European Charter on Regional or Minority Languages'.[399]

As adopted on 10 July 1999, the Law on the Use of Languages of National Minorities grants inhabitants in municipalities with a minority population of 20 % or more according to the last census the right to use their mother tongue in official communication with the municipality and to the bodies of the State administration and local self-government.[400] However, the Slovak Center for Legal Analyses, the Kalligram Foundation, pointed out in a 2003 report on the Implementation of the European Charter of Regional or Minority Languages in the Slovak Republic (hereafter: Kalligram Report), that 'the use of minority language is not completely granted even in municipalities where the 20 % threshold is met, because municipal authorities are not covered by the law on the use of

[396] Monitoring Committee, Doc. No. 8496, 6 September 1999, sub 124.
[397] *Ibid.*, sub 125.
[398] Advisory Committee Opinion on Slovakia, 2001, sub 36 and at p. 19.
[399] Slovak Comment, 2001, sub 7.
[400] Section 2(1) and (3) of Act No. 184/1999 Coll.

minority languages'.[401] The Kalligram Report gives the example of the Trnava region, 'where Trnava regional parliament did not approve the usage of Hungarian minority language even though the Hungarian minority population here forms 23 %. The law is not applicable, because in Trnava city itself the Hungarian minority population does not reach the necessary threshold of 20 %.' According to the Kalligram Report, this problem 'is generally present in the case of regional administration bodies that are located in municipalities where none of the minorities of ethnic groups reach the necessary 20 % threshold, even though within the region in general, as well as in many individual municipalities within the region, this rate is reached'.[402]

With regard to the language used by the authorities of territorial self-administration and the authorities of public and legal institutions, the text of the Act on the State Language of the Slovak Republic is very strict: 'In the course of accomplishment of their duties, the State authorities and State organizations, the authorities of territorial self-administration and the authorities of public and legal institutions, the State language shall be, by those authorities, used compulsorily on the whole territory of the Slovak Republic. Demonstration of commensurate knowledge of the State language by word of mouth and writing is a qualification for being taken into service, or for entering a similar occupational relationship, as well as a prerequisite for accomplishing work agreed within specified job description of a public and legal authority.'[403]

However, this position has been slightly modified by the recent Law on the Use of Languages of National Minorities establishing that 'the body of public administration and its employees are obliged to use in official communication the State Language, and under condition established by this law and specific legal acts they may use also a minority language. The body of public administration and its employees are not obliged to be proficient in a minority language'.[404]

Considering the fact that the drafting of the Law on the Use of Languages of National Minorities has been a political issue for a long time,

[401] Center for Legal Analyses - Kalligram Foundation, Report: Implementation of European Charter of Regional or Minority Languages in Slovak Republic (hereinafter: Kalligram Report), April 2003, pp. 1-2.

[402] *Idem.*

[403] § 3 sub 1 Act No. 270/1995 Coll. Emphasis added.

[404] Section 7 (1) Act No. 184/1999 Coll.

the limited scope of present text is not surprising. Contrary to the expectations and proposals of the Hungarian Coalition Party, it does not cover a number of other issues concerning the use of minority languages, notably in the field of pre-school education, the system of primary and secondary schools, culture,[405] its use in judicial proceedings, and its use in the media.

As far as these issues are concerned, the general point of departure remains the Act on the State Language of the Slovak Republic, which states that 'mutual contact of the courts with citizens, court proceedings, administrative proceedings, verdicts and minutes of courts and of administrative authorities, shall all be conducted and issued in the State language'.[406] And, Paragraph 7 sub b states: 'the rights of persons pertaining to national minorities and ethnic groups (...) resulting from specific regulations[407] remain untouched by this law'.

11.4 The Use of One's Minority Language in Judicial Proceedings (Article 10 (3) Framework Convention)

Article 10 Paragraph 3 Framework Convention deals with the right to use a minority language in judicial (criminal) proceedings. The guarantee in this Article does not extend beyond the second Paragraph of Article 5 of the ECHR which states that '[e]veryone who is arrested shall be informed promptly, in a language which he understands, of the reasons for his arrest and of any charge against him'. Article 6 Paragraph 3 ECHR contains a similar provision, but adds the right 'to have the free assistance of an interpreter if he cannot understand or speak the language used in court'.[408]

In Slovakia, the right to use a minority language in official proceedings is regulated by several specific legal acts, such as the Courts and Judges Act[409] section 7 (3): 'Everyone may act before the court in his

[405] Section 5 (1) and (2) Act No. 184/1999 Coll.

[406] Section 7 sub a Act No. 270/1995 Coll.

[407] Act No. 141/1961 Coll., on Penal Criminal Proceedings, § 2, section 14; Act No. 36/1967 Coll., on Experts and Interpreters; Edict No. 37/1967 of the Ministry of Justice of the Slovak Republic, on Administrating the Law on Experts and Interpreters in the Wording of the Subsequent Regulations.

[408] Article 6 (3) sub e ECHR.

[409] Act No. 335/1991 Coll.

own language. The law determines when the costs connected with the services of an interpreter are paid by the State.' Similar legal norms are found in the Civil Procedure Act[410] section 18: 'Parties in civil court proceedings have the same standing. They have the right to act before the court in their mother tongue. The court is obliged to provide them with the same opportunities for the exercising of their rights.' The Criminal Court Proceedings Act[411] section 2 (14) states: 'Everyone is entitled to use his mother tongue before bodies acting in criminal proceedings' and the Act on the Organization of the Constitutional Court of the Slovak Republic and Proceedings before it and the Position of Its Judges[412] section 23: 'Physical persons may use their mother tongue at oral trials or other negotiations. The costs of interpreting are borne by the Constitutional Court of the Slovak Republic.'

However, this right, as well as many other minority rights, depends on the fulfilment of the 20 % rate. According to the Kalligram Report there are cases where the official proceedings at a regional level take place in the Hungarian language and subsequently, for example during the appeal, proceedings are moved to the national level where the minority population rate does not reach the necessary 20 % and for this reason the decision of the competent body at the higher level cannot be delivered in the Hungarian language. The Kalligram Report concludes that in such cases

> 'a legal principle being broken, that of the unity of administrative (but also judicial) proceedings.(...) The principle is not respected in so far that the first level proceeding conducted in minority language is in some cases followed by appellate proceeding, where the minority language cannot be used because of the non-fulfilment of the 20 % rate. The first and the appellate level of proceeding are conducted in different circumstances, which might even give rise to constitutional concerns.'[413]

Further important shortcomings of Slovak legislation with regard to the use of languages of national minorities during official proceedings are, according to the Kalligram Report, the fact that minority languages cannot be used during the so-called specialized State administration proceed-

---

[410] Act No. 70/1992 Coll.
[411] Act No. 158/1992 Coll.
[412] Act No. 38/1993 Coll.
[413] Kalligram Report, 2003, pp. 1-2.

ings (such as tax or customs proceedings); the weak awareness on the part of State officials concerning the issue of the use of minority languages; the fact that official pre-printed forms very often used in official proceedings are not available in the language of the relevant national minority; and, 'last but not least, that the commitment of Slovak Republic to publish the most important legal documents in language of national minority is not performed by the State itself, but is mostly supported by private financial sources'.[414]

11.5 Names and Surnames (Article 11 (1) Framework Convention)

According to Article 11 of the Framework Convention, the Parties 'undertake to recognise (...) the right to use his or her surname (patronym) and first names in the minority language and the right to official recognition of them, according to modalities provided for in their legal system'.

As far as the use of names and surnames in the mother tongue is concerned, Slovakia brought its legislation into line with the Framework Convention by adopting the Act on Names and Surnames of 24 September 1993[415]. According to the second paragraph (1) 'A person born on the territory of the Slovak Republic may be given more than one name including a foreign name, (...) but not more than three names'. Further, the Names and Surnames Act[416], also makes it possible to enter a foreign name, or more names, in the Register. At the same time, this enables the use of a foreign name in its Slovak form on the basis of registration in the Register. This registration is not regarded as an application for permission to modify a surname, as regulated by a special law. The Names and Surnames Act meets the demands of persons belonging to national minorities by allowing them to rechoose – and enter in the Register – their name in their mother tongue, or foreign language. In this way, this Act harmonized the legal regulation with the guaranteed constitutional rights of these citizens. In section 7, the above Act also makes it possible – on the basis of free choice – to use a foreign name in its Slovak form. This is

[414] *Idem.*
[415] Act No. 257/1993 Coll., became effective on 1 January 1994.
[416] Act No. 300/1994 Coll.

facilitated by the Act on the State Language of the Slovak Republic Section 3 sub 6, stating that 'every citizen of the Slovak Republic has a right to alter, free of charge, his first name and his family name into a Slovak orthographic form'.

Unlike Bulgaria, Slovakia has never had a name-changing campaign imposed and brutally enforced by the State. Consequently, the issue of minority names is less controversial and problematic in Slovakia. Nevertheless, the Advisory Committee, according to its Opinion of 2000, 'received disturbing reports suggesting that the Slovak form of a surname is still imposed in some instances on women belonging to national minorities'.[417] The Slovak Government's reaction, in its Comment to this Opinion, is that 'it would appreciate to be given a more concrete reference to the cases the Advisory Committee referred to (...) in order to be able, when necessary, to take due measures'.[418]

11.6 Denomination of Communities (Article 11 (3) Framework Convention)

Article 11 of Framework Convention deals, in its second Paragraph, with the right of persons belonging to minorities 'to display in his or her minority language signs, inscriptions and other information of a private nature visible to the public'. The third Paragraph states that, '[i]n areas traditionally inhabited by substantial numbers of persons belonging to a national minority, the Parties shall endeavour, in the framework of their legal system, including, where appropriate, agreements with other States, and taking into account their specific conditions, to display traditional local names, street names and other topographical indications intended for the public also in the minority language when there is a sufficient demand for such indications'.

The Act on the State Language of the Slovak Republic states in § 3 sub 3 (d) that 'official names of municipalities and their districts, denomination of the streets and other public places, other geographical names, as well as the data in the layout of the State map works, including the land-

[417] Advisory Committee Opinion on Slovakia, 2000, sub 37.
[418] Slovak Comment, 2001, sub 8.

registry maps, are conducted in the Slovak language; denomination of municipalities in other languages is regulated by a separate law'.[419]

Such a separate law is the Act on the Denomination of Communities in the Languages of National Minorities as of 7 July 1994,[420] according to which, 'communities in which members of a national minority constitute at least 20 % of the inhabitants may on separate road signs marking the beginning and the end of the community be denominated in the language of the national minority'.[421] The limitation of the use of the minority language to signs which mark the beginning and end of the municipality is clearly more restrictive that Article 11 para. 3 of the Framework Convention, which provides for wider use (town districts, street names, other topographical names).[422] However, to some extent, this discrepancy has been rectified with the adoption of the Law on the Use of Languages of National Minorities[423]. According to its Section 3 (1) 'the municipality on its territory, in those municipalities referred to in Section 2 para. 1, *may*[424] display street names and other local topographical indications also in a minority language'.

Disputable is Section 2 of the Act on the Denomination of Communities in the Languages of National Minorities[425], stating that 'in official communications, especially in public documents, stamps of community and cartographic works names of communities are exclusively used in the official language'. Apparently, Slovakia has used the margin of appreciation left in Article 11 Paragraph 3 of the Framework Convention Section 2 in such a way that it does not leave any possibility for the use of the minority language in the mentioned situations.

As far as the implementation of these provisions in practice is concerned, no specific cases or information have been found by the author of this study. It must be mentioned, however, that a 20 % threshold is re-

---

[419] Act No. 191/1994 Coll. See also, Act No. 184/1999 Coll., Section 2 (5): In the municipality referred to in para. 1, the name of the body of public administration shall also be denominated in a minority language.

[420] Act No. 191/1994 Coll.

[421] Section 1 § 1 of Act No. 191/1994 Coll.

[422] See: Revised paper containing common analysis, findings and recommendations of the European Commission, OSCE HCNM and Council of Europe Secretariat concerning the legal regulations and status of minority languages in Slovakia, 5 March 1998.

[423] Act No. 184/1999 Coll.

[424] Emphasis added A.M.

[425] Act No. 191/1994 Coll.

quired for the implementation of these rights in practice. As already pointed out in the context of other minority rights with a 20 % threshold, the implementation of such rights depends on the results of population censuses, on changeable administrative borders and on the concentration of minority populations within more crucial towns and municipalities (where decisions are taken with regard to culture and education).

11.7 Conclusion

During the last decade several important events have taken place in Slovakia: the Constitution was adopted in 1992, the Slovak Republic was born in 1993, the ratification of the Europan Convention on Human Rights and accession to the Council of Europe took place in 1993, the ratification of the Framework Convention in 1998, a new government was installed in 1998, and a new president was chosen in 1999.

As said, it was only in 1998 that Mečiar's regime came to an end and it might be too early to draw any conclusions concerning the subsequent governments. However, some tendencies can already be pointed to. The changes on the national political scene in Slovakia have certainly changed and improved the situation of the minorities. The political changes opened the way for the implementation of international standards in national legislation (see, for instance, the new Act on the Use of Minority Languages, which was adopted in 1999). These developments took place relatively recently and the political heritage of more than six years of prime minister Mečiar's regime has not yet been wiped out.[426]

However, the Slovak Government seems to be satisfied concerning the way in which it has fulfilled its obligations with regard to the protection of minorities following from the Framework Convention. According to the Slovak Government itself the Slovak Republic

> 'protects the existence of national minorities within its territory. The protection of the rights of persons belonging to national minorities is essential to stability, democratic security and peace in Europe. As a pluralist and genuinely democratic society, the Slovak Republic not only respects the ethnic,

[426] Vladimir Mečiar won the first round of the presidential elections in 2004, but his competitor Ivan Gasparovic won with 59.91% of the votes the second round runoff on 17 April 2004.

cultural, linguistic and religious identity of each person belonging to a national minority, but also creates appropriate conditions enabling these persons to express, preserve and develop this identity. The Slovak Republic endeavours to create a climate of tolerance and dialogue between national minorities, the Government and the majority population, which is necessary to enable cultural diversity to be a source of enrichment for the whole society, not of division.(...)'.[427]

Also the Council of Europe is rather positive and optimistic with regard to the fulfilment of Slovakia's international obligations:

> 'National minorities enjoy a relatively high level of protection. The Slovak Republic has ratified the Framework Convention for the Protection of National Minorities and has honoured its commitment under paragraph 9 of the Opinion No. 175 (1993) by granting to every person belonging to a minority the right to use his/her surname and first names in his/her mother tongue and, in the regions in which substantial numbers of a national minority are settled, the right for the persons belonging to this minority to display in their language local names, signs, inscriptions and other similar information, in accordance with the principles contained in Recommendation 1201 (1993).'[428]

Further, also the adoption of the Law on the Use of Minority Languages in official communications is welcomed by the Council of Europe,[429] although it is noted that 'other problems resulting from the State language law, with regard to freedom of expression, as well as the use of minority languages in other settings, notably education, still need to be regulated'.[430]

As far as the implementation of international obligations concerning the use of minority languages in Slovak legislation is concerned, it can be concluded that, although Article 34 of the Slovak Constitution mentions the use of minority languages, it is in reality the Law on the State Language which determines the status of minority languages: minority languages are exceptions to the general rule that the Slovak language is the State language; the use of minority languages must be regulated in spe-

---

[427] Slovak State Report, 1999, p. 4.

[428] Monitoring Committee, Doc. No. 8496, 6 September 1999, sub 135.

[429] *Ibid.*, sub 136.

[430] COE PA Recommendation No. 1419 (1999), Honouring of Obligations and Commitments by Slovakia.

cific separate laws. Some of these specific laws extend further than the Framework Convention requires (for instance, minority schools are partly financed from the State budget[431]) and others offer insufficient protection (such as the regulations on the use of minority languages in official proceedings)

The Law on the Use of Languages of National Minorities has slightly mitigated the influence of the law on the State Language, but its scope is too limited. Especially the use of minority languages in education and in court proceedings has not been addressed in this law. These aspects are regulated by many separate laws.

Nevertheless, the adoption of the recent Law on the Use of Languages of National Minorities might also have an important psychological aspect: it shows that the use of minority languages is not necessarily an exception to the use of the State language, but that, especially in areas where more than 20 % of the population belong to a minority, it is a right which makes, at least in this respect, the minority equal to the majority. For minorities it is important to reach this 20 % threshold as it implies several important minority rights. That is the reason why, during the last census in May 2001, the different minority groups called on their members to 'declare themselves'.

In general, it can be said that Slovakia's national legislation complies to a large extent with the standards following from Articles 10 and 11 Framework Convention,[432] but that the Act on the State Language disturbs this picture, notwithstanding the recent Law on the Use of Minority Languages which has, to a certain extent, mitigated the effect of the Act on the State Language. The Minority Languages Law, however, does not address the issue of minority education and the use of minority languages in legal proceedings; these matters are regulated by separate Acts.[433]

The implementation of national legislation in practice is in many cases unproblematic. For instance, the use and registration of names and surnames in minority languages does not cause major problems. Further, there are rights, such as the denomination of street names or even the use of minority languages in contacts with the authorities, which are, technically speaking, not difficult to implement, provided there is enough po-

---

[431] See Chapter 12.

[432] Monitoring Committee, Doc. No. 8496, 6 September 1999, sub 116.

[433] Advisory Committee Opinion on Slovakia, 2000, sub 55.

litical will and awareness on the part of the authorities. The greatest problem with the implementation of these rights is the fact that they are linked to the 20 % threshold. This threshold is difficult to establish in some areas and with regard to some minorities (e.g. the Roma). This situation might lead to a situation in which rights exist on paper, but not in practice. Moreover, as the report by the Slovak Kalligram Foundation pointed out: 'the use of minority language is not completely granted even in municipalities where the 20 % threshold is met, because municipal authorities are not covered by the law on the use of minority languages. At the same time, municipal authorities (as public, but not State authorities) are key players in the sphere of rights of national minorities – they are those competent for example in the sphere of education and culture.'[434]

The next Chapter will discuss the issue of educational rights of minorities and will evaluate these rights on the basis of cases concerning Hungarian minorities in Slovakia and Romania, and the Roma in Slovakia, Romania and Bulgaria.

[434] Kalligram Report, 2003, pp. 1-2.

Chapter 12
EDUCATIONAL RIGHTS

12.1 Introduction

Educational rights are a concern for many minorities in Slovakia[435], Romania and Bulgaria. This Chapter, however, will discuss this problem with special emphasis on the Hungarian minorities in both Slovakia and Romania, and the Roma in Slovakia, Romania and Bulgaria.

It must be noted, however, that Article 12 (3) which contains the right of access to education, has to some extent already been dealt with in Part II on non-discrimination with regard to the Roma minority. Since the implementation of these rights does not constitute a major problem with regard to other minorities, this will not be separately discussed in this Chapter. However, Article 12 (2) dealing with, *inter alia*, 'adequate opportunities for (...) access to textbooks' will be discussed according to its relevance in given cases.

Articles 13 and 14 of the Framework Convention contain several, partly overlapping, provisions on education. Article 13 deals with the establishment of minority schools, Article 14 (1) with the right to learn the minority language and Article 14 (2) with the right to receive instruction in the minority language. This latter right will appear to be the most troublesome for States to realize.

---

[435] As far as other minorities are concerned, the Kalligram Report provides the following data: 'the Ukrainian minority has its base of education for teachers at Prešov University, where the Department of Ukrainian Language and Literature operates. This department provides three kinds of studies for its students: Bc. in Ukrainian language; Mgr. in Slavonic philology of Ukrainian language and literature, respectively pedagogy together with Ukrainian language and literature in combination with another subject. Ruthenians have no such base. Czechs and Polish did not articulate such demands. Carpathian Germans started to show interest for establishing study for preparation of teachers for first four grades of elementary schools and there is some cooperation with UKF in Nitra. Representatives of national minorities are studying at other universities, faculties and departments of Slovak higher education. [Statistics show, however,] that representation of university students of none of the minorities reaches the level that would correspond with its representation within the population of this country.' See, Kalligram Report, 2003, pp. 3-4.

12.2 Slovakia

12.2.1 The Right to Set Up Minority Schools (Article 13 Framework Convention)

Article 13 Framework Convention contains the right of minorities to set up and to manage their own private educational and training establishments. The scope of this right is limited by two conditions: first, these schools are subject to the requirements of the overall education system, and, second, the exercise of this right shall not entail any financial obligation for the State. However, the possibility of such contribution is not excluded.[436]

In Slovakia, Article 42 (3) of the Constitution states that: 'Schools other than State schools may be established, and instruction in them provided, only under conditions defined by law. Such schools may charge a tuition fee.' With regard to further implementation in national legislation, the Advisory Committee of the Framework Convention pointed out that this provision of the Constitution is implemented in national legislation in only one very general provision: Article 3 of Act No. 29/1984 on the Network of Primary and Secondary Schools (the Schools Act) regulating the following: 'Citizens of Bohemian, Hungarian, German, Polish and Ukrainian (Ruthenian) nationality are ensured the right to education in their own language to an extent proportional to the interests of their national development.'[437]

Upon the Advisory Committee's conclusion that Slovakia had limited legislative provisions concerning education in the national minority languages[438], the Slovak Government replied that it 'respectfully recommends to pay attention to that part of the Implementation Report which stated the highly developed national minority education system comprising more that 700 schools at various levels of education that have been established on the basis of the valid Slovak legislation'. Further, the Slovak government noted that 'the implementation process of the Convention includes not only legislative provisions and guarantees but mainly

[436] Explanatory Report to the Framework Convention, sub 73.
[437] Advisory Committee Opinion on Slovakia, 2000, sub 43.
[438] *Idem.*

practical implementation at the institutional level which has a traditionally high standard in Slovakia'.[439]

Although Slovakia's attitude seems quite exceptional compared to other States where implementation usually seems to stop at the level of national legislation, it should be realized that implementation without a proper legislative basis hides the danger of arbitrariness and discrimination. However, as long as there is no proof of this,[440] Slovakia's fervour in establishing minority schools can only be welcomed.

Also in another respect, Slovakia shows a great deal of fervour in implementing its international and constitutional obligations: as follows from Slovakia's report all schools with a minority language as the language of instruction, schools where the minority language is taught or schools with Slovak as the language of instruction are a part of the SR's education system and are financed from the State budget. Besides State schools, the law allows the establishment of private and church schools which are financed from the State budget.[441] With these financial regulations[442] the Slovak Republic clearly goes further than the requirements set by Article 13 Paragraph 2 of the Framework Convention.

12.2.2 The Right to Receive Instruction in the Minority Language (Article 14(2) Framework Convention)

For areas inhabitated by persons belonging to national minorities traditionally or in substantial numbers, Article 14 (2) of the Framework Convention provides in very cautiously formulated terms, that 'the Parties shall endeavour to ensure (...) that persons belonging to [national] minorities have adequate opportunities for being taught the minority language or for receiving instruction in this language'. Paragraph 3 reiterates that these rights should be implemented 'without prejudice to the learning of the official language or the teaching in this language'.

In line with Article 14 (2), but in much more concrete, Article 34 of the Slovak Constitution states that 'citizens belonging to national minori-

---

[439] Slovak Comment, 2001, sub 11.

[440] The educational rights of the Roma will be dealt with separately in section 12.4.

[441] Slovak State Report, 1999, p. 31.

[442] Ordinance No. 113/1991 Coll., on the Provision of Subsidies to Private Schools from the State Budget, section 2 (3).

ties or ethnic groups also have, under conditions defined by law, a guaranteed right to education in their own language.

The above-mentioned Act on the Network of Primary and Secondary Schools (the Schools Act) section 3 (1) is especially relevant in the context of Article 14(2) Framework Convention, where it says that: 'training and education are carried out in the State language. Citizens of Bohemian, Hungarian, German, Polish and Ukrainian (Ruthenian) nationality are ensured the right to education in their own language to an extent proportional to the interests of their national development.'

However, § 4 of the Act on the State Language of the Slovak Republic seems to underscore especially the third paragraph of Article 14 of the Framework Convention and, thus, the importance of the official language. It states that 'education of the State language is compulsory at all the elementary schools and high schools; a language other than the State language shall be a language of instruction and of examination in an extent administered by specific regulations.'[443]

In this context Article 12 (2) Framework Convention should also be mentioned stating, *inter alia*, that Parties 'shall provide adequate opportunities for (...) access to textbooks (...). In Slovak legislation this provision has been implemented as follows:

> 'In § 4 sub 4 of the Act on the State Language of the Slovak Republic it is regulated that: '[t]extbooks and instructional texts used in the educational and instruction process in the Slovak Republic are issued in the State language, with the exception of textbooks and instructional texts intended for education in the Languages of national minorities, ethnic groups and other foreign languages. Their usage is administered by special regulations.'[444]

Such special regulation is, for instance, a law of 1999 providing that the pedagogical documentation in grammar schools and in secondary schools will be in the State language and that the pedagogical documentation in the schools with a minority language of instruction will be bilingual, in the State language and in the language of the particular minority.[445] According to the Slovak State Report, 'textbooks for all types of primary

---

[443] Act No. 29/1984, § 3 and 3a, in the wording of Act No. 171/1990 and Act No. 230/1994.

[444] Act No. 29/1984; Instruction of the Government of the Slovak Republic No. 282/1994, SL, On Usage of Textbooks and Instructional Texts.

and secondary schools are purchased from the Ministry of Education budget. No special funds for the needs of schools with a minority language as the language of instruction are excluded. Textbooks and exercise books for schools with a minority language as the language of instruction are continuously approved, published and distributed to schools'.[446]

With regard to the implementation of these provisions in practice, the different Slovak governments have demonstrated a flexible attitude. In March 1997 the Undersecretary of Education (in Mečiar's Government) sent a circular to the heads of the school districts making it known that in Hungarian schools the Slovak language should be taught exclusively (this was later changed to 'mainly') by ethnic Slovak teachers; that in communities where the Hungarian community exceeds 40 % of the total population the teachers in Slovak schools should receive supplementary pay; that all communities which include a Hungarian population and where there is no school or there is no Slovak school, wherever possible a Slovak school should be opened, but not a Hungarian one.[447] Fortunately for the minorities in Slovakia, the next (1998) government in which the Hungarian Coalition Party (SMK) took part, declared in its program that it 'will guarantee the raising of the educational standard of citizens belonging to national minorities to the national average, and will address the issue of training teachers for schools teaching in minority languages, and theologians, cultural and educational employees in minority languages through the creation of an appropriate institutional level within existing universities'.[448]

More specifically, this government intended to: i) bring the level of education of citizens belonging to national and ethnic minorities on an par with the national average; ii) enhance the training of teachers for schools where a minority language is used as the language of instruction; iii) improve the quality of Slovak language teaching at schools where Hungarian is the language of instruction.

---

[445] Act No. 5/1999, adopted on 13 January 1999, amending Act No. 29/1984 on the System of Primary and Secondary Schools, State Language Act No. 270/1995 and Act No. 542/1990 on State Administration in Education and School Self-administration.

[446] Slovak State Report, 1999, pp. 28-29.

[447] The circular cites governmental decrees Nos. 459/95, 768/95 and 845/95. See also <www.slovakia.org/society-hungary.htm>.

[448] *Programové vyhlásenie vlády Slovenskej republiky*, Úrad vlády SR, Bratislava, 1998, p. 20.

One of the first specific measures which the new coalition government actually took was to reintroduce bilingual school report cards at schools where the language of instruction was not Slovak.[449] Under the previous government such certificates had been replaced by Slovak ones. In connection with this issue, two head masters of Hungarian minority schools who opposed the new regulations were dismissed on 15 March 1998. The next government reinstated them, however.[450]

As follows from the Slovak Report, at present, depending on the specific characteristics of individual minorities, the State and the intensity of their national awareness, as well as tradition, the education of national minorities takes place at:

1) schools with a minority language as the language of instruction, where all the subjects are taught in the mother tongue of minorities and the State language is taught as a compulsory subject – schools with Hungarian as the language of instruction, mostly primary schools and high schools,

2) schools with a minority language as the language of instruction, where only some subjects are taught in the mother tongue of minorities and some in the State language – schools with Ukrainian and German as the language of instruction,

3) schools where a minority language is taught, where the mother tongue and literature are taught in the mother tongue of minorities on the basis of the requirements of the parents and all other subjects are taught in the State language – schools with Ukrainian, Ruthenian and German as the language of instruction.[451]

Slovakia declared in its report of 1999 that 'all schools where the language of instruction is a national minority language are staffed with

---

[449] Act No. 5/1999 of 13 January, amending Act No. 29/1984 on the System of Primary and Secondary Schools, State Language Act No. 270/1995 and Act No. 542/1990 on State Administration in Education and School Self-administration was adopted. Article III, section 11 (2) reads as follow: 'School reports for students of primary schools and students of secondary schools are issued in the State language. Students of primary schools and students of secondary schools in which a national minority language is the language of instruction are issued bilingual school reports, in the State language and in the language of the relevant national minority.'

[450] Monitoring Committee, Doc. No. 8496, 6 September 1999, sub 130.

[451] Slovak State Report, 1999, p. 31.

qualified teachers[452], whose professional growth and qualification is secured by legislation through various forms of training at the level of the State Pedagogical Institute in Bratislava and methodical centers in the SR'.[453] Nevertheless, Vladislav Rosa (from 1991 to 1995 the Chief Inspector of Schools in the Slovak Republic) is pessimistic: According to him the situation in Slovak education and in science and research is critical, and the system has been reduced to a basic level of functioning because of severe financial restrictions. Therefore, 'one can only hope that most of these [above-mentioned political] intentions will gradually be implemented and that the policy statement will not again become a pile of empty promises'.[454]

12.3 Romania (Article 14 Framework Convention)

As described in Chapter 9, the problems of the Hungarians in Romania focus on the issue of teaching in and of the Hungarian language. The rights mostly demanded by the Hungarian minority in Romania: the right to learn the mother tongue and the right to be taught in the mother tongue, are laid down in Article 14 (1) and (2) Framework Convention.These rights have been incorporated in the national legislative framework of Romania. In 2001, the Advisory Committee welcomed 'the fact that Article 32 of the Romanian Constitution [of 1991] and the Education Act expressly guarantee members of national minorities the right to learn and be taught in their mother tongue', and noted 'that in Romania, both teaching of and instruction in minority languages exist'[455]

In fact, the legal framework for mother tongue education seems to comply with international norms: Chapter XII of Act No. 84/1995 on

[452] However, the same Report admits that 'in order to decrease the high number of unqualified teachers in primary schools, the Romany Culture Department of the Nitra Pedagogical University (now called the University of Constantine Philosopher) established a separate department in Spisska Nova Ves in the 1995/96 academic year. Under the coordination of the Romany Culture Department, this department secures, inter alia, the study of non-teaching subjects "Social and Educational Work" focused on Romany culture and training courses for young Romany women and unemployed Roma.'

[453] Slovak State Report 1999, p. 28.

[454] Vladislav Rosa, 'Education and Science' in: Slovakia 1998-1999, Meseznikov, Grigorij, Ivantyšyn, Nicholson (eds.), *A Global Report on the State of Society*, pp. 276-277.

[455] Advisory Committee Opinion on Romania, 2001, sub 61.

education deals exclusively with teaching for persons belonging to national minorities. According to this Act, 'persons belonging to national minorities have the right to study and be educated in their mother tongue at all levels and in all types of educational establishment, as well as in all subjects for which there is a sufficient demand, as provided for in law'.

Ministerial Order No. 3113/2000 facilitates access to the study of the mother tongue for pupils belonging to national minorities who, with their parents or legal guardians, choose instruction in Romanian, while keeping the mother tongue as an additional study subject. And also for higher education there is an appropriate regulatory framework (see Section 123 of Act No. 84/1995).[456]

12.3.1 The Right to Learn the Mother Tongue (Article 14 (1) and (2) Framework Convention): the Case of the Csangos

Article 14, first Paragraph, provides that 'the Parties undertake to recognize that every person belonging to a national minority has the right to learn his or her minority language'. The second Paragraph imposes on States a very carefully formulated positive obligation to endeavour to ensure adequate opportunities, *inter alia*, for being taught the minority language. As follows from the above description of the legislative framework in Romania, there is a good legal basis to implement these rights. The following particular example of the Csangos shows how these rights find their way into practice.

The Csangos are a non-homogenous group of Roman Catholics forming an enclave near the border with Moldavia near Iaşi. This ethnic group is a relic from the Middle Ages that has survived in Moldavia, in the eastern part of the Romanian Carpathians. Csangos speak an early form of Hungarian and are associated with ancient traditions, and a great diversity of folk art and culture. However, the Csango language is about to vanish within a few generations: despite the provisions of the Romanian law on education and repeated requests from parents there is no teaching of the Csango language in the Csango villages. As a consequence, very few Csangos know how to write their mother tongue.

In general, the Csangos make no political demands, but merely want to be recognised as a distinct culture and ask for assistance in safeguarding

[456] Romanian Comment, 2002, sub 64.

their culture and language. According to the Parliamentary Assembly of the Council of Europe, assistance from the Council of Europe is justified, and therefore the Assembly, *inter alia*, recommends the following measures: the possibility to be educated in the mother tongue should be ensured in accordance with the Romanian Constitution and the legislation on education. In the meantime, classrooms should be made available in local schools and teachers working in the villages teaching the Csango language should be paid; there should be an option for Roman Catholic services in the Csango language in the churches in Csango villages and the possibility for the Csangos to sing hymns in their own mother tongue; an information campaign should be launched in Romania concerning the Csango culture and the advantages of co-operation between the majority and minorities; finally, the unique linguistic and ethnographical features of the Csangos should be appropriately recorded.[457]

The demands and ambitions of the Csangos clearly have the interest and support of the Council of Europe. Further, Articles 12 to 14 of the Framework Convention and the Language Charter, as soon as they are ratified by Romania, fully apply to their situation. Notwithstanding this international legal support the future of the Csango language and culture is not certain. From international standards to factual improvement is still a long way to go.

12.3.2 The Right to be Taught in the Mother Tongue (Article 14 (2) Framework Convention): the Case of Other Minorities

Unlike the Csangos, who demand the right to learn their mother tongue, the ambitions of other minorities extend further: the right to receive instruction in their mother tongue as laid down in the second Paragraph of Article 14 Framework Convention. Also with this right, the main problem is not with its implementation in national legislation (see above), but with its implementation in practice.

In its Comment, the Romanian Government underlines the efforts and measures of, *inter alia*, the Ministry of Education and Research to develop and diversify the network of units where teaching is in the mother tongue. For instance, new classes were opened for Turkish, Ukrainian

[457] COE PA Recommendation No. 1521 (2001), on the Csango minority culture in Romania.

and German children in various regions in 2000. In accordance with the new Education Act, a section using Turkish as the language of teaching has been opened at Medgidia University, and three new sections using Hungarian for teaching purposes were opened at Oradea Private University in 2000. Some documents are already being drafted in Hungarian or German at Babes-Bolyai University in Cluj, where Romanian, Hungarian and German sections coexist. In the 2001-2002 academic year a new private university was due to be operating in Miercurea Ciuc, with financial support from the Republic of Hungary.[458]

However, the implementation of these regulations encounters some practical problems, such as the shortage of qualified teachers and minority-language textbooks, especially for the Armenian Croat, Polish, Serb, Slovak, Turkish and Tatar minorities. This makes it difficult for schools attended by children from national minorities to provide full education of the same standard as that provided in Romanian. This may discourage parents from sending their children to schools where most subjects are taught in the minority language.[459] This practice interferes with the provisions in Article 12 (2) and (3) Framework Convention: the obligation of States to promote equal opportunities for access to education and access to textbooks.

Also the Advisory Committee observed that, for instance, in the 1999-2000 school year, it appeared that only some minorities benefited to some extent from instruction in minority languages and that there were reports that certain classes, particularly in Ukrainian and Croat schools, were not taught in the minority language, but in Romanian. Further, the Advisory Committee noted that, in the past, some minorities, such as the Turks, the Tatars, the Russians and the Bulgarians, were also taught in their own languages, but that this seems 'no longer to be the case today'.[460]

As far as higher education is concerned, the Advisory Committee welcomed 'the existing possibilities for persons belonging to national minorities, as well as the recent positive developments that have led to the possibility, introduced by Article 123 of Act No. 151/1999, of establishing multicultural institutions, where languages other than Romanian can be used in the teaching'.[461] Further, the Advisory Committee welcomed 'a

[458] Romanian Comment, 2002, sub 64.
[459] Advisory Committee Opinion on Romania, 2001, sub 53.
[460] *Ibid.*, sub 61, 62, and 64.
[461] *Ibid.*, sub 55.

continuing dialogue between the Romanian authorities and those concerned that could help to find a solution that would correspond to the aspirations of the Hungarian and German minorities in the matter of higher education'.[462]

12.3.3 **The Hungarian Minority**

At present, an important issue between Hungarians and the Romanian State is the establishment of a Hungarian language State university. Although there is a private Hungarian university financed by Hungary, the aim of the Hungarians in Romania is to re-establish the Bolyai University in Cluj-Napoca, which was 'voluntarily merged'[463] in 1959 with the Romanian Babeş University. As a consequence, the number of subjects that could be studied in the Hungarian language drastically shrank. At present, at the Babeş-Bolyai University as well as at the University of Medicine and Pharmacy in Târgu Mureş and the Drama Academy in Târgu Mureş only some of the classes are taught in the minority languages of Hungarian, German and Romanes.[464] Contrary to the Babeş-Bolyai University the 'new' Hungarian University should be a real mixed, multilingual university. However, such a university is still controversial: in 2000 almost 40 % of the inhabitants of Transylvania said they would 'on no condition' agree to the setting up of a university with Hungarian as a teaching language.[465]

12.3.4 **Conclusion**

For most minorities their mother tongue constitutes a crucial element of their identity. For many decades minorities in Romania had to live under severe physical and cultural repression. Many people died, others fled or were sold abroad. Notwithstanding, but maybe also due to, efforts to assimilate them, the Hungarians in Romania re-emerged after 1989 as one

---

[462] *Idem.*

[463] In protest against the further destruction of Hungarian culture in Romania the Hungarian pro-rector of the university committed suicide. Cathy O'Grady, Zoltán Kántor, Daniela Tarnovschi, *Hungarians of Romania*, CEDIME-SE, p. 49.

[464] <http://www.ubbcluj.ro/ubb-en/pr-acad/programe-academice.html>.

[465] Ethnocultural Diversity Resource Center (EDRC), *Ethnobarometer, Interethnic Relations in Romania*, Cluj, 2000, p 51.

of the largest and most determined minorities. Determined, in particular, to preserve their language. Romania seems to be fairly co-operative as far as minorities are concerned, especially the larger ones, certainly concerning instruction in minority languages. However, practical problems with teachers and textbooks often frustrate good intentions.

Unlike the Csangos, whose modest demands fit within the scope of the provisions of the Framework Convention, the Hungarians in Transylvania have aspirations which extend beyond this Convention, such as autonomy and a Hungarian State University. Both claims seem justifiable from the point of view of history and by the large number of Hungarians living in Romania. However, historical and numerical justifications for minority rights do not give rise to sympathy, but rather to suspicion on the part of the majority.

12.4 Educational Rights of the Roma in Slovakia, Romania and Bulgaria

Article 12 paragraph 3 Framework Convention (equal access to education in general) with regard to the Roma has been discussed in the context of Part II on non-discrimination. It was concluded that, for several reasons, only a very small percentage of Roma children attend school regularly. This section will discuss the position of the Roma in the light of Article 14(2) of the Framework Convention: their right to instruction in their own language, Romanes.

12.4.1 **Slovakia**

Although some experts claim that providing the option of Roma language[466] education could improve education levels in Roma communities[467], at present few Roma enjoy access to education in Romanes. Roma

[466] The codification of the Roma Language occurred in 1971 when the language committee of the Union of Gypsies – Roma in Slovakia accepted the binding written form of the Slovak dialect of the Romani language. Since the transcription of Romani languages in different countries varied, the International Romani Union approved the unified variant of the Romani language at its IVth Congress in Warsaw in 1990. See, Vašečka, 1999, p. 411.

[467] This is disputed in the last UNDP Report where 'bilingualism is likely, at best, to be a mixed blessing'. 'Bilingualism can only be an asset if it goes hand in hand with profi-

representatives emphasise that even if State-supported education in Romanes is not feasible at present, children should be able to use their mother tongue at school without feeling ashamed; the development of a strong network of Roma assistants and the introduction of language courses in Romanes would be a first step. Roma history and culture are not yet part of the regular curricula of elementary and secondary schools. Instead, in Slovakia the Ministry of Education has added an one-hour course on discrimination in the general curriculum, but Roma activists claim that this is insufficient to counter widespread discriminatory attitudes.[468]

A number of factors have been mentioned to explain why Roma children have not received education in their native language:

- Slovak legislation, until 1991, classified the Roma only as a socially dependent group of citizens,
- No school network has offered education in the Roma language. According to the Slovak Report, the Roma language is used in nursery schools and in preparatory primary school classes with a high concentration of Roma pupils using it as a support language. It is also used at the secondary school of arts in Kosice and at the Romany Culture Department at the University of Constantine Philosopher Nitre and its separate department in Spisska Nova Ves. Education in Romanes in primary schools and ordinary secondary schools is lacking.
- The Roma themselves are uncertain as regards the use of their language in education. Asked, 'What would be the best way to provide your children with access to education equal to what the children from the majority have?', most of the responding Roma parents believe that the only sustainable way to provide their children with equal access to education is by encouraging integration, rather than by segregating them from the majority.[469]

---

ciency in the official language, as a second language in addition to, not in place of, the official one. If Roma language is perceived as a substitute rather than as a supplement to majority language proficiency, it will reduce educational and employment opportunities and will promote further isolation, and subsequent ghettoization, of the community.' UNDP, 2002, p. 59.

[468] OSI AP Report on Slovakia, 2002, pp. 576-577.

[469] UNDP, 2002, p. 57

- The need for education in Romanes is questioned; according to the UNDP, the argument that Roma children's access to quality education can be improved by teaching at least some subjects in Roma languages reflects the assumption that these languages are widely known and used by these children. Even assuming that differences between various Roma dialects are negligible, data on the issue are uncertain. Data show that, on average, only 54 % of the respondents state that they use Roma at home, with the highest incidence in Bulgaria. Therefore the UNDP concludes that 'bilingual education strategies may not be appropriate' and that 'the easier exchange of cultural codes in the schools [by using the State language] may instead be more important'.[470]

As mentioned in section 12.2, in Slovakia the – feeble – legal basis for minority schools and education in minority languages is Article 34 of the Constitution and Article 3 of the Act on the Network of Primary and Secondary Schools (the Schools Act). This latter Article does not mention the Roma minority among the minorities whose 'right to education in their own language to an extent proportional to the interests of their national development' it ensures. Education of the Roma minority in Romanes is, therefore, almost non-existent in Slovakia.[471]

The Slovak Report to the Advisory Committee of 1999 emphasises the importance of education for the Roma in the Slovak language instead of Romanes. To achieve this, recourse is taken to pre-school education. The Ministry of Education aims 'to stabilize and renew the operation of nursery schools, particularly in settlements with a high concentration of Roma children, with an emphasis on their education in the Slovak language and the creation of conditions for training 5-6 year old children and children with postponed school attendance, using all available forms for their preparation for entry into primary schools'.[472]

To support the reinforcement of knowledge of the Slovak language – as the State language in the Slovak Republic – the Ministry of Education has approved and secured the publication of spelling books in Romanes

[470] *Ibid.*, pp. 61-62.

[471] See also the Advisory Committee Opinion on Slovakia, 2000, sub 39, 40, and 44. The Slovak Government denies this: Slovak Comment, 2001, sub 12.

[472] Slovak State Report, 1999, p. 27.

and the Slovak language for primary school pupils. Students from the Roma minority who meet the conditions for further study at secondary schools can study at any secondary school in Slovakia. Conditions have been created especially for Roma students to study at the Secondary Pedagogical School in Levoca, and the Secondary School of Arts and Conservatory in Košice.[473] Further, the Kalligram Report mentions that the basis for university studies for the education of Roma is provided by Konštantín Philosopher University (UKF) in Nitra, where in 1990 the Department of Roma Culture was established. In cooperation with other faculties, UKF provides study for future teachers for the first four grades of elementary schools focusing on Roma culture together with social work focusing on the Roma community.[474]

As described in Chapter 4.4 the general right to education (Article 12 Framework Convention) of the Roma minority is under great pressure. A very small percentage of Roma children attend school regularly. This is not only the result of government failure, but also of social problems within some Roma communities. However, as far as the right of the Roma minority to the teaching of and education in their own language is concerned, one can conclude that this right is almost non-existent in practice. The policy of the Slovak government is to integrate the Roma into Slovak society. There are no ordinary primary and secondary schools where Roma children can be educated in, at least a part of the subjects, their own language.[475] This is, in contrast to other large (Hungarian) and small (German) minorities who do have the possibility to attend schools where their minority language is taught.

The difference between, for instance, the educational rights of the Hungarians, on the one hand, and the Roma, on the other, is a symptom of other more fundamental differences between these two minority groups: the Hungarians are politically well organized; they have clear demands with regard to a Hungarian State university and (cultural) autonomy; they have for a long time been in the role of the oppressor in the region where they live and are now backed by a strong kin-State Hungary which even enacted the Hungarian Status Law to protect Hungarian identity abroad; and they are not economically and socially marginalised.

---

[473] Monitoring Committee, Doc. No. 8496, 6 September 1999, sub 136 – 138.
[474] Kalligram Report, 2003, pp. 3-4.
[475] Rooker, 2002, pp. 239-240.

Concerning most Roma almost the opposite can be said: they are not politically organized; they do not have clear demands with regard to education in their own language at any level; they are not backed by a strong kin-state; they have never been in the role of the oppressor in Slovakia; and they are economically and socially marginalised.

In the case of the Roma minority in Slovakia the feeble legislative basis for minority education (consisting of Article 34 of the Slovak Constitution and Article 3 of the Act on the Network of Primary and Secondary Schools), as criticised by the Advisory Committee, turns out to be discriminatory and arbitrary. Whereas Slovakia showed a great deal of fervour in establishing minority language schools for all minorities mentioned in the Schools Act, and considered a further legislative basis to be unnecessary, the Roma minority are left without national legislation and without schools with education in Romanes.

12.4.2 **Bulgaria**

Also in Bulgaria, although it is possible to receive instruction in Romanes, the emphasis is on instruction in the Bulgarian language. According to the Bulgarian Constitution, Article 36 (1), 'the study and use of the Bulgarian language is a right and obligation of every Bulgarian citizen'. The second Paragraph provides that 'Citizens whose mother tongue is not Bulgarian shall have the right to study and use their own language alongside the compulsory study of the Bulgarian language'.

As far as education in and of Romanes in concerned, this language can be studied up to four hours pr week as an optional course in schools. Moreover, after 1997 Romani can be studied in Bulgarian schools. In recent years, some elements of multicultural education in the field of music, literature and history have also been introduced. The St. Kliment Ohridski Sofia University and the New Bulgarian University have instituted special courses in Roma culture and folklore.[476] Unfortunately, in its recent State Report the Bulgarian Government had to admit that 'despite efforts in the early 1990s to introduce Roma in first grade in some minority schools, Roma as a mother tongue is practically not studied. Tuition started in 1992 with about 4000 Roma children, but by 1999, their

[476] Maria Spirova, *Roma of Bulgaria*, CEDIME-SE, pp. 27-29.

number dropped about 500. Some of the difficulties are related to the lack of textbooks, a shortage of trained teachers and teaching aids for the higher classes.'[477] On the other hand, the extent to which the Roma value mother tongue education might have declined as a consequence of the general approach of the government to integrate Roma in the culture and language of the majority.

12.4.3 **Romania**

The most far-reaching measures to enable instruction of Romanes can be found in Romania. The Romanian Ministry of Education established the option for Romanes and history classes in primary and secondary schools in 1999 and this measure has been implemented in some schools where pupils study Romanes for three to four hours per week. Classes in Romanes can be established upon parental request. In the sixth and seventh grades, parents may also request an hour per week of 'history and traditions of the Roma'. Some associations representing members of the Roma minority have requested that instruction be given in the Roma language. After consulting in local communities the parents whose children would have been given instruction in Romanes, it was concluded that there was no real desire for Roma children to have all their instruction given in the Roma language: 'The parents' attitude may be based on the fact that they consider that instruction in Romanian or Hungarian, as appropriate, provides a better foundation for the satisfactory economic and social integration of their children'.[478]

Nevertheless, the Ministry of Education and Research has supported increasing the number of Roma language teachers. As result of these efforts, the process of teaching Romanes has greatly expanded. There are at present some 200 Roma/Gypsy teachers using mother-tongue Romanes/ Gypsy as the medium of instruction (3-4 hours per week). The number of pupils studying in their mother tongue (Romanes) has risen from 780 to 11 000. Additional classes have been created, and the number of reserved places in higher education (150 each year) has risen. Since 1998 Bucharest University has had a Roma language and literature section.

---

[477] Bulgarian State Report, 2003, p. 65.
[478] Romanian Comment, 2002, sub 63.

Even travelling schools have been set up to provide initial education for the nomad population of Roma origin.[479]

12.4.4 **Conclusion**

As described in Chapter 4, the Roma minorities equally in Slovakia, Romania and Bulgaria face great obstacles with regard to access to education, Article 12 (3) Framework Convention. However, remarkably, there are considerable differences between the way and extent to which the three States in question implement Article 14(2) in their national legislation and in practice, especially with regard to their Roma minority.

Whereas in Romania teaching for Roma children in and of their mother tongue is rooted not only in national legislation but also in reality; for Slovakia, and to a certain extent also for Bulgaria, instruction in the State language has priority in the case of the Roma. In fact, the implementation of both Article 12 (equal access to education) and 14 of the Framework Convention seems to place Slovakia and Bulgaria with a choice: integration or separation? The UNDP described the situation as follows: 'poor knowledge of majority languages is a potent constraint on access to education. Providing Roma children with additional opportunities to improve their command of the majority language is therefore a precondition for improving their access to education. Roma-language instruction is not a substitute for good command of majority languages. Reliance on Roma languages as educational instruments may be ineffective and could even contribute to the further isolation of Roma communities. Bilingualism can be both an asset and a segregating factor.'[480]

This conclusion is not consistent with the general ideal as laid down, for instance, in Article 14 of the Framework Convention that education in and the teaching of minority languages is something which is valuable and worth pursuing. In fact, Article 12, concerning equal access to education, and Article 14, containing the right to instruction in the minority language, interfere with each other as far as education for the Roma is concerned. As described in Chapter 4, for Roma minorities in Slovakia, Romania and Bulgaria, the main impediments to access to education ap-

---

[479] Romanian Comment, 2002, sub 56; OSI AP Report on Romania, 2002, pp. 517-518.

[480] UNDP, 2002, pp. 61-62.

pear to be poverty (lack of food) and insufficient knowledge of the State language. The practical result of this situation is that the right to have instruction in the minority language has to yield to the possibility to have any education at all (in the State language). Most policy measures, such as pre-school education and summer courses for Roma teachers, are beneficial to the integration of the Roma in the language and culture of the majority. However, in the case of the Roma the line between integration and assimilation is very thin.[481]

[481] See Article 5 par. 2 Framework Convention.

Chapter 13
CONCLUSIONS CONCERNING LINGUISTIC RIGHTS

For most minorities their mother tongue constitutes a crucial element of their identity. Several standards on the UN level and regional level aim to protect the linguistic rights of minorities, and most of these documents have been ratified by Slovakia, Romania and Bulgaria. A central article on the UN level with regard to cultural -including linguistic- rights is Article 27 ICCPR, which, in a certain sense, serves as a safety-net provision for minorities from all over the world: after ratification by the State , the First Protocol to the ICCPR gives individuals belonging to a minority group the possibility to file a complaint against their State before the Human Rights Committee.[482]

A completely different approach to the protection of the (linguistic) rights of minorities can be found in the Framework Convention and the Language Charter. As described, the provisions in these two instruments leave a considerable margin of discretion to States with regard to the implementation of their obligations. The implementation of these rights is monitored by a system of State Reports. The Framework Convention explicitly takes into account possible financial, administrative and technical difficulties associated with the use of minority languages in relations with public authorities and with the instruction of or in minority languages. The Language Charter, although also flexibly formulated, gives more details concerning objectives and principles on which the Parties are expected to base their policies, legislation and practice.

In the case of such conventions which leave a wide margin of discretion to States a crucial question for minorities is how States use this margin: flexibility for States usually means, for minorities, non-uniformity and dependence on national regulations.

In Slovakia the Hungarian minority demands several linguistic rights and educational rights. Article 34 of the Slovak Constitution gives a broad constitutional basis for these demands. The linguistic rights, such

[482] See the extensive case-law of the HRC on Article 27.

as the right to street names in the language of the minority, are regulated by the Law on the Use of Minority Languages and the, somewhat controversial,[483] Law on the State Language. In general, both the Council of Europe[484] and the Slovak Government[485] seem to be satisfied concerning the way in which Slovakia has fulfilled its obligations with regard to the protection of minorities following from Articles 10 and 11 Framework Convention. With regard to the practical implementation of national legislation an important obstacle appears to be the 20 % threshold, which is difficult to establish in some areas and with regard to some minorities (e.g. the Roma).[486]

With regard to educational rights, Slovakia has used its measure of discretion in a particular way: it has been passed on from the Constitution to national legislation and finally into practice. In the case of educational rights, not mentioned in the Law on the Use of Languages of National Minority, the implementation of Article 34 of the Slovak Constitution occurs on the basis of only one provision: Article 3 of the Act on the Network of Primary and Secondary Schools. This broad provision excludes Roma from the list of minorities entitled to educational rights and further leaves a large margin of discretion to State and local authorities dealing with educational matters. For the Hungarian and some other minorities in Slovakia this has resulted in a relatively high number of educational institutions where the minority language can be taught and/or is the language of instruction.[487] However, for the Roma, this wide measure of discretion on every level – international, constitutional, legislative and local – has resulted in an almost complete lack[488] of educational institutions where Romanes is the language of instruction or where this language can be taught, not only as a support language.[489]

In Bulgaria, 'Roma as a mother tongue is practically not studied'.[490] As described in Chapter 4, several measures have been taken, within the

---

[483] COE PA Recommendation No. 1419 (1999), Honouring of Obligations and Commitments by Slovakia.

[484] Monitoring Committee, Doc. No. 8496, 6 September 1999, sub 135.

[485] Slovak State Report, 1999.

[486] Kalligram Report, 2003, pp. 1-2.

[487] Slovak State Report, 1999, pp. 31-39; Slovak Comment, 2001, sub 10-12.

[488] An exception is the secondary school of arts in Kosice and the Romany Culture Department at the University in Nitre, Slovak State Report, 1999, p. 32.

[489] Slovak State Report, 1999, p. 32, Slovak Comment, 2001, sub 12.

[490] Bulgarian State Report, 2003, p. 65.

framework of a desegregation program, to increase the number of children who attend Bulgarian schools. In Bulgaria the right to equal access to education prevails over the right to education in the minority language. Desegregation and integration in Bulgarian culture and society is the main policy towards Roma in Bulgaria.

To a certain extent, Slovakia's and Bulgaria's integrative policy towards the Roma shows similarities. Both States are faced with the dilemma between Article 12 (access to education) and 14 (education in the mother tongue) Framework Convention and prefer to implement Article 12. Both States emphasize the importance of knowledge of the State language in the case of the Roma and in both States education in Romanes is almost non-existent.

However, the difference between these two States is that in Bulgaria the choice to desegregate the Roma seems to be inspired by the conviction that this will improve the position of the Roma in Bulgaria. Bulgaria's State Report of 2003 describes quite openly the problems of and with the Roma minority and gives an overview of the objectives and measures which the government is taking and will take in order to change this situation.[491]

In Slovakia the scope and seriousness of problems concerning the Roma population are widely known thanks to reports by international and national non-governmental organizations. The overall attitude and tone of the Slovak government in, for instance, its State Report and Comment on the Opinion of the Advisory Committee, remains one of denial and blaming the Roma themselves.[492] Instead of openness and cooperativeness with regard to these huge problems, which Slovakia shares with many other States, self-confidence with regard to their minority policy and nationalistic sentiments seem to prevail in Slovakia.

Finally, another – separate – approach towards education in a minority language is also possible and workable: in Romania mother-tongue education is an important issue for the Hungarian minority, but also for the Csango and some other, smaller minorities, such as the Croats and Ukrainians. The implementation of international standards in Romanian national legislation is considered to comply with international norms.[493] In

---

[491] Bulgarian State Report, 2003, pp. 65-68.

[492] See, for instance, Slovak Comment, 2001, sub 3, 5, 6, 9, 12.

[493] Advisory Committee Opinion on Romania, 2001, sub 61; Romanian Comment, 2002, sub 64.

general, Romania seems rather co-operative towards minorities, especially the larger ones, as far as instruction in the minority language is concerned. Practical problems with the implementation often concern the availability of text books and teachers. With regard to the educational rights of the Roma, Romania's efforts to implement these rights have led to considerable positive results. Many Roma pupils are studying in the Roma language or have an opportunity to learn this language at school.

Part IV
CONCLUDING REMARKS

Chapter 14
CONCLUSIONS, OBSERVATIONS AND RECOMMENDATIONS

14.1 Purpose and Overview of this Study

The purpose of this study has been to assess how the standards of the Framework Convention function in reality. The principles laid down in the Council of Europe Framework Convention for the Protection of National Minorities, which entered into force more than five years ago, had to pass several stages – national legislation, State policy and practice and, finally, 'reality' – before being able to realize the aim of the Framework Convention to 'protect within their respective territories the existence of national minorities'.[494] This study has described and analysed the practical results of the obligations and commitments concerning the protection of minorities following from the Framework Convention in the case of Slovakia, Romania and Bulgaria.

These three States have been selected for this study because they have several aspects in common, which enabled, to a certain extent, a comparison of problems and approaches. Slovakia, Romania, and Bulgaria have in common the fact that they have several relatively large groups of national minorities with a kin-state (the Hungarians and Germans in Romania and Slovakia, the Turks in Bulgaria). Further, all three States have a large Roma community, a difficult socio-economic situation, a recent communist past, and finally, all three States are Member States of the Council of Europe and have ratified the Framework Convention.

In this study, the situation of minorities in Slovakia, Romania and Bulgaria has been described and evaluated with respect to two specific principles: Part II discussed the principle of non-discrimination. Part III dealt with the principle of the protection of linguistic rights. Both principles are embodied in the provisions of the Framework Convention, the international document on which this study focused. However, where necessary, the influence and context of other international documents has also been taken into account.

---

[494] Preamble to the Framework Convention.

The two principles mentioned have been examined with regard to 'State practice' and 'reality'. This meant with regard to 'State practice' that national Constitutions, national legislation and, where possible, other administrative or legal measures taken by the State with regard to minorities have been analysed. With regard to 'reality' this meant that – on the basis of reports by experts, non-governmental organizations, and interviews – the actual situation of the minorities in question has been assessed.

14.2 Problems with the Determination of 'Reality'

The 'realities' of the minority groups mentioned in this study – the Roma in Slovakia, Romania and Bulgaria, the Hungarian minority in Slovakia and (including the Csangos) in Romania, the Muslims in Bulgaria and the Germans in Slovakia – were all representative as cases of violations of the principle of non-discrimination, of the principle of the protection of linguistic rights, or of both principles.

It must be noted, however, that the perception of what 'reality' actually is, varies considerably. 'Reality' as described in the different State Reports and Comments to the Council of Europe looks much better than 'reality' described in reports by the European Roma Rights Center or Amnesty International, which, in turn, is different from the 'reality' as experienced by separate individuals belonging to a minority group. Further, 'reality' is sometimes difficult to establish when government officials or medical personnel (for instance, in hospitals in Eastern Slovakia where forced sterilization of Romani women takes place) deny practices which are documented by several national and international NGOs. In some cases, the large discrepancies between these sources of information proved the relevance of my own fact-finding journeys.

The different international monitoring mechanisms, like the system of State Reports to the Council of Europe, aim to look behind national legislation and to reveal 'reality', or practice, but sometimes States confine themselves to a description of (ir)relevant national legislation and do not say anything about the way in which this legislation functions in practice. Moreover, it takes years for some States (Bulgaria's Report of 2000 appeared in 2003) to fulfil their reporting obligations to the Council of Europe. This makes reporting systems as a means to establish the functioning or implementation of international norms in practice rather ineffective and indecisive.

Further, as mentioned, the implementation of minority rights in practice often depends on the 20 % threshold, thus on the results of population censuses. Moreover, these results can be manipulated by changing administrative and territorial divisions. As described in Chapter 2, the results of population censuses do not always match reality, especially in the case of the Roma. This means that the whole system of minority right is built on quicksand.

The existence of a discrepancy between reality and standards is obvious for anyone interested in the situation of minorities (especially in the situation of the Roma in the States mentioned). However, the above-mentioned factors make it very difficult to establish the exact scope of the discrepancy. This considerably complicates the development of policy and measures on the national and international level concerning the protection of minorities.

14.3 General Conclusion: Varying Discrepancies

As said, this study intended to assess the use of international principles on minority rights for minorities in Slovakia, Romania and Bulgaria. From the analysis of both the principle of non-discrimination as well as the principle concerning the protection of linguistic rights, it became clear that there is a certain – large or small – discrepancy between the international standards and reality. However, it also appeared that the exact scope of this discrepancy is difficult to establish and, moreover, that its scope varies according to which minority group is concerned.

In Part I, the standard of non-discrimination as laid down in international and national legal standards has been discussed with regard to the Roma minority in Slovakia, Romania and Bulgaria, the Muslim minority in Bulgaria, and in relation to the Beneš Decrees affecting the Hungarians and the German minority in Slovakia. It appeared that, notwithstanding international standards and implementation mechanisms discrimination still flourishes in many different forms and degrees. This is not a very surprising conclusion when one realises that some discriminatory measures are still in force (like the Beneš Decrees in Slovakia) or have only recently been abolished but have left traces in the attitude of the people towards minorities (for instance, the name-changing campaign in Bulgaria), and that some anti-discrimination policies and measures in the States mentioned are of a very recent date (like the different Roma programs) and have not yet proven their value in practice.

Part III of this study concerned different linguistic rights, in particular of the Hungarian minority in Slovakia and Romania and of the Roma. It appeared that the principles of Articles 10 and 11 Framework Convention are relatively easy to implement and do not cause major problems (for instance the denomination of Communities), but that these rights are built on a feeble basis: the population census in Slovakia and Romania.

However, it appeared that educational rights, and especially the realization of education in the minority language (Article 14 (2)), might have a strong political and symbolic value, and that the implementation of these rights (for instance, the establishment of a Hungarian University in Romania) is hampered by this fact. Except for universities, the overall picture with regard to the educational rights of the non-Roma minorities in Slovakia and Romania is rather positive. However, as far as educational rights of the Roma minorities are concerned, it became very clear that Romania has adopted a 'separatist' approach by permitting and enabling education in Romanes, and that Slovakia and Bulgaria have adopted an 'integrative' approach to this issue, by giving absolute priority to education in the Slovak and Bulgarian languages. Although the underlying intentions of the latter States might be good, especially in Bulgaria the success of the desegregation programs seems convincing, it might lead to a contradiction: the protection of a minority by the destruction of its cultural identity.

14.4 Can States Overcome the Discrepancies?

Are the different measures, Roma plans, and programs drafted by successive governments of the States in question and by Roma NGOs enough to overcome these discrepancies? The recommendations in the annual EU Accession Monitoring Reports criticise the efforts of States on the same points: a larger budget should be allocated for the implementation of the different measures; more commitment should be shown, not only at the highest governmental levels, but, rather at the lowest level: in municipalities, local administration, mayors. Finally, a greater effort must be made to expose different forms of discrimination (such as racially-motivated violence against Roma prisoners) by government officials and police officers.

Thus, more money is needed from States (in fact, some States have already started to enlarge their annual budget for the implementation of minority measures), more commitment and greater efforts (so far, only Bulgaria has admitted that violence against Roma by police officers occurs). Further, although it is clear that the full rights of the Roma, including the complete elimination of social discrimination, cannot be immediately achieved, States should be urged to (further) develop appropriate strategies for the gradual elimination of discrimination. In these strategies both the Roma and other sectors of civil society should be involved and States should set benchmarks for what should be achieved during different stages in that strategy.

Having said that, is it enough to overcome the difference between reality and standards? It is obvious and easy to blame States for violations of their treaty obligations. However, it should be realised that the States mentioned have assumed these obligations relatively recently, that most of these States are still carrying the burden of a harsh communist regime in the near past, and that they are confronted with economic depression. These factors are not excuses for human rights violations, but they might explain some of the slowness at governmental level and mental inertia at the level of ordinary citizens (for instance, hospital personnel in Eastern Slovakia who still continue with forced sterilizations of Romani women) in implementing the (new) international and national standards, especially those regarding non-discrimination.

14.5 Can International Organizations Overcome the Discrepancies?

Inherent in a document drafted on the international level, as a compromise between many States, is a certain generality. The consequence in the case of the Framework Convention is that it does not fit all minorities; its standards do not link up with the specific needs of the different minorities. On the one hand, the priority for the Roma seems to be non-discrimination and basic social rights (clean drinking water and access to healthcare); the realization of other rights, like the linguistic rights of Article 14 Framework Convention, seems to be far out of reach for most Roma. In fact, the needs of the Roma are much more fundamental than the kind of rights offered by the Framework Convention. The situation of the Roma should rather be improved by the implementation of rights laid down in international documents like the UN Covenant on the Elimination of All Forms of Discrimination, the EU Race Equality Directive and, especially, the UN Covenant on Economic, Social and Cultural Rights.

On the other hand, the ambitions of the Hungarian minorities in Slovakia and Romania are a Hungarian language university and the restoration of cultural and territorial autonomy. Both issues surpass the standards of the Framework Convention. For them, the standards of the Framework Convention constitute an absolute minimum. The Csangos, finally, desire more protection for their language and culture. In fact, only this latter minority falls within the scope of the Framework Convention. The Framework Convention seems to have its greatest value for small, not too ambitious, middle-class minorities.

Minorities and majorities differ, international principles differ, the priorities and needs of minorities differ, and State approaches towards minorities differ. This raises the question whether the Framework Convention is an appropriate instrument to address all minorities and all minority problems. Already in Chapter 2, with regard to Article 3 of the Framework Convention ('the right (not) to declare that one belongs to a minority'), one of the conclusions was that international standards are unrealistic and unattainable: they are too far, too high. This conclusion was also drawn at the end of Part II concerning non-discrimination: especially where the Roma are concerned the situation seems hopeless

One way to 'bridge the gap' would be to lower the high standards. This seems unthinkable from the perspective of international morality, but is, unfortunately, a fact in international reality: by accepting Slovakia as a member in 2004, the European Union has lowered its accession requirements with regard to human rights. On the question of what counted for accession to the Europan Union, law or its implementation in practice, the EU seems to have a pragmatic, though not very optimistic, vision: what now counts are, according to Verheugen, 'credible strategies' for Roma integration, since 'it would be an illusion to believe that social and cultural discrimination against the Roma can be eliminated before membership, (...) it will take decades to achieve that'.[495] This approach might

[495] RFE/RL Newsline Vol. 5, No. 168, Part II, 5 September 2001.

be called realistic, but it might also be conceivable that a great part of the motivation of States to improve the situation of minorities, and especially the difficult and complex situation of the Roma, will disappear as soon as the goal of EU accession has been achieved.[496]

Another way to 'bridge the gap' would be to adopt only specific and concrete provisions in international documents. Where the more concrete linguistic rights are concerned, the international standards appear to be more realistic and attainable. Except for several practical (lack of teachers, books) and political ('minority' universities remain an issue) problems, the standards of the Framework Convention are rather clear and can easily be transposed in more concrete national legislation, and concentrated on the local situation. Contrary to linguistic rights, which are obligations of result, the standard of non-discrimination, as an obligation of conduct, is much more complex, vague, and, unfortunately, contrary to the 'natural' attitude of many people. Very often, this standard is more difficult to fully understand and implement not only by the State but, especially, by ordinary people: it is in shops, restaurants, cinemas, public transportation, work and schools, that discrimination of the Roma takes place. However, it appeared that States are much more prepared to adopt, and understand the use of, national anti-discrimination legislation when 'inspired' by an international document with great moral and legal value, like Protocol No. 12 to the ECHR, or with political or economic consequences, like the EU Race Directive. The Framework Convention will probably need a judicial monitoring mechanism in order to become 'inspiring' enough for States to lead to concrete measures, and in order to become really functional for minorities who need it.

14.6 Function of the Framework Convention

What is the function of the Framework Convention for minorities whose reality is infinitely far removed from these standards? According to Istvan Horvat of the Research Center for Interethnic Relations in Cluj,

[496] Compare, for instance, the way in which Romania and Bulgaria have implemented the EU Race Directive, long before their accession to the EU will become a fact, and the insurmountable problems Slovakia – a certain member of the EU in the near future – seems to be coping with as regard the implementation of this Directive in national legislation.

'the Framework Convention does not impose solutions, it inspirits'.[497] International standards can have such an 'inspiring' role, as, for instance, in the case of the children from Fakultete, the Roma ghetto near Sophia, who filed a claim against their State for not providing them with adequate school education and were even prepared to take the case to the European Court of Human Rights (see Chapter 4, section 4.4). The Framework Convention could have such a function as well, but it lacks an individual claims mechanism or a system for direct complaints at the international level.

To States the Framework Convention provides direction for their legislation, measures and policy concerning minorities. The monitoring system of the Framework Convention – the State Reports, Advisory Opinions of the Advisory Committee and Comments on these Opinions – are in line with this function of the Convention. For States, international standards in the form of a *framework* convention is very convenient: the standards mark the general direction of national legislation and policy, but are not specific enough to hamper States in the phase of detailed implementation. This can be seen as one of the positive sides of a *framework* convention: the feasibility of concrete measures and the needs of the minorities in question, which can best be estimated on the national level. A drawback of this *framework* system is, however, that it gives States the possibility to 'hide' behind the margin of discretion and to implement their treaty obligations only partially, which means, only in national legislation and not further in practice, or superficially, thus, not in compliance with the intention of the convention.

In sum, the overall picture of protection of minorities by means of a *framework* Convention is as follows: the Framework Convention cannot directly reach the subjects or beneficiaries of its provisions, but only through the intermediary of the State in question, and vice-versa, the beneficiaries, minorities or victims in question cannot directly reach the international level with their claims or complaints concerning violations of their rights by their State.

Undoubtedly, the conclusion of the Framework Convention for the Protection of Minorities between many States (some unwilling), was a political achievement. However, it should be asked whether the interests

[497] Interview with Istvan Horvat, Research Center for Interethnic Relations, Cluj, 22 November 2001.

of minorities are best served by the present form of protection by the international community. All the above-mentioned elements, and in particular the fact that part of its standards cannot be implemented in 'reality', make the role of the Framework Convention in fact a rather limited one: it serves, at most, as a source of inspiration. This seems to be not a very satisfying role for the international community, but it is the role that it has explicitly chosen by adopting a *framework* Convention.

However, real improvements in the situation of minorities and workable practical measures appear to come from below and cannot be imposed from above. As the example of the different Roma plans illustrates, in this picture the role of the State, and especially that of the international community, is primarily a budgetary one.

14.7 Observations and Recommendations

14.7.1 **General**

1. States should be reminded of the fact that, notwithstanding international and national efforts to improve the situation of minorities, there is still (wide) discrepancy between international standards concerning minorities and the reality which minorities face in everyday life.
2. It should be realized that the discrepancy between international standards concerning minorities and the reality which minorities face in everyday life, in many cases remain hidden behind fairly good national legislation. Therefore, States should be urged to provide more information concerning (the effects of) the implementation of national legislation in the factual and actual living conditions of the minorities concerned in their State Reports.
3. The gap between reality and international standards varies according to the minority concerned. This fact should be taken into account during the development of (new) minority standards at the regional and international level.
4. The Framework Convention seems to have its greatest value for small, not too ambitious, middle-class minorities.
5. States and the international community should also realize that, especially in the case of the Roma, this discrepancy is too wide in the

sense that international standards are practically unattainable and, consequently, risk losing their meaning and effectiveness.

6. States should be aware that the fact that the Framework Convention leaves them a margin of discretion also implies that the States themselves are responsible for filling this margin and for making the international standards effective.
7. Governments which lack the political will to support international and national legislation concerning the protection of minorities should be reminded that such an attitude will ultimately lead to an increase in social and (national and international) political unrest.

14.7.2 **Non-discrimination**

8. Not all rights and standards are equally suitable for being laid down in a Convention which is formulated in the form of a framework. While laying down an international standard concerning non-discrimination the margin of appreciation for States should be kept as narrow as possible.
9. There is a need to convince national and especially local authorities in Slovakia, Romania, and Bulgaria of the use, necessity and inevitability of combating discrimination and, consequently, of the implementation measures.
10. States are much more prepared to adopt, and understand the use of, national anti-discrimination legislation when 'inspired' by an international document with great moral and legal value, like Protocol No. 12 to the ECHR, or with political or economic consequences, like the EU Race Directive.
11. The problem of discrimination does not lie in the sphere of the implementation of international standards in national legislation, but in the transformation of national legislation into concrete and effective measures. Therefore the international and national focus should be on improving and monitoring this latter stage of implementation.
12. The existence of racially motivated violence by public officials is still being denied by most of the governments concerned. In order to bring about the necessary change of mentality human rights training programs and seminars for public officials (such as police officers) are indispensable. States should be urged to organize such training and seminars themselves or to invite international human rights experts to do so.

13. International monitoring systems concerning human rights and minorities' rights should be more alert as to national policies which take advantage of and stir up negative sentiments among the population against minorities. The resulting prejudices and resentment among the various ethnic groups can be very harmful and difficult to eliminate, also in the longer term.

14.7.3 **Linguistic Rights**

14. Contrary to the standard of non-discrimination, the international standards concerning linguistic rights fit very well within the format of a framework Convention. The financial, administrative and technical difficulties associated with the use of minority languages in relations with public authorities and with the instruction of or in minority languages can best be regulated on the national or local level.
15. States and international organizations should pay more attention to the fact that, on the level of national legislation as well as in national policy, there is a tendency towards (unjustified) discrimination among different minorities in the attribution, implementation and realization of linguistic and educational rights.
16. States, supported by international organizations, should invest much more in the quality of education in schools in Roma neighbourhoods.
17. The integrative policy which gives absolute priority to education in the Slovak and Bulgarian languages will not only have an impact on the knowledge of Roma children's mother tongue, but also on their self-esteem and cultural identity. Both States and international organizations involved should seriously reconsider and discuss the feasibility of such effects of integrative policies (as, for instance, is reflected in the Bulgarian desegregation programs) towards Roma.

14.7.4 **Roma**

18. The very serious situation of the Roma communities in many Eastern and Central European States not only calls for more international involvement, but also for more cooperation and an exchange of experiences and expertise between States which face similar problems.

19. The results of population censuses do not always match reality; especially in the case of the Roma their number is usually much higher. States should take this fact into account when developing policy and budgetary measures concerning the Roma.
20. Investing in the improvement, where necessary, and implementation of the different Roma Programs is probably the most efficient way to improve the situation of the Roma in the short and longer term.. More international support should be given to, and more international funding should be invested in, the realization of the aims of the Roma programs in the respective States.
21. Although it is clear that the full rights of the Roma, including the complete elimination of social discrimination, cannot be immediately achieved, States should be urged to (further) develop appropriate strategies for the gradual elimination of discrimination. In these strategies States should set benchmarks for what should be achieved during different stages in that strategy.
22. In order to improve the effectiveness of implementation measures, the Roma (and other minorities) should be involved and consulted in the development of programs or decisions concerning their situation.
23. The margin of appreciation which the Framework Convention leaves to States can only be adequately filled in with regard to minorities whom the State is willing and able to protect. Therefore, a difficult and complex problem like the situation of the Roma needs a separate international instrument which specifically focuses on the rights, problems, and needs of the Roma minorities in Europe and which provides States with practical and workable guidelines and rules concerning the protection of the Roma.
24. States and the Council of Europe should be alert as to the integrative and assimilative policy towards the Roma which has been adopted by some States (and which is also reflected, to a certain extent, in the policy of the European Union).

BIBLIOGRAPHY

Andreescu, Gabriel, Strasbourg Ombudsperson for National Minorities, Romania, Shadow Report: October 1999, <www.minelres.lv/reports/romania/romania_NGO.htm>.

Anăstăsoaie, V., Tarnovschi, D., (eds.), *Roma Projects in Romania, 1990-2000,* Ministry of Public Information National Office for the Roma Cluj-Napoca, 2001.

Arndt, V., Der Zweite Präsident Edvard Beneš, Helmuth-Block-Verlag, Magdeburg, 1992.

Bakker, Edwin, *Minority Conflicts in Slovakia and Hungary?*, Labyrint Publications, Capelle a/d IJssel, 1997.

Bedard, Tara, 'Romanian Roma: Two years After the Adoption of the Government Strategy, No visible Change', in: *Roma Rights*, No. 1-2, 2003.

Bulgarian Helsinki Committee, 'Human Rights in Bulgaria in 2001', in: *Obektiv*, Special Issue, March 2002, <www.bghelsinki.org>.

Bulgarian Helsinki Committee, Report Submitted Pursuant to Article 25 Paragraph 1 of the Framework Convention for the Protection of National Minorities, Adopted by the Committee of Ministers on 30 September 1998, at the 642nd meeting of the Ministers' Deputies, <www.bghelsinki.org>.

Bulgarian Helsinki Committee, Alternative Report to the Report Submitted by Bulgaria Pursuant to Article 25 Paragraph 1 of the Framework Convention for the Protection of National Minorities, Sophia, November 2003, <www.bghelsinki.org>.

Bútorová, Zora; Gyárfášová, Ol'ga, and Marián Velšic, 'Public Opinion', in: Meseznikov, Grigorij, Ivantyšyn, Nicholson (eds.), *Slovakia 1998-1999, A Global Report on the State of Society*, Bratislava, 1999.

Cahn, Claude, 'Roma Rights and Anti-Discrimination Law', in: *Roma Rights*, No. 1-2, 2003.

Center for Legal Analyses – Kalligram Foundation, Report: Implementation of European Charter of Regional or Minority Languages in Slovak Republic, April 2003,<www.cla.sk>.

Culic, I., Horváth, I., Stan, C., *Reflections on Differences, Focus on Romania*, Limes, Cluj, 1999.

Daftary, Farimah, Gál, Kinga, *The New Slovak Language Law: Internal or External Politics?*, ECMI, Flensburg, 2000.

Daskalovski, Zhidas, *Different people, different destinies: Transylvanian Hungarians*, CST Transylvania, <www.rrz-uni-hamburg.de/AEGEE/CST-TRANS/e_zhidas.html>.

DOSTÁL, Ondrej, 'Národnostné menšiny', in: Kollár, Miroslav, Meseznikov, Grigorij (eds.), *Slovensko 2000, Súhrnna správa o stave spoločnosti*, Bratislava, 2000, pp. 175-189.

DURAY, Miklos, *Hungarians Nation in Slovakia*: <www.slovakia.org/society-hungary.htm>.

EUROPEAN CENTRE FOR MINORITY ISSUES, *Implementing the Framework Convention for the Protection of National Minorities*, ECMI Report No. 3, Flensburg, 1999.

EUROPEAN COMMISSION, 2000 Regular Report from the European Commission on Slovakia's Progress Towards Accession, 8 November 2000.

EUROPEAN ROMA RIGHTS CENTER, *Sudden Rage at Dawn, Violence Against Roma in Romania*, 1996, <www.errc.org/publications/reports/index.shtml>.

European Roma Rights Center, *Time of the Skinheads; Denial and Exclusion of Roma in Slovakia*, 1997, <www.errc.org/publications/reports/index.shtml>.

EUROPAN ROMA RIGHTS CENTER, *State of Impunity, Human Rights Abuse of Roma in Romania*, 2001, <www.errc.org/publications/reports/index.shtml>.

EUROPEAN ROMA RIGHTS CENTER, Comment Concerning the Slovak Republic for Consideration by the United Nations Human Rights Committee at its 78th Session, 14 July – 8 August 2003, (ERRC, 2003).

EUROPEAN ROMA RIGHTS CENTER, Joint Statement of the European Roma Rights Center (ERRC) and the International Helsinki Federation for Human Rights (IHF) to the OSCE Conference on Discrimination, Racism and Xenophobia, Vienna, 4-5 September 2003. PC.DEL.106/03, 11 September 2003.

FÜLE, Ján, 'Media', in: Meseznikov, Grigorij, Ivantyšyn, Nicholson, Tom (eds.), *Slovakia 1998-1999, A Global Report on the State of Society*, Bratislava, 1999, pp. 375-394.

GERGELY, D., Morteanu, M., *Human Rights Department, Discrimination and Violence Cases*, Romani Criss, Roma Center for Social Intervention and Studies, January-October 2001.

HRUBALA, Jan, 'Legal analysis of national and European anti-discrimination legislation', part of a joint project entitled *Implementing Europan Anti-Discrimination Law*, ERRC, Interights, Migration Policy Group, 2001, p. 12.

HUMAN RIGHTS WATCH, World Report 2001: Bulgaria: Human Rights Developments, <http://www/hrw.org/wr2k1/europe/bulgaria.html>.

ILIEVA, Margarita, 'The Bulgarian Draft Anti-Discrimination Law: An Opportunity to Make Good on the Constitutional Promise of Equality in a Post-Communist Society', in: *Roma Rights*, No. 1-2, 2003.

IORDACHE, Romanita and Tabacu, Andreea, 'Not Yet Viable: Anti-discrimination Action in Romania', in: *Roma Rights*, No. 1-2, 2003.

JUDT,Tony, 'Romania: Bottom of the Heap', *New York Review of Books*, Vol. 48, No. 17, Nov. 1, 2001.

KANEV, Krassimir, 'Changing Attitudes Towards the Ethnic Minorities in Bulgaria and the Balkans, 1992-1997,' in: '*Ethnicity and Nationalism in East Central Europe and the Balkans*', Thanasis D. Sfikas and Christopher Williams (eds.), Aldershot, Ashgate, 1999, pp.197-236.

DE KEERSMAEKER, G., 'Hongarije en de Hongaarse minderheden in Slowakije en Roemenië', in: *NoordZuid Cahier*, December 1997.

KOINOVA, Maria, *Muslims of Bulgaria,* Center for Documentation and Information on Minorities in Europe- Southeast Europe (CEDIME-SE).

KUSÝ, Miroslav, 'L'udské práva', in: Kollár, Miroslav, Meseznikov, Grigorij (eds.), *Slovensko 2000, Súhrnna správa o stave spoločnosti*, Bratislava, 2000, pp.163-174.

LENKOVA, Marianna 'Black& White v/s Diversity, The Image of the Roma in the Balkan Media', *Greek Helsinki Monitor,* <www.greekhelsinki.gr/english/articles/montpellier-marianna.html>.

LENKOVA, Marianna, *Turks of Bulgaria,* Center for Documentation and Information on Minorities in Europe- Southeast Europe (CEDIME-SE).

MALANCZUK, P., *Akehurst, Modern Introduction to International Law*, Seventh Revised Edition, Routeledge, London, 1997.

MATES, Pavel, *The New Slovak Constitution*, RFE/RL Research Report, Vol 1, No. 43, 30 October 1992.

MEIJKNECHT, Anna, *Towards International Personality: The Position of Minorities and Indigenous Peoples in International Law*, Intersentia, Antwerp, 2001.

MINISTRY OF LABOUR, Social Affairs and Family of the Slovak Republic, *Conceptual Intends of the Government of the Slovak Republic for Solution of the Problems of Romany Population under Current Social and Economic Conditions*, Bratislava, 1997.

NASTASĂ, L, Levente, S. (eds.), *Interethnic Relations in Post-Communist Romania,* Ethnocultural Diversity Resource Center, Cluj-Napoca, 2000.

O'GRADY, Cathy; Kántor, Zoltán; Tarnovschi, Daniela, *Hungarians of Romania*, Center for Documentation and Information on Minorities in Europe – Southeast Europe (CEDIME-SE).

O'MAHONY, John, 'In the ghetto', *Guardian Unlimited*, 3 November 2001.

OPEN SOCIETY INSTITUTE, *Monitoring the EU Accession Process: Minority Protection,* Central European University Press, Budapest, 2001.

OPEN SOCIETY INSTITUTE, *Monitoring the EU Accession Process: Minority Protection in Slovakia*, 2001, (OSI AP Report on Slovakia, 2001).

OPEN SOCIETY INSTITUTE, *Monitoring the EU Accession Process: Minority Protection in Slovakia*, 2002, (OSI AP Report on Slovakia, 2002).

OPEN SOCIETY INSTITUTE, *Monitoring the EU Accession Process: Minority Protection. Minority Protection in Bulgaria*, 2001, (OSI AP Report Bulgaria, 2001).

OPEN SOCIETY INSTITUTE, *Monitoring the EU Accession Process: Minority Protection. Minority Protection in Bulgaria*, 2002, (OSI AP Report Bulgaria, 2002).

OSCE, Summary: *Seminar on Roma in the OSCE Area*, 14-15 June 2000, Bratislava, The Hague, 2000.

OSCE, *Report on the Situation of Roma and Sinti in the OSCE Area*, HCNM, The Hague, 2000.

PENTASSUGLIA,G., *Minorities in International Law*, Strasbourg, Council of Europe Publishing, 2002.

PISAROVA, Martina, 'Anti-discrimination law on agenda again', in: *The Slovak Spectator*, 22-28 September 2003.

RESEARCH CENTER FOR INTERETHNIC RELATION, *Ethnobarometer, Interethnic Relations in Romania*, May-June 2000.

ROMANI BAH-FOUNDATION, *Annual Report 2000-2001*, Sofia.

ROMANI CRISS, *Human Rights department Discrimination and Violence Cases*, January-October 2001.

ROMANI CRISS, *Piatra Neamt Case, documenting report* by D. Gergely and M. Morteanu.

ROOKER, Marcia, *The International Supervision of Protection of Romany People in Europe*, Nijmegen University Press, Nijmegen, 2002.

ROSA, Vladislav, 'Education and Science' in: Meseznikov, Grigorij, Ivantyšyn, Nicholson (eds.), *Slovakia 1998-1999, A Global Report on the State of Society*, Bratislava, 1999, 259-278.

SIMPSON, Fiona, '*Developing Support Structures for Ethnic Minorities in Slovakia*', GeoJournal 50, pp. 127-131, 2000.

SPIROVA, Maria, *Roma of Bulgaria*, Center for Documentation and Information on Minorities in Europe- Southeast Europe (CEDIME-SE).

SPOLU INTERNATIONAL FOUNDATION, *Breaking the Vicious Circle, Lessons Learned from Experience in Social Inclusion of Roma Communities Through Participation*, Sofia, 2000.

TROEBST, Stefan, *The Council of Europe's Framework Convention for the Protection of National Minorities Revisited*, European Centre for Minority Issues, Flensburg, 1998.

UNITED NATIONS DEVELOPMENT PROGRAM (UNDP), *Avoiding the Dependency Trap*, Bratislava, 2003.

UNITED NATIONS DEVELOPMENT PROGRAM (UNDP), *National Report on Human Development: Slovakia 1998*, Bratislava, 1998.

VANCOUVER SOCIETY, Human Rights for Minorities in Central Europe – *Study Paper on the Beneš Decrees*, Conference on the Beneš Decrees, 28 November – 1 December 2001, Komárno/Révkomárom, Slovak Republic.

VAŠEČKA, Michal, 'The Roma', in: Meseznikov, Grigorij, Ivantyšyn, Nicholson (eds.), *Slovakia 1998-1999, A Global Report on the State of Society*, Bratislava, 1999, pp. 395- 415.

WEBER, R., *Report on the Measures to Combat Discrimination in the 13 Candidate Countries (VT/2002/47), Country Report Romania*, Migration Policy Group, Brussels, 2003.

YANAKIEV, Yantsislav, *Integration of Ethnic Groups in the Military the Case of Bulgaria*, Paper presented during a workshop on 'Military and Society' held in Prague, 15-19 November 2002, organized by the Working Group on Military and Society of the Geneva Centre for the Democratic Control of Armed Force.

ZEMAN, Z. and Klimek A., *The life of Edvard Benes 1884-1948*, Clarendon Press, Oxford, 1997.

ZOON, I., *On the Margins, Roma and Public Services in Romania*, Open Society Institute, New York, 2001 (Zoon, 2001 Romania).

ZOON, I., *On the Margins, Roma and Public Services in Romania, Bulgaria, and Macedonia*, Open Society Institute, New York, 2001. (Zoon, 2001).

ZOON, I., *On the Margins, Roma and Public Services in Slovakia*, Open Society Institute, 2001 (Zoon, 2001 Slovakia).

COUNCIL OF EUROPE DOCUMENTS

Parliamentary Assembly (COE PA)

Opinion No. 161 (1992), on the application by Bulgaria for membership of the Council of Europe, adopted on 5 May 1992.

Opinion No. 175 (1993), on the application by the Slovak Republic for membership of the Council of Europe, adopted on 29 June 1993.

Opinion No. 176 (1993) on the Application by Romania for Membership of the Council of Europe, adopted on 28 September 1993.

Order No. 488 (1993), on the Honouring of Commitments Entered into by New Member States.

Resolution No. 927 (1989), on the Situation of the Ethnic and Muslim Minority in Bulgaria.

Resolution No. 1123 (1997), on the Honouring of Obligations and Commitments by Romania.

Resolution No. 1196 (1999), on the Honouring of Obligations and Commitments by Slovakia.

Resolution No. 1211 (2000), on the Honouring of Obligations and Commitments by Bulgaria.

Resolution No. 1335 (2003) on the Preferential Treatment of National Minorities by the Kin-state: the Case of the Hungarian Law on Hungarians Living in Neighbouring Countries of 19 June 2001.

Motion concerning the Hungarian Law on Hungarians Living in Neighbouring Countries of 19 June 2001, Doc. No. 9153, 28 June 2001.

Recommendation No. 1109 (1989), on the Situation of Refugees of Bulgarian Nationality in Turkey.

Recommendation No. 1114 (1989), on the Situation of Minorities in Romania.

Recommendation No. 1326 (1997), on the Honouring of Obligations and Commitments by Romania.

Recommendation No. 1442 (2000), on the Honouring of Obligations and Commitments by Bulgaria.

Recommendation No. 1521 (2001), on the Csango Minority Culture in Romania.

Advisory Committee on the Implementation of the Framework Convention for the Protection of National Minorities (Advisory Committee)

Report submitted by the Slovak Republic pursuant to Article 25 paragraph 1 of the Framework Convention for the Protection of National Minorities, ACFC/SR(1999)008, received 4 May 1999.

Report submitted by Romania pursuant to Article 25 paragraph 1 of the Framework Convention for the Protection of National Minorities. ACFC/SR(1999)011, received 24 June 1999.

Report submitted by Bulgaria pursuant to Article 25 paragraph 1 of the Framework Convention for the Protection of National Minorities. ACFC/SR(2003)001, received 9 April 2003.

Opinion on Slovakia of the Advisory Committee on the Framework Convention for the Protection of National Minorities. ACFC/INF/OP/I(2001)001, adopted on 22 September 2000.

Opinion on Romania of the Advisory Committee on the Framework Convention for the Protection of National Minorities, ACFC/INF/OP/I(2002)001, adopted on 6 April 2001.

Comment of the Government of the Slovak Republic to the Opinion of the Advisory Committee on the Implementation of the Framework Convention for the Protection of National Minorities in Romania. GVT/COM/INF/OP/I(2001)001, published 6 July 2001.

Comment of the Government of Romania to the Opinion of the Advisory Committee on the Implementation of the Framework Convention for the Protection of National Minorities in Romania. GVT/COM/INF/OP/I(2002)001, published 10 January 2002.

Committee on the Honouring of Obligations and Commitments by Member States of the Council of Europe (Monitoring Committee)

Doc. No. 7795, 11 April 1997, Honouring of Obligations and Commitments by Romania, (rapporteur: Jansson).

Doc. No. 8496, 6 September 1999, Honouring of Obligations and Commitments by Slovakia, (rapporteurs: Magnusson, Sinka).

Doc. No. 8616, 26 January 2000, Honouring of Obligations and Commitments by Bulgaria (rapporteurs: Atkinson and Gjellerod).

Committee on Legal Affairs and Human Rights

AS/Jur (1996) 7, 18 January 1996, Consideration on the Act of the Slovak Republic on its State Language in the light of the standards of the Council of Europe by Dr. Heinz Tichy.

Committee of Ministers (CM)

Reply from the Committee of Ministers to Parliamentary Assembly Recommendation 1419 (1999), 12 January 2000, CM/Del/Dec (99)692/2.1a, GR-EDS(99)60, 66.

Reply from the Committee of Ministers to Parliamentary Assembly Recommendation 1442 (2000), 15 March 2000, CM/Del/Dec(2000)701/2.1a, GR-EDS(2000)12 Rev.,16 Rev.

Resolution of the Committee of Ministers on the Implementation of the Framework Convention for the Protection of National Minorities by Slovakia, Resolution, ResCMN(2001)5, adopted on 21 November 2001.

Resolution of the Committee of Ministers on the implementation of the Framework Convention for the Protection of National Minorities by Romania. Resolution, ResCMN (2002)5, adopted on 13 March 2002.

European Court of Human Rights

Case Relating to Certain Aspects of the Laws on the Use of Languages in Education in Belgium (Merits), EurCourtHR, Judgment of 23 July 1968, Series A, No. 6.

Assenov and Others v. *Bulgaria*, EurCourtHR, Appl. No. 24760/94, Judgment of 28 October 1998.

Velikova v. *Bulgaria*, EurCourtHR, Appl. No. 41488/98, Judgment of 18 May 2000.

Hasan and Chaush v. *Bulgaria*, EurCourtHR, Appl. No. 30985/96, Judgment of 26 October 2000.

Boris Stankov and the United Macedonian Organization Ilinden v. *Bulgaria,* application nos. 29221/95 and 29225/95, EurCourtHR, Judgment of 2 October 2001.

Anguelova v. *Bulgaria*, EurCourtHR, Appl. No. 38361/97, Judgment of 13 June 2002.

Annex I
COUNCIL OF EUROPE FRAMEWORK CONVENTION FOR THE PROTECTION OF NATIONAL MINORITIES

The member States of the Council of Europe and the other States, signatories to the present framework Convention,
Considering that the aim of the Council of Europe is to achieve greater unity between its members for the purpose of safeguarding and realising the ideals and principles which are their common heritage;
Considering that one of the methods by which that aim is to be pursued is the maintenance and further realisation of human rights and fundamental freedoms;
Wishing to follow-up the Declaration of the Heads of State and Government of the member States of the Council of Europe adopted in Vienna on 9 October 1993;
Being resolved to protect within their respective territories the existence of national minorities;
Considering that the upheavals of European history have shown that the protection of national minorities is essential to stability, democratic security and peace in this continent;
Considering that a pluralist and genuinely democratic society should not only respect the ethnic, cultural, linguistic and religious identity of each person belonging to a national minority, but also create appropriate conditions enabling them to express, preserve and develop this identity;
Considering that the creation of a climate of tolerance and dialogue is necessary to enable cultural diversity to be a source and a factor, not of division, but of enrichment for each society;
Considering that the realisation of a tolerant and prosperous Europe does not depend solely on co-operation between States but also requires transfrontier co-operation between local and regional authorities without prejudice to the constitution and territorial integrity of each State;

Having regard to the Convention for the Protection of Human Rights and Fundamental Freedoms and the Protocols thereto;

Having regard to the commitments concerning the protection of national minorities in United Nations conventions and declarations and in the documents of the Conference on Security and Co-operation in Europe, particularly the Copenhagen Document of 29 June 1990;
Being resolved to define the principles to be respected and the obligations which flow from them, in order to ensure, in the member States and such other States as may become Parties to the present instrument, the effective protection of national minorities and of the rights and freedoms of persons belonging to those minorities, within the rule of law, respecting the territorial integrity and national sovereignty of states;
Being determined to implement the principles set out in this framework Convention through national legislation and appropriate governmental policies,
Have agreed as follows:

SECTION I

Article 1
The protection of national minorities and of the rights and freedoms of persons belonging to those minorities forms an integral part of the international protection of human rights, and as such falls within the scope of international co-operation.

Article 2
The provisions of this framework Convention shall be applied in good faith, in a spirit of understanding and tolerance and in conformity with the principles of good neighbourliness, friendly relations and co-operation between States.

Article 3
1 Every person belonging to a national minority shall have the right freely to choose to be treated or not to be treated as such and no disadvantage shall result from this choice or from the exercise of the rights which are connected to that choice.
2 Persons belonging to national minorities may exercise the rights and enjoy the freedoms flowing from the principles enshrined in the present framework Convention individually as well as in community with others.

Section II

Article 4

1 The Parties undertake to guarantee to persons belonging to national minorities the right of equality before the law and of equal protection of the law. In this respect, any discrimination based on belonging to a national minority shall be prohibited.
2 The Parties undertake to adopt, where necessary, adequate measures in order to promote, in all areas of economic, social, political and cultural life, full and effective equality between persons belonging to a national minority and those belonging to the majority. In this respect, they shall take due account of the specific conditions of the persons belonging to national minorities.
3 The measures adopted in accordance with paragraph 2 shall not be considered to be an act of discrimination.

Article 5

1 The Parties undertake to promote the conditions necessary for persons belonging to national minorities to maintain and develop their culture, and to preserve the essential elements of their identity, namely their religion, language, traditions and cultural heritage.
2 Without prejudice to measures taken in pursuance of their general integration policy, the Parties shall refrain from policies or practices aimed at assimilation of persons belonging to national minorities against their will and shall protect these persons from any action aimed at such assimilation.

Article 6

1 The Parties shall encourage a spirit of tolerance and intercultural dialogue and take effective measures to promote mutual respect and understanding and co-operation among all persons living on their territory, irrespective of those persons' ethnic, cultural, linguistic or religious identity, in particular in the fields of education, culture and the media.
2 The Parties undertake to take appropriate measures to protect persons who may be subject to threats or acts of discrimination, hostility or violence as a result of their ethnic, cultural, linguistic or religious identity.

Article 7

The Parties shall ensure respect for the right of every person belonging to a national minority to freedom of peaceful assembly, freedom of association, freedom of expression, and freedom of thought, conscience and religion.

Article 8

The Parties undertake to recognise that every person belonging to a national minority has the right to manifest his or her religion or belief and to establish religious institutions, organisations and associations.

Article 9

1 The Parties undertake to recognise that the right to freedom of expression of every person belonging to a national minority includes freedom to hold opinions and to receive and impart information and ideas in the minority language, without interference by public authorities and regardless of frontiers. The Parties shall ensure, within the framework of their legal systems, that persons belonging to a national minority are not discriminated against in their access to the media.

2 Paragraph 1 shall not prevent Parties from requiring the licensing, without discrimination and based on objective criteria, of sound radio and television broadcasting, or cinema enterprises.

3 The Parties shall not hinder the creation and the use of printed media by persons belonging to national minorities. In the legal framework of sound radio and television broadcasting, they shall ensure, as far as possible, and taking into account the provisions of paragraph 1, that persons belonging to national minorities are granted the possibility of creating and using their own media.

4 In the framework of their legal systems, the Parties shall adopt adequate measures in order to facilitate access to the media for persons belonging to national minorities and in order to promote tolerance and permit cultural pluralism.

Article 10

1 The Parties undertake to recognise that every person belonging to a national minority has the right to use freely and without interference his or her minority language, in private and in public, orally and in writing.

2 In areas inhabited by persons belonging to national minorities tradition-

ally or in substantial numbers, if those persons so request and where such a request corresponds to a real need, the Parties shall endeavour to ensure, as far as possible, the conditions which would make it possible to use the minority language in relations between those persons and the administrative authorities.
3 The Parties undertake to guarantee the right of every person belonging to a national minority to be informed promptly, in a language which he or she understands, of the reasons for his or her arrest, and of the nature and cause of any accusation against him or her, and to defend himself or herself in this language, if necessary with the free assistance of an interpreter.

Article 11
1 The Parties undertake to recognise that every person belonging to a national minority has the right to use his or her surname (patronym) and first names in the minority language and the right to official recognition of them, according to modalities provided for in their legal system.
2 The Parties undertake to recognise that every person belonging to a national minority has the right to display in his or her minority language signs, inscriptions and other information of a private nature visible to the public.
3 In areas traditionally inhabited by substantial numbers of persons belonging to a national minority, the Parties shall endeavour, in the framework of their legal system, including, where appropriate, agreements with other States, and taking into account their specific conditions, to display traditional local names, street names and other topographical indications intended for the public also in the minority language when there is a sufficient demand for such indications.

Article 12
1 The Parties shall, where appropriate, take measures in the fields of education and research to foster knowledge of the culture, history, language and religion of their national minorities and of the majority.
2 In this context the Parties shall inter alia provide adequate opportunities for teacher training and access to textbooks, and facilitate contacts among students and teachers of different communities.
3 The Parties undertake to promote equal opportunities for access to education at all levels for persons belonging to national minorities.

Article 13

1 Within the framework of their education systems, the Parties shall recognise that persons belonging to a national minority have the right to set up and to manage their own private educational and training establishments.

2 The exercise of this right shall not entail any financial obligation for the Parties.

Article 14

1 The Parties undertake to recognise that every person belonging to a national minority has the right to learn his or her minority language.

2 In areas inhabited by persons belonging to national minorities traditionally or in substantial numbers, if there is sufficient demand, the Parties shall endeavour to ensure, as far as possible and within the framework of their education systems, that persons belonging to those minorities have adequate opportunities for being taught the minority language or for receiving instruction in this language.

3 Paragraph 2 of this article shall be implemented without prejudice to the learning of the official language or the teaching in this language.

Article 15

The Parties shall create the conditions necessary for the effective participation of persons belonging to national minorities in cultural, social and economic life and in public affairs, in particular those affecting them.

Article 16

The Parties shall refrain from measures which alter the proportions of the population in areas inhabited by persons belonging to national minorities and are aimed at restricting the rights and freedoms flowing from the principles enshrined in the present framework Convention.

Article 17

1 The Parties undertake not to interfere with the right of persons belonging to national minorities to establish and maintain free and peaceful contacts across frontiers with persons lawfully staying in other States, in particular those with whom they share an ethnic, cultural, linguistic or religious identity, or a common cultural heritage.

2 The Parties undertake not to interfere with the right of persons belonging to national minorities to participate in the activities of non-governmental organisations, both at the national and international levels.

Article 18

1 The Parties shall endeavour to conclude, where necessary, bilateral and multilateral agreements with other States, in particular neighbouring States, in order to ensure the protection of persons belonging to the national minorities concerned.

2 Where relevant, the Parties shall take measures to encourage transfrontier co-operation.

Article 19

The Parties undertake to respect and implement the principles enshrined in the present framework Convention making, where necessary, only those limitations, restrictions or derogations which are provided for in international legal instruments, in particular the Convention for the Protection of Human Rights and Fundamental Freedoms, in so far as they are relevant to the rights and freedoms flowing from the said principles.

SECTION III

Article 20

In the exercise of the rights and freedoms flowing from the principles enshrined in the present framework Convention, any person belonging to a national minority shall respect the national legislation and the rights of others, in particular those of persons belonging to the majority or to other national minorities.

Article 21

Nothing in the present framework Convention shall be interpreted as implying any right to engage in any activity or perform any act contrary to the fundamental principles of international law and in particular of the sovereign equality, territorial integrity and political independence of States.

Article 22

Nothing in the present framework Convention shall be construed as limiting or derogating from any of the human rights and fundamental freedoms which may be ensured under the laws of any Contracting Party or under any other agreement to which it is a Party.

Article 23

The rights and freedoms flowing from the principles enshrined in the present framework Convention, in so far as they are the subject of a corresponding provision in the Convention for the Protection of Human Rights and Fundamental Freedoms or in the Protocols thereto, shall be understood so as to conform to the latter provisions.

SECTION IV

Article 24

1 The Committee of Ministers of the Council of Europe shall monitor the implementation of this framework Convention by the Contracting Parties.
2 The Parties which are not members of the Council of Europe shall participate in the implementation mechanism, according to modalities to be determined.

Article 25

1 Within a period of one year following the entry into force of this framework Convention in respect of a Contracting Party, the latter shall transmit to the Secretary General of the Council of Europe full information on the legislative and other measures taken to give effect to the principles set out in this framework Convention.
2 Thereafter, each Party shall transmit to the Secretary General on a periodical basis and whenever the Committee of Ministers so requests any further information of relevance to the implementation of this framework Convention.
3 The Secretary General shall forward to the Committee of Ministers the information transmitted under the terms of this Article.

Article 26

1 In evaluating the adequacy of the measures taken by the Parties to give effect to the principles set out in this framework Convention the Commit-

tee of Ministers shall be assisted by an advisory committee, the members of which shall have recognised expertise in the field of the protection of national minorities.
2 The composition of this advisory committee and its procedure shall be determined by the Committee of Ministers within a period of one year following the entry into force of this framework Convention.

SECTION V

Article 27
This framework Convention shall be open for signature by the member States of the Council of Europe. Up until the date when the Convention enters into force, it shall also be open for signature by any other State so invited by the Committee of Ministers. It is subject to ratification, acceptance or approval. Instruments of ratification, acceptance or approval shall be deposited with the Secretary General of the Council of Europe.

Article 28
1 This framework Convention shall enter into force on the first day of the month following the expiration of a period of three months after the date on which twelve member States of the Council of Europe have expressed their consent to be bound by the Convention in accordance with the provisions of Article 27.
2 In respect of any member State which subsequently expresses its consent to be bound by it, the framework Convention shall enter into force on the first day of the month following the expiration of a period of three months after the date of the deposit of the instrument of ratification, acceptance or approval.

Article 29
1 After the entry into force of this framework Convention and after consulting the Contracting States, the Committee of Ministers of the Council of Europe may invite to accede to the Convention, by a decision taken by the majority provided for in Article 20.d of the Statute of the Council of Europe, any non-member State of the Council of Europe which, invited to sign in accordance with the provisions of Article 27, has not yet done so, and any other non-member State.

2 In respect of any acceding State, the framework Convention shall enter into force on the first day of the month following the expiration of a period of three months after the date of the deposit of the instrument of accession with the Secretary General of the Council of Europe.

Article 30

1 Any State may at the time of signature or when depositing its instrument of ratification, acceptance, approval or accession, specify the territory or territories for whose international relations it is responsible to which this framework Convention shall apply.

2 Any State may at any later date, by a declaration addressed to the Secretary General of the Council of Europe, extend the application of this framework Convention to any other territory specified in the declaration. In respect of such territory the framework Convention shall enter into force on the first day of the month following the expiration of a period of three months after the date of receipt of such declaration by the Secretary General.

3 Any declaration made under the two preceding paragraphs may, in respect of any territory specified in such declaration, be withdrawn by a notification addressed to the Secretary General. The withdrawal shall become effective on the first day of the month following the expiration of a period of three months after the date of receipt of such notification by the Secretary General.

Article 31

1 Any Party may at any time denounce this framework Convention by means of a notification addressed to the Secretary General of the Council of Europe.

2 Such denunciation shall become effective on the first day of the month following the expiration of a period of six months after the date of receipt of the notification by the Secretary General.

Article 32

The Secretary General of the Council of Europe shall notify the member States of the Council, other signatory States and any State which has acceded to this framework Convention, of:

a. any signature;

b. the deposit of any instrument of ratification, acceptance, approval or accession;

c. any date of entry into force of this framework Convention in accordance with Articles 28, 29 and 30;
d. any other act, notification or communication relating to this framework Convention.

In witness whereof the undersigned, being duly authorised thereto, have signed this framework Convention.

Done at Strasbourg, this 1st day of February 1995, in English and French, both texts being equally authentic, in a single copy which shall be deposited in the archives of the Council of Europe. The Secretary General of the Council of Europe shall transmit certified copies to each member State of the Council of Europe and to any State invited to sign or accede to this framework Convention.

Annex II
CENSUS RESULTS

Slovakia 2001:[498]
Slovakia's total population in 2001: 5,379,455 (5,274,335 in 1991)
Slovak: 4,614,854 (85.8 %)
Hungarian: 529,528 (9.7 %)
Romany: 89,920 (1.7 %)
Czech: 44,620 (0.8 %)
Ruthenian:24,201 (0.3 %)
Ukrainian:10,814 (0.2 %)
Other (German,Moravian, Silesian, Croatian, Jewish, Polish, Bulgarian): 0.1 %

Romania 2002:[499]
Romania's total population in 2002: 21,680,974 (22,760,449 in 1992)
Romanian: 19,399,597 (89.5 %)
Hungarians: 1,431,807 (6.6 %)
Roma: 535,140 (2.5 %)
Other: (German, Swabian and Saxon, Ukrainian, Russian, Lipoveni, Turkish, Serbian, Tatar, Slovakian, Bulgarian, Jewish, Croatian, Czech, Polish, Greek, Armenian):312,489 (<1 %)
Unknown: 1,941

Bulgaria 2001:[500]
Bulgaria's total population in 2001: 7,908,901 (8,472,724 in 1991)
Bulgarians: 6,655,210 (83.9 %)
Turks: 746,664 (9.4 %)
Roma: 370,908 (4.7 %)
Others (Macedonians, Jews, Armenians, Russians, Karakachani, Greeks, Vlachs, Romanians and others): 69,204 (1 %)
Not stated: 62,100 (<1 %)
Unknown: 24,807 (< 0.5 %)

---

498 <www.statistics.sk/webdata/english/census2001/tab/zu.htm>.

499 Romanian Statistical Yearbook 2002: <www.insse.ro/indexe.htm>.

500 <www.nsi.bg/Census_e/Ethnos.htm>.

INDEX